UNCERTAIN LEGACIES

**Federal Budget Policy
from Roosevelt through Reagan**

UNCERTAIN LEGACIES

Federal Budget Policy
from Roosevelt through Reagan

DENNIS S. IPPOLITO

UNIVERSITY PRESS OF VIRGINIA
CHARLOTTESVILLE AND LONDON

THE UNIVERSITY PRESS OF VIRGINIA
Copyright © 1990 by the Rector and Visitors
of the University of Virginia

First published 1990

Library of Congress Cataloging-in-Publication Data
Ippolito, Dennis S.
    Uncertain legacies : federal budget policy from Roosevelt through
Reagan / Dennis S. Ippolito.
        p.   cm.
    Includes bibliographical references and index.
    ISBN 0-8139-1287-3
    1. Budget—United States—History—20th century.   2. Government
spending policy—United States—History—20th century.   I. Title.
HJ2051.I66   1990
353.0072'2'09043—dc20   90-36590
                                                             CIP

Printed in the United States of America

For Nancy Christine and Courtney

Contents

Tables and Figures

Tables

Figures

Preface

This book examines the development of federal budget policy from the New Deal through the Reagan presidency. Its starting point is the severity of current budget-control problems, particularly deficits and debt. Its thesis is that the question of how to balance the budget (and at what level) is inseparable from basic, long-standing policy issues. It is essential, therefore, to bring a historical perspective to bear on the disagreements over spending priorities and tax policy that have frustrated one budget-control effort after another.

Recent reforms in federal budgeting have focused on institutional procedures. While procedural reforms perhaps have improved the decision-making process, they obviously have failed to resolve the budget policy conflicts that continue to generate large deficits and growing debt. These conflicts, moreover, are more complex than the conventional ideological diagnoses that "spending is out of control" or "taxes are too low." Instead, important changes in the composition of both the spending and revenue sides of the budget have made it increasingly difficult to control the balance between them.

Budget-control problems need to be analyzed first in terms of policy. Once the relevant policy issues have been identified, it becomes possible to evaluate budget process reforms in a meaningful fashion. A presidential line-item veto, for example, is unlikely to contribute in any significant way to improved budget control, since it cannot affect the automatic spending that drives much of the budget. By the same token, neither the executive nor congressional budget process has been adapted to the reality of modern budgeting, in which indexing of a wide range of programs simultaneously forces spending up and revenues down.

This book, then, attempts to provide a coherent overview of how (and why) budget policy has changed, with attendant information on major programmatic and fiscal issues. It explores the link between these changes and presidential or congressional initiatives, with an emphasis on the president's influence over the basic components of budget policy. Finally, it attempts to integrate policy and institutional analysis, examining not only what role presidential budgets have played but also what role they should play in the budget process. In 1921 the president was given a central responsibility in the budget process for some clearly stated reasons. It is perhaps time to review these reasons and to suggest how decision-making processes might be made more congruent with policy realities and institutional responsibilities.

During the course of this study, I have received valuable assistance from a number of organizations and individuals. Many years ago, the Earhart Foundation sponsored a project on presidential power which eventually evolved into this research. Michael Greve helped to arrange continuing support that has been most helpful. Southern Methodist University recently provided a research leave which allowed me to complete my work.

My debts to individuals are many. I am grateful to other scholars, including two anonymous reviewers, who have graciously shared their expertise. My colleagues in the Department of Political Science at SMU have provided an exceptional environment in which to work. Mary McComas has worked on this manuscript for a very long time, with great skill, patience, and commitment.

UNCERTAIN LEGACIES

Federal Budget Policy
from Roosevelt through Reagan

1

Budget Control in Perspective

Budgets are important at all levels of government, but the federal budget has achieved the lofty status of political drama. At the beginning of each year, the president's budget is released in a flood of publicity, as if it truly were the "Budget of the United States Government" rather than simply his recommended budget program. Congress then proceeds through its complex and cumbersome budget process, which insures that policy disagreements with the president will be fought and refought over many months. Before each side's victories and defeats can even be totaled up, it is time for a new budget round to begin.

The budget is treated, in sum, as commensurate with governing—a critical measure of presidential influence and the key to a president's success or failure. For quite some time, the verdicts have ranged from the dismal to the apocalyptic, primarily because the deficit has served as an almost universal litmus test. Near the end of the Reagan presidency, a spokesman for a prestigious business task force on the budget termed the president's deficit record "a cancer eating away at the vitals of the nation."[1] A widely respected government affairs journal concluded that while Ronald Reagan had secured much of his original agenda—"lower taxes, higher defense outlays, and the political advantage of forcing opposition Democrats to make painful spending choices"—his victories had come "at a fearful price."[2]

For three decades, deficits have been the norm, and their magnitude has reached extremely high levels. For fiscal years 1983–86, the annual deficit averaged over $200 billion. Despite a sharp deficit decline in FY 1987, the annual average for fiscal years 1987–1989 was over $150 billion. The gross federal debt more than tripled during the 1980s and now stands at approximately $3 trillion. Net interest on the debt now exceeds $170 billion annually, over three times its cost in FY 1980. One out of every seven spending dollars in the budget is required to pay interest on the publicly held debt, and almost the same proportion of net interest outlays is needed to finance foreign-held debt.[3]

As a standard against which to assess budget control, however, an exclusive focus on deficits may be misleading. There is a good deal of uncertainty about the impact that deficits have on the economy, as well as even more fundamental disagreement about the appropriate measurement of budget deficits and public debt.[4] Robert Eisner, among others, has warned that the politics of the deficit issue makes it difficult to examine economic effects dispassionately: "The federal deficit has become in some circles the hottest political issue since Vietnam. Democrats and Republicans echo each others' proclamations of disaster and largely restrict their differences to their proposed remedies, and the casting of blame. Scoring political points has replaced almost all efforts at sober economic analysis."[5] The overwhelming emphasis on deficits and debt also makes sober political analysis more difficult. The deficit is an important budgetary fact, but neither its economic nor its political implications are altogether simple and straightforward.

Chronic deficits do not necessarily signify a failure of the budget process. The policy disagreements that have frustrated recent efforts to balance the budget, for example, are far from trivial. Fiscal conservatives, who once deplored deficits as close to immoral, now have accepted them as the price for financing the Reagan tax cuts and defense buildup. Liberals, whose attitudes toward deficits have usually been ambivalent, have chosen to protect their favored spending programs regardless of deficits. One can disagree with these positions, but they represent deliberate and defensible budget policy choices.

A helpful step in analyzing the political implications of deficits is to provide some perspective. The size of deficits needs to be measured accurately. The trends that have caused the gap between spending and revenues to widen need to be identified. In particular, the composition as well as the size of the federal budget has changed dramatically over the past several decades, creating serious obstacles to short-term budget control. It is important to recognize that the basic foundation of annual budget control—comprehensiveness, predictability, and balance—has eroded at least in part because of automatic formulas that govern major portions of spending and tax policy. Bringing the budget into balance is a much more difficult policy task than it was two or three decades ago.

Budget Conflict and the Deficit Dilemma
The federal budget's high visibility and salience are recent phenomena.[6] In 1921 the Budget and Accounting Act assigned to the president the responsibility for transmitting to Congress estimates of expenditures and

proposed appropriations necessary "in his judgment" for support of the government.[7] From this point through the 1960s, the federal budget process rarely merited special attention. The president's budget was more influential, but paradoxically less controversial, than it is today, with Congress usually content to make only modest changes in presidential spending requests.[8] Tax policy was comparatively stable as well, since revenue requirements were defined by spending commitments.[9]

Through most of this period, the institutional responsibilities of the president and Congress were recognized by both sides as separate and distinct. Congress did not replicate the president's work, nor did it assert coequal policy leadership. It did reserve, and frequently exercise, the right to say no to presidential requests. It occasionally passed a spending or tax bill over a presidential veto. As Louis Fisher has described this budget system, "The president took responsibility for the aggregates, and Congress lived within those totals while rearranging the priorities. In short, each branch did what it was well suited for."[10]

Over the past two decades, important components of the budget, most notably defense, have become much more politicized, and this politicization has carried over into the budget process.[11] The budget reforms that Congress adopted in 1974 mandated congressional budget resolutions that were to serve as alternatives to the president's budget.[12] According to former Speaker of the House James C. Wright, Jr., budget resolutions are much more than alternatives: "The congressional budget resolution . . . , of course, is the budget. . . . Congress makes the budget; the President does not."[13] The post-1974 budget system has sharpened conflicts over the size, composition, and financing of the budget. The budget highlights congressional challenges to presidential fiscal policy and spending priorities, and it is uniquely useful for this purpose in that it must come up every year.

The budget's high standing on the political agenda reflects a declining consensus on policy and on presidential versus congressional powers. Whether policy disagreement has heightened institutional disagreement or vice versa, there seems to be little question that budget conflict has shifted to a new level:

> The other democracies agree on objectives; they just lack the means; America has the means but differs over the ends. And that difference matters because the separation of powers institutionalizes these differences by giving the opposing sides independent platforms from which to carry on their struggle.

None of the other nations with which we compare ourselves experienced prolonged difficulty in agreeing on a budget, or fought essentially the same issues over and over again with the same high intensity and as little conclusiveness as have Americans. By any measure—time, intensity, dissensus, historical or contemporary comparison—the budgetary battles of our time are extraordinary.[14]

The catalyst for continued budget wars has been the deficit problem. The persistence and, more important, the growth of budget deficits have been at the core of charges that the budget is out of control, or that the budget process is fatally flawed, or that the president and Congress lack the political will to make difficult but necessary decisions.

Concern over deficits is not a strictly modern preoccupation in the United States. As James Savage has pointed out, "From the earliest days of the republic the idea of balancing the federal government's budgets has played a central role in American political life."[15] The deficit issue has become more compelling, however, as departures from the balanced budget rule have become commonplace and as the political system's inability to restore that rule has become frustrating and embarrassing.

Despite the lack of compliance, the balanced budget rule continues to occupy an honored place in presidential politics. The Reagan administration, for example, took office in 1981 with one of the most ambitious budget programs since the New Deal, promising at the outset that its proposals would lead "surely and predictably, toward a balanced budget" by 1984.[16] Four years earlier, Jimmy Carter had unveiled an Economic Recovery Program designed to balance the budget by 1981.[17]

Carter's deficit record was no better than his predecessor's, while Reagan's stands as the worst in history. These are, however, hardly aberrations. Deficits have been growing steadily since the 1930s, during peacetime and wartime and under both Democrats and Republicans. Since FY 1930, there have been only nine balanced budgets, the most recent being in FY 1969. Measured in current dollars, cumulative deficits rose to unprecedented levels during the 1970s and 1980s (see table 1.1). In real terms (constant dollars), deficit growth has been somewhat less ominous, but the numbers are still rather startling. The annual average real deficit for the 1980s is actually on a par with that from World War II and more than double the annual average for the 1970s.

Measured against economic growth, the deficit and public debt buildups remain relatively high. Up until twenty years ago, peacetime deficits never exceeded 3 percent of gross national product (GNP) in any single

Table 1.1. Budget Deficits, Fiscal Years 1930-89 (in billions of dollars)

| Fiscal Years | Number of Deficits | Current Dollars | | Constant Dollars (FY 1982) |
		Net Deficits[a]	Annual Average	Annual Average
1930-39	9	$ 20.9	$ 2.1	NA
1940-49	7	177.6	17.8	$129.1
1950-59	7	17.4	1.7	6.9
1960-69	8	56.5	5.6	18.2
1970-79	10	365.0	36.5	61.7
1980-89[b]	10	1573.5	157.3	143.9

SOURCES: *Historical Tables, Budget of the United States Government, Fiscal Year 1990* (Washington, D.C.: GPO, 1989), pp. 19-20; *Budget of the United States Government, Fiscal Year 1990* (Washington, D.C.: GPO, 1989), p. 10-45.
[a] Total deficits minus total surpluses, administrative budget basis for fiscal years 1930-34; unified budget basis for fiscal years 1935-89.
[b] Fiscal year 1989 is estimated.

year and usually were well below this level. For the entire fiscal 1950–69 period, which encompassed the Korean War and the peak spending years for Vietnam, deficits averaged less than 1 percent of GNP on an annual basis (see table 1.2). After the Vietnam War, this average started to climb and by the late 1970s had reached 3 percent. During fiscal years 1983–86, annual deficits exceeded 5 percent of GNP, while for Reagan's entire tenure the average was only slightly lower. Because of mounting deficits, the post–World War II decline in publicly held debt as a percentage of GNP was reversed in the 1970s, and this reversal then accelerated over the next decade.

While no one applauds this deficit and debt record, its economic consequences are hotly disputed. There can be no argument, however, about the increased cost of servicing the debt. Because interest rates have moved upward over the past several decades, the financing costs for even stable debt levels would have risen. With interest rates and debt levels going up simultaneously, net interest costs have jumped to more than 3 percent of GNP, more than double the GNP share for most of the post–World War II period. As a point of comparison, the ratio of defense

Table 1.2. Deficits, Debt, and Interest Costs, Fiscal Years 1940–89

	Annual Average Percentage of GNP		
Fiscal Years	Deficit	Publicly Held Debt	Net Interest
1940–44	15.3	59.8	0.9
1945–49	4.6	98.6	1.8
1950–54	0.4	66.7	1.5
1955–59	0.5	52.1	1.2
1960–64	0.7	44.2	1.3
1965–69	0.9	34.4	1.3
1970–74	1.2	27.2	1.4
1975–79	3.6	27.4	1.6
1980–84	4.2	30.3	2.5
1985–89[a]	4.1	41.6	3.2

SOURCE: *Historical Tables, Budget of the United States Government, Fiscal Year 1990*, pp. 17-18, 46-52, 144-45.
[a] Fiscal year 1989 is estimated.

spending to net interest outlays was about seven to one before the Vietnam buildup. The ratio now is less than two to one.

Direct budget costs are an important consequence of deficit and debt expansion. Responding to this problem and to growing concerns about the economic and political repercussions of chronic deficits, President Reagan and Congress joined in support of the Balanced Budget and Emergency Deficit Control Act of 1985 (popularly known as Gramm-Rudman-Hollings, or GRH). This legislation established an automatic deficit-reduction procedure designed to balance the budget by fiscal 1991, but a key portion of the law was declared unconstitutional by the Supreme Court in 1986.[18] The following year, the president and Congress agreed to amendments restoring the automatic budget cuts, or sequestration, to Gramm-Rudman-Hollings and extending the deficit-reduction schedule through FY 1993. Despite this legislation, serious questions remain about the prospects for a balanced budget in the near future.[19]

Very large differentials between spending and revenues are not simply a function of the 1981 Reagan tax cuts, or the Reagan defense buildup, or other recent budget changes. The composition of federal spending and federal receipts has been shifting for decades, and these shifts make it virtually impossible to eliminate the current deficit without major policy reversals. Long-term spending and revenue trends have narrowed politically acceptable policy options.

The Growth of Spending

Over the past half century, federal outlays have risen from several billion dollars annually to well over one trillion dollars, and most of this increase has taken place since 1970. Just twenty years ago, federal outlays totaled less than $200 billion. Between fiscal years 1970 and 1980, spending more than tripled, to almost $600 billion. By the end of the 1980s, another $500 billion had been added to the yearly total. Increases of such magnitude naturally have encouraged the perception that spending control has deteriorated greatly, if not entirely disappeared. The spending-control problem is indeed serious, but its severity differs greatly across spending categories.

Measuring Growth

Factors such as inflation and economic growth need to be taken into account when analyzing spending growth, as well as other parts of the budget. The necessity for distinguishing real increases from nominal increases is basic, since inflation-generated budget growth and policy-generated budget growth are quite different problems with very different solutions. In addition, an important dimension of the real magnitude of government is the size of the economy supporting its activities. If spending growth is at or below economic growth, the government's relative size is not increasing even though its expenditures may be going up sharply. The budget's explosive growth becomes less imposing when these perspectives are introduced, and the perception that spending control has deteriorated becomes harder to support.

As shown in table 1.3, outlay growth has been very high for quite some time, whether measured in current dollars or constant dollars. Real growth has been lower than nominal growth, as might be expected, but the surprising point is that the rate of increase in real growth has actually slowed. Overall real growth for the 1980s was less than 30 percent, about on a par with the 1970s and well below that for the 1950s and 1960s.

Comparing spending to GNP also shows the long-term nature of budget growth. Spending has outpaced economic growth by a wide margin since the beginning of the New Deal, with the outlays-GNP level climbing from less than 5 percent to well over 20 percent (see table 1.4).

Table 1.3. Current and Constant Dollar Outlays, Fiscal Years 1930–89 (in billions of dollars)

Fiscal Year	Total Outlays	
	Current Dollars	Constant Dollars (FY 1982)
1930	$ 3.3	NA
1939	9.1	NA
Percentage increase	176%	
1940	9.5	$ 83.2
1949	38.8	202.5
Percentage increase	308%	143%
1950	42.6	220.5
1959	92.1	346.9
Percentage increase	116%	57%
1960	92.2	340.4
1969	183.6	510.4
Percentage increase	99%	50%
1970	195.6	509.4
1979	503.5	660.2
Percentage increase	157%	30%
1980	590.9	699.1
1989 (est.)	1137.0	902.4
Percentage increase	92%	29%

SOURCES: *Historical Tables, Budget of the United States Government, Fiscal Year 1990*, pp. 19–20; *Budget of the United States Government, Fiscal Year 1990*, p. 10–45.

By the early 1950s, however, spending as a percentage of GNP was already double pre–World War II levels, and a major upward shift in the relative size of the federal sector had already taken place. While current levels are higher than during the 1950s or 1960s, the proportional change since then has been comparatively modest.

Decelerating spending growth—both in real terms and relative to economic growth—hardly suggests deteriorating spending control. It

Table 1.4. Outlays as a Percentage of GNP, Fiscal Years 1930-90 (in billions of dollars)

Fiscal Year	Total Outlays	Percentage of GNP
1930	$ 3.3	3.6%
1935	6.4	8.9
1940	9.5	9.9
1945	92.7	43.6
1950	42.6	16.0
1955	68.4	17.7
1960	92.2	18.2
1965	118.2	17.6
1970	195.6	19.8
1975	332.3	21.8
1980	590.9	22.1
1985	946.3	23.9
1990 (est.)	1,151.8	21.0

SOURCES: U.S. Bureau of the Census, *Historical Statistics of the United States, Colonial Times to 1970*, pt. 1 (Washington, D.C.: GPO, 1975), p. 224; *Historical Tables, Budget of the United States Government, Fiscal Year 1990*, pp. 19-20.

should be pointed out, however, that decelerating growth does not mean reduced spending. The modern version of budget control, with its emphasis on rates of growth, bears little resemblance to its pre–New Deal counterpart. During the 1920s, for example, government outlays actually dropped, the budget was in surplus each year, and about one-third of the $23 billion World War I public debt increase was erased.

The Great Depression and World War II altered this fiscal approach permanently. With social welfare and peacetime defense components added to the budget, policymakers have usually assumed year-to-year increases. Their disagreements have been over rates of growth. (The latest manifestation of this approach is the use of baselines to measure future growth. The current services baseline, for example, is defined as "the estimated budget outlays and proposed budget authority that would be included in the budget . . . if programs and activities . . . were carried on . . . at the same level as the current year without a change in policy."[20] Using baseline spending projections, it is entirely possible to "cut" the budget for a future fiscal year and at the same time to see spending grow during that year.)

Even if the spending-GNP level remains stabilized, however, the budget will be far from balanced. Indeed, unless receipts grow more rapidly than GNP, or spending grows less rapidly, the gap between receipts and outlays will remain (see figure 1.1). And if the GNP gap were to remain constant, the deficit would grow larger in dollar terms.

The spending-control solution to deficits is further complicated by the changing composition of federal outlays. The budget would currently be balanced, for example, if spending were about 19 percent of GNP. This percentage is exactly the average for the 1960s. Since then, the sources of spending growth have changed, however, making very difficult the task of returning to that earlier GNP level.

Budget Composition

The primary impetus for budget growth has switched several times since the New Deal (see figure 1.2). The initial stage in the development of the modern budget was the enactment of social welfare and other domestic spending programs during the 1930s. Then for nearly three decades after the United States entered World War II, defense needs provided the momentum behind budget expansion. During the early 1970s, social welfare expenditures displaced defense as the largest component of the budget. Since then, the portion of the budget devoted to defense and to nondefense discretionary spending ("all other") has been steadily shrinking.

This point is underscored by GNP comparisons. As percentages of GNP, both defense and discretionary spending have dropped sharply since the early 1960s (see figure 1.3). These reductions have been more than offset, however, by the growth of social welfare programs ("entitlements and other mandatory spending") and net interest. Since fiscal 1980, these have averaged nearly 14 percent of GNP, approximately double their combined GNP level during the 1960s.

Nearly two-thirds of the spending-GNP base, then, is accounted for by programs not directly controlled by the budget process. Interest outlays are determined by the amount of debt that must be refinanced in a given year along with interest rates prevailing at that time. For immediate deficit-reduction purposes, the GNP share represented by interest is simply unavailable.

Social welfare outlays can be cut, but the constraints are fairly formidable. Eligibility and benefit levels can be revised by Congress. Factors

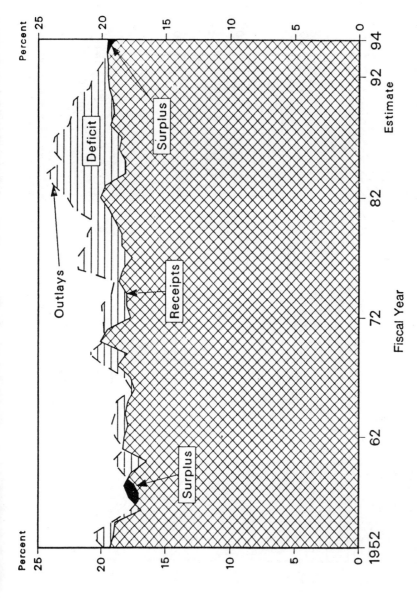

Figure 1.1. Budget totals as percentages of GNP, fiscal years 1952–94. Source: *Historical Tables. Budget of the United States Government, Fiscal Year 1990* (Washington, D.C.: GPO, 1989), p. 8. Estimates for fiscal years 1989–94 are based on the Reagan administration's fiscal 1990 budget proposals.

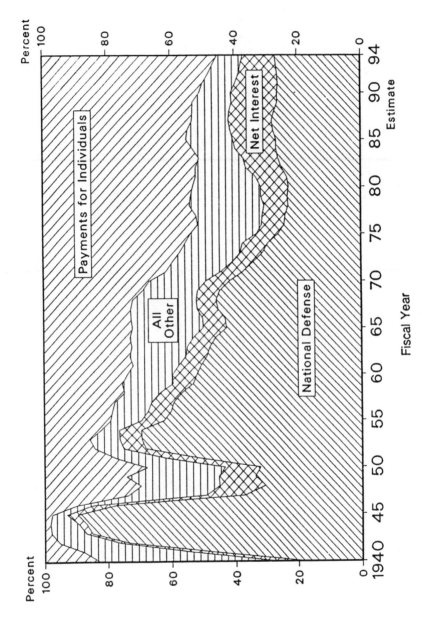

Figure 1.2. Percentage composition of federal outlays, fiscal years 1940-94. Source: *Historical Tables, Budget of the United States Government, Fiscal Year 1990*, p. 12. Estimates for fiscal years 1989-94 are based on the Reagan administration's fiscal 1990 budget proposals.

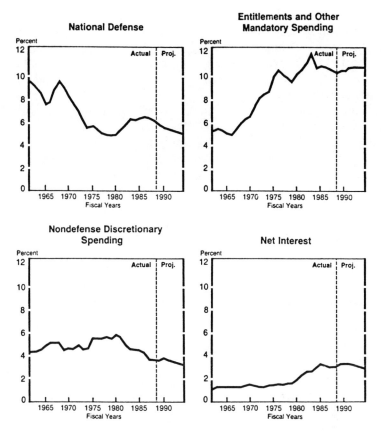

Figure 1.3. Outlays for major spending categories as a percentage of GNP, fiscal years 1962-94. Source: Congressional Budget Office, *The Economic and Budget Outlook: Fiscal Years 1990-1994* (Washington, D.C., 1989), p. 58.

such as demographic patterns and rates of inflation also affect entitlement outlays but are not controlled by Congress. While some entitlements were trimmed during the 1980s, the major ones, such as social security and medicare, continued to expand very rapidly. From FY 1981 through FY 1989, total "payments for individuals" rose by just over $200 billion.[21] Most of this increase was accounted for by just three programs: social security (up more than $90 billion); medicare (up nearly $50 billion); and federal civil and military retirement (up almost $20 billion). In FY 1989, these three programs accounted for approximately 70 percent of total payments for individuals.

The shape of the spending budget presents an obvious dilemma. There has already been a very sharp cutback in the GNP levels for defense and discretionary domestic spending, which now account for only about one-third of the budget. The budget process has managed to hold long-term spending in these categories below economic growth and overall budget growth rates.

Where budget control has failed, by contrast, has been in a relatively small number of very popular and very costly programs. It is not at all clear that this failure is rooted in the budget process or in the timidity of elected officials or in the politicization of budget policy. Indeed, steps have been taken to depoliticize these programs. Social security benefit increases were indexed to the cost of living in 1972 partly in order to eliminate the problem of election-year increases by the president and Congress. In 1985 social security was formally shifted "off-budget," again partly to insulate the program from political manipulation.[22] Significant portions of the medicare program are also indexed, and the hospital insurance part of medicare is also scheduled for off-budget status in 1993.[23] Depoliticizing the fastest-growing and largest segments of the budget, however, means that the unequal competition for budgetary resources will continue.

Budget Receipts and Tax Policy

Unlike spending, budget receipts have roughly paralleled economic growth for several decades. Only four times in the past fifty years has the level of budget receipts exceeded 20 percent of GNP, and two of those occasions were during World War II. For each of the past four decades, the average annual budget receipts–GNP level has fluctuated within a narrow range (see table 1.5).

The overall pattern obscures, however, two important points about tax policy. First, and again unlike spending, tax cuts have been periodically enacted whenever the rate of growth in receipts has begun to outstrip economic growth by a significant margin. Second, the results of long-term revisions in tax policy have been to shift the composition of tax receipts away from general revenues and toward social security levies. In FY 1960 individual income taxes were 8.0 percent of GNP. The FY 1990 estimate is 8.5 percent. By comparison, social insurance taxes (primarily social security) have risen from 2.9 percent to 7.1 percent of GNP over this same period. The combined tax burden on individuals has shifted upward, but virtually none of the revenue increment is available to support general government activities.

The Reagan tax cuts of 1981 reduced total receipts below 20 percent

Table 1.5. Receipts as a Percentage of GNP, Fiscal Years 1950-89

Fiscal Years	Annual Average Percentage of GNP
1950–59	17.5
1960–69	18.2
1970–79	18.3
1980–89[a]	19.0

Source: *Historical Tables, Budget of the United States Government, Fiscal Year 1990*, pp. 19-20.
[a] Fiscal year 1989 is estimated.

of GNP, and they have remained below this level. In addition, the composition of receipts pre-Reagan and post-Reagan has important implications. As shown in table 1.6, the relative level of social insurance taxes climbed almost without interruption during the Reagan presidency. Corporation income taxes fluctuated but finally returned to pre-Reagan levels. The prospects for future upward growth in either of these receipts categories are slim. Payroll tax increases have already been accelerated twice in little more than a decade, and large social security surpluses are now projected through the 1990s. The Tax Reform Act of 1986 substantially raised corporate taxes, accounting for the projected growth in the corporation income tax–GNP level over the next several years.

This growth in other taxes leaves individual income taxes as the main revenue source with which to bridge the outlays-receipts differential. The indexing of tax policy during the Reagan presidency, however, means that any future increases will have to be deliberate. Individual income tax brackets, the standard deduction, and personal exemptions are now adjusted annually for inflation, thereby eliminating inflation-boosted tax increases.[24] The revenue impact of indexing is substantial. The Congressional Budget Office (CBO) estimates, for example, that repeal of indexing would boost revenues by nearly $150 billion over the fiscal 1990–94 period.[25]

The elimination of "invisible" tax increases for individuals is important, since statutory tax increases would have to be very broad-based in order to raise substantial revenues. Moreover, since individual income

Table 1.6. Receipts by Major Source, Fiscal Years 1961-90 (as percentages of GNP)

Fiscal Year	Individual Income Taxes	Corporate Income Taxes	Social Insur- ance Taxes & Contributions	Excise Taxes	Other	Total Revenues
1961	8.0	4.0	3.2	2.3	0.7	18.2
1962	8.2	3.7	3.1	2.2	0.7	17.9
1963	8.1	3.7	3.4	2.2	0.7	18.1
1964	7.7	3.7	3.5	2.2	0.8	17.9
1965	7.3	3.8	3.3	2.2	0.9	17.4
1966	7.5	4.1	3.5	1.8	0.9	17.7
1967	7.7	4.3	4.1	1.7	0.9	18.7
1968	8.1	3.4	4.0	1.7	0.9	18.0
1969	9.4	3.9	4.2	1.6	0.9	20.1
1970	9.1	3.3	4.5	1.6	1.0	19.5
1971	8.2	2.5	4.5	1.6	1.0	17.7
1972	8.2	2.8	4.6	1.3	1.1	18.0
1973	8.1	2.8	4.9	1.3	0.9	18.0
1974	8.4	2.7	5.3	1.2	1.0	18.6
1975	8.0	2.7	5.6	1.1	1.0	18.3
1976	7.7	2.4	5.3	1.0	1.0	17.6
1977	8.2	2.8	5.5	0.9	1.0	18.4
1978	8.3	2.8	5.6	0.8	0.9	18.4
1979	8.9	2.7	5.7	0.8	0.9	18.9
1980	9.1	2.4	5.9	0.9	1.0	19.4
1981	9.6	2.0	6.1	1.4	1.0	20.1
1982	9.5	1.6	6.4	1.2	1.1	19.7
1983	8.7	1.1	6.3	1.1	0.9	18.1
1984	8.1	1.5	6.5	1.0	0.9	18.1
1985	8.5	1.6	6.7	0.9	0.9	18.6
1986	8.3	1.5	6.8	0.8	1.0	18.4
1987	8.9	1.9	6.8	0.7	0.9	19.3
1988	8.4	2.0	7.0	0.7	0.9	19.0
1989 (est.)	8.3	2.1	7.1	0.7	0.9	19.1
1990 (est.)	8.5	2.1	7.1	0.6	0.9	19.3

SOURCE: *Historical Tables, Budget of the United States Government, Fiscal Year 1990*, pp. 28-29.

taxes account for well under half of the total receipts, they obviously would have to be raised disproportionately to effect a major deficit reduction.

A substantial upward shift in budget receipts is not impossible. Its likelihood is diminished, however, by some of the same constraints that affect spending. A large portion of the spending budget is indexed, which means that outlays will rise automatically with inflation. This indexation makes spending control more difficult. Tax policy is also indexed, in part, but the effect is to keep this side of the budget from automatically outstripping economic growth. What was once possible—budget balance through revenue increases without policy change—can no longer occur.

Budget Reform and Budget Theory

One can argue against apocalyptic judgments of the spending and revenue trends of the past several decades, particularly insofar as those judgments focus on the economic effects of deficits. A much stronger critical case can be mounted against deficits on the point that their growth and persistence constitute a political failure. Despite agreement across the political spectrum that deficits should, and indeed must, be eliminated, the executive branch and Congress have failed thus far to come up with a solution. The Gramm-Rudman-Hollings approach, in fact, acknowledges this failure by substituting formulas for political decisions. Assuming that Gramm-Rudman-Hollings eventually works, which is a huge assumption, the issue of how the political process can then deal responsibly with future budget policy will still remain.

Budget Reform

One response to the perception of political failure has been growing support for some type of budget process reform. At one extreme, constitutional amendments have been advocated that would mandate balanced budgets or would limit the growth in government spending or taxation.[26] Throughout his presidency, Ronald Reagan coupled his support for a constitutional budget limit with his advocacy of a line-item veto which would allow the president to veto portions of appropriations bills.[27] Since the 1974 congressional budget reforms, there has also been constant pressure to refine and strengthen the congressional process. Even defenders of the 1974 budget act now acknowledge that serious weaknesses in congressional budgeting must be remedied.[28]

The umbrella of budget reform covers two different types of problems. First, there is the problem of designing a budget process which will work effectively in the executive branch and Congress, while at the same time conforming to the constitutionally prescribed separation of powers. Second, there is the problem of budget policy outcomes, defined as excessive spending, inadequate revenues, or chronic deficits.

For much of our history, budget reform at the federal level attempted to achieve budget policy goals by changing the budget process. After the Civil War, for example, Congress gave broad powers over spending to newly created appropriations committees in order to bring budgets into surplus and thereby to reduce the debt incurred during wartime. A similar strategy was employed after World War I, and it was reinforced by provisions for a presidential budget.[29]

The connection between process and policy objectives in these cases was almost automatic, because of an underlying consensus on the norms governing budgeting. The most important of these norms was the belief that budgets had to be balanced, except during emergencies such as war. This goal meant, in practice, that spending had to be restrained by policymakers, since taxes were likely to be controlled by the political process. In order to control spending, authority to make spending decisions had to be centralized—with the president or with the appropriations committees— and that authority had to be reasonably comprehensive, extending to most of the spending done by government.

With a consensus on norms linking process and policy, budget reform efforts enjoyed at least temporary success. After both the Civil War and World War I, expenditures were tightly controlled, budgets were in surplus, and wartime debts were cut significantly. Eventually, these reforms were undercut by new fiscal pressures, but they demonstrated the efficacy of adapting the budget process to specific budget policy problems.

This adaptation was conspicuously absent, however, from the most important budget reform of the modern era—the 1974 Congressional Budget and Impoundment Control Act. The procedures and organization established by the 1974 budget act were designed to strengthen congressional influence over budget policy, not to achieve a specific budget policy objective. The 1974 reforms were intended to be "policy neutral."[30] Their objective was to make Congress "a more respected institution and a more effective partner in Government" by improving the manner in which it made budgets.[31] As defined by the Senate Rules and Administration Committee, congressional budget reform meant adding "a new and comprehensive budgetary framework to the existing decision-making process, with minimum disruption to established methods and procedures."[32]

The spending-control and deficit problems that initially catalyzed the reform debates of the early 1970s were not resolved by the final legislative product.[33] In the end, there was no consensus on the necessity for spending restraint. The growing portion of the budget that circumvented the annual appropriations process continued to be insulated. Neither was there a consensus that the budget had to be balanced, which meant that deficits could be justified as economic stimulus policy. Centralized, comprehensive control over spending, which had been the primary component of earlier budget reforms, was subordinated in 1974 to procedures relating to spending priorities, fiscal policy management, and independent congressional budgeting.

Budget Theory

The direction that budget reform took in 1974 has produced policy results that have proved unsatisfactory to both parties and to virtually the entire political spectrum. The deficit problem has grown worse. The comprehensiveness and predictability of the annual budget have diminished. Conflicts over budget policy have consumed more and more of each year's legislative process.

While the 1974 reforms were not derived from a particular theory of budgeting, they implicitly rejected a view of budgeting and decision making which had been widely accepted for many years. Aaron Wildavsky's theory of "budgetary incrementalism" had described a budget process in which decisions proceeded from "a historical base, guided by accepted notions of fair shares, . . . [were] fragmented, made in sequence by specialized bodies, and coordinated through repeated attacks on problems and through multiple feedback mechanisms."[34]

Budgetary incrementalism was a way of making decisions which allowed policymakers to cope with the otherwise overwhelming complexity of the budget. It was also tied, however, to a general agreement on policy goals:

> Calculations were made, conflict diffused, and yet, wonder of wonders, budgets were passed on time while revenues and expenditures stayed within hailing distance.
>
> A bottom-up decentralized process . . . required widespread agreement on the norms of balance and comprehensiveness. A commitment to budget balance meant acceptance of a de facto spending limit. . . . Adherence to the norm of comprehensiveness meant that almost everything was in the same pot. When restraints had to be exercised in the name of balance, therefore,

neither substantial revenues nor expenditures were outside the purview of the political authorities for ratcheting up or down.[35]

Both the budget process and budget policy, however, have moved away from the incrementalist model. The circle of congressional participation in budget decision making has expanded greatly, making it more difficult to make binding decisions. The intense politicization of budget policy decisions is now routine. Conflict between the executive branch and Congress is protracted and almost continuous.

The divorce of budget policy from incrementalism has been even more pronounced. With the erosion of the balanced budget norm, tax policy has moved from a framework of periodic, marginal adjustments to one of frequent and occasionally dramatic changes. Within the spending portion of the budget, growth rates across program categories and over time have varied enormously. The decline in real defense spending during the early 1970s was followed by the largest peacetime defense buildup of the post–World War II era. Discretionary domestic programs, whose costs had mounted rapidly during the 1970s, were cut back significantly under Reagan. The costliest and fastest-growing social welfare programs, such as social security and medicare, have largely escaped spending-control efforts. By contrast, the costs of social welfare programs to assist low-income groups have fluctuated widely over the past two decades.

Recent budget policy reflects a complexity and variety of change which cannot be adequately explained by incrementalist theory. As a result, analysts have stressed the importance of applying certain distinctions to the study of the budget process and budget policy. The first of these is an institutional one that acknowledges essential differences between executive branch and congressional budgeting.[36] The second is a recognition that different components of budget policy respond differently to political, economic, and other external influences on budget policy.[37]

These distinctions define the approach of this book. Its purpose is to illuminate current budget policy issues by placing them in a historical context. Modern budget policy can be traced back to the New Deal, and the evolution of spending and tax policies over the ensuing half century helps to explain how and why we find ourselves in a fiscal dilemma. In order to add coherence to the analysis, a consistent emphasis is placed on the president's role in shaping budget policy. By focusing on what different administrations have accomplished (or failed to accomplish) over an extended period, it should be possible to assess the strengths and weaknesses of executive budgeting.

Finally, the underlying assumption of this book is that reform of the budget process is inseparable from budget policy changes. As Wildavsky has argued, "There would be no point in tinkering with the budgetary machinery if, at the end, the pattern of outcomes was precisely the same as before."[38] The basic fiscal issues—how to balance the budget and at what level—are inseparable from policy choices. The budget process cannot produce satisfactory results when there are fundamental, unresolved disagreements over spending priorities and tax policy. Before we can realistically debate reforms in process or procedures, we need to understand the policy issues that these reforms must be able to resolve.

I

**Tax Policy and
Balanced Budgets**

2

The Destabilizing of Tax Policy

From the tax side of the budget, the explanation for deficits appears simple. The willingness to pay for government services is exceeded by the demand for services. Further, the public's professed abhorrence of deficits is less threatening to policymakers than the potential pitfalls of raising taxes or cutting services. As Susan Hansen has concluded, one of the few clear, consistent findings about public opinion on taxes is that "people of course prefer lower to high taxes and demand more government services at lower tax rates. Although puzzled economists may ask, 'Does the public really believe that services can be provided for free?' the answer clearly is that many do."[1]

Despite its intuitive attraction, this explanation presents some problems. First, peacetime federal budgets were balanced nearly half the time during the two decades from the end of World War II until the beginning of the Vietnam War, and the deficits that otherwise occurred were usually quite small. In most cases, deficits amounted to less than 1 percent of GNP. Second, the share of federal receipts from individual income taxes and social insurance taxes rose by nearly 25 percent. Third, despite this shift toward politically sensitive revenue sources, the level of budget receipts (again measured against GNP) remained relatively stable. In FY 1969, when the budget was last balanced, receipts exceeded 20 percent of GNP, only slightly below their World War II peak.

Analyses of tax policy during this halcyon period have emphasized the importance of an incremental decision-making process in maintaining a close approximation between spending and tax levels. During the Truman and Eisenhower administrations, presidential opposition to tax reductions stabilized the tax system.[2] Within Congress, powerful and autonomous revenue committees, particularly Ways and Means, usually reinforced presidential arguments for budget balance over tax reduction. Congressional decision making was not very democratic, but the policy outcome of this closed process was stable and reasonably responsible tax policy.[3] Indeed, the 1969 tax bill, arguably one of the most progressive pieces of tax legislation ever enacted, was largely fashioned by the Nixon administration and a conservative House Ways and Means Committee. As summarized by Catherine Rudder, Ways and Means was a "control committee"—"a small, elite body operating behind closed doors . . . under closed rules . . . [following] norms of restrained partisanship, 'responsible legislating,' and apprenticeship"; Ways and Means not only dominated the House but also was "a substantial restraining influence on the Senate."[4]

It should be emphasized, however, that certain conditions facilitated an incremental decision-making process and incremental changes in tax policy. There was no need during the late 1940s and 1950s to raise taxes in order to maintain high revenue levels. Instead, simply moderating reductions from the wartime tax structure kept revenues in line with spending. Economic growth, coupled with low inflation rates, also moderated pressures to adjust rate structures and exemption levels. The 1969 tax bill was the first major tax reform since the end of World War II, and it was necessitated by the twin spending pressures of Vietnam and new domestic program commitments.

The confluence of facilitating economic conditions and an incremental decision-making process which restrained partisan and short-term pressures allowed the "guardians of the Treasury" in Congress and the executive branch to hold the line on revenue reductions.[5] This stability in tax policy disintegrated, however, during the 1970s, as the economy and the tax process changed radically. Economic growth slowed, while inflation climbed. Spending, driven in part by high inflation, exceeded economic growth. Income tax liabilities rose faster than real income, as inflation pushed individuals into higher tax brackets.

As the political pressures to reduce taxes mounted, the old restraints gave way. The president's role in the budget process was no longer an exclusive or dominant one after Watergate. Within Congress, the democratization of procedures and fragmentation of the committee system produced a tax process which was much more open to constant change and to organized interests.[6] The increased responsiveness of tax policy decision making made it much more difficult to resist ad hoc claims and to maintain the integrity of the tax system.

The public's growing dissatisfaction with rising tax burdens was not directed just at the federal government. State governments also faced numerous challenges, symbolized most notably by the passage of Proposition 13 in California in 1978.[7] This voter initiative, passed by a better than two-to-one margin with a record-setting turnout, mandated significant cutbacks in property taxes. The taxpayer's revolt it ostensibly symbolized spread to other states and to the federal government.

By the late 1970s, tax policy had slipped its moorings. The budgetary nexus between spending and taxation had been cut. Institutional barriers against tax reduction had been weakened. The increased political responsiveness of the tax policy process had produced not only inadequate revenues but also growing dissatisfaction inside and outside government.

The 1970s produced erratic and bizarre policy results. A series of tax reform bills cut the tax base, while at the same time marginal rates for many taxpayers increased. For low-income taxpayers, the declining value of personal exemptions and sharply increased payroll taxes offset reduced income tax liabilities. Tax expenditures grew in numbers and revenue impact. A weakened presidency and a democratized Congress produced tax policy that was definitely less stable and arguably less fair than was the case during the 1950s and 1960s.

Spending and Tax Policy

The structure of tax policy responds to changes in the size and growth of the spending side of the budget. For example, enormous increases in revenue demands, and hence significant changes in tax policy, have occurred during major wars. The Civil War and World Wars I and II all had a dramatic, long-term impact on the federal tax system. The most recent revenue shift—the explosive growth of payroll taxes since the 1960s—is an exception to the war-financing pattern but not to the more general relationship between spending growth and tax policy.

Consumption Taxes

Except for a brief period at the time of the Civil War, the federal government was able to do without income taxes for well over a century. From 1789 until the Civil War, customs duties were usually sufficient to cover the modest spending of the federal government.[8] While customs duties could finance low, stable budgets, they could not raise additional large sums quickly and easily. In order to meet the unprecedented financing demands of the Civil War, the government was forced to levy excise taxes, an individual income tax, and estate and gift duties. These new taxes produced hundreds of millions of dollars in new revenue, but spending grew so rapidly, reaching a peak of $1.3 billion in fiscal 1866, that very heavy borrowing was also required. The total federal debt by the end of the war was $2.75 billion. Customs duties, which had supplied 95 percent

Table 2.1. Federal Expenditures and Receipts, Fiscal Years 1870–1915 (in millions of dollars)

Fiscal Year	Total Expenditures	Total Receipts	Percentage of Total Receipts Supplied by Custom Duties/ Excise Taxes
1870	$ 309.6	$ 411.2	74%
1880	267.6	333.5	92
1890	318.0	403.1	92
1900	520.9	567.2	91
1910	693.6	675.5	89
1915	746.1	683.4	79

SOURCE: *Historical Statistics*, pt. 2, pp. 1106, 1108, 1114.

of total receipts in 1860, were generating less than one-third of total receipts six years later.

Postwar spending shifted to a higher peacetime level, in part because of interest costs on the debt. In the late 1860s these costs averaged more than $135 million annually, well above total federal expenditures in any prewar year.[9] To meet this additional spending, excise taxes (primarily affecting alcohol and tobacco) were continued, but other war taxes, including the income tax, were allowed to expire. The combination of customs duties and excise taxes proved sufficient to support spending levels for the next fifty years, primarily because spending grew very slowly. From 1870 to 1915, spending increased by less than $450 million, with customs duties and excises generally keeping pace (see table 2.1). Even after the federal income tax was implemented, consumption taxes continued to supply three-fourths of total receipts.

Income Taxes: Stage One

The federal individual income tax received constitutional sanction in 1913.[10] It was then enacted as a relatively minor part of a tariff reform and reduction bill sponsored by the Wilson administration and implemented later that year. Its high exemption level ($4,000 for a married couple) required few individuals to pay any tax at all. Further, the maximum rate was set at only 7 percent, despite attempts by Progressives in the House and Senate to set much steeper marginal rates.[11] The first permanent income tax did not produce major revenues, nor did it redistribute income. It was simply a supplementary revenue source tied to tariff reduction.

World War I quickly altered the level and composition of budget receipts. For fiscal years 1911–15, total budget receipts were $3.5 billion. For fiscal years 1916–20, the total was over $17 billion, and even this increase was overwhelmed by the financing demands of the war. Peak wartime spending reached $18.5 billion in fiscal 1919, and the total federal debt grew by more than $23 billion over the course of the war.

The transition in tax policy during the war was accomplished through a series of revenue bills boosting individual and corporate tax revenues. The corporate tax rate was raised, and both a capital stock tax and an excess profits tax were imposed on corporations.[12] Personal exemptions for individual taxpayers were lowered, and marginal rates on income were raised. There were other tax initiatives, including higher excises and a new federal inheritance tax, but the corporate and individual tax levies had the greatest impact.

From 1916 to 1919, corporate and individual tax revenues rose from less than $345 million to almost $3.5 billion.[13] Individual income taxes, which had produced $68 million in 1915, generated almost $1.3 billion just four years later. Over that same period, the number of returns went from fewer than 340,000 to over 5.3 million. With the top marginal rate having been raised from 7 percent to 77 percent, there was a high degree of progressivity in rates and in actual liability.[14]

The transformation of the income tax from a minor to a major revenue source was not altogether divorced from redistributive notions or at least from considerations of ability to pay. Nevertheless, revenue demands were by far the dominant consideration. The federal government moved away from almost total dependence on consumption taxes not because of their regressivity but rather because they could not provide the very large infusions of revenue necessary to finance the war.

The shift from consumption to income taxes, then, was not greatly affected by normative theories or principles of taxation. The next important shift—from an income tax with a relatively narrow reach to a mass income tax system—was likewise the result of expediency. World War II, like World War I, generated very sharp and immediate spending increases, which necessitated, in turn, a far-reaching expansion of the tax system.

The period between the wars did not produce changes of comparable magnitude. It did provide, however, two radically different approaches to income taxation. The first was a forerunner of contemporary supply-side tax theories, stressing the negative economic and revenue effects of high tax rates. The second, which very gradually emerged during the New Deal, emphasized the redistributive objectives of income tax policy.

Andrew Mellon and Tax Policy Incentives. The 1920s was a period of sustained budget control in the United States, with spending held stable and the budget in surplus, usually by substantial amounts. In addition, four tax reduction bills were enacted, with Secretary of the Treasury Andrew Mellon playing the pivotal role in revising tax policy.

Mellon's views on taxation offered an intriguing blend of conservative ideology and pragmatism. According to Mellon, higher rates did not automatically produce higher revenues. Along with many of his contemporaries, Mellon was convinced that very high rates were counterproductive, encouraging evasion or channeling capital to tax-favored or nontaxable investments (such as tax-exempt bonds). This view had, in fact, been argued by Mellon's predecessor in the Wilson administration, and Woodrow Wilson himself had challenged the efficacy of high peacetime rates.[15] There was a widely shared belief that regardless of other considerations, a progressive rate structure along the lines of the World War I tax system would inevitably be undermined, with adverse effects on revenues.

For Mellon, however, "other considerations" reinforced the revenue argument. High tax rates, he believed, reduced individual incentive and struck at the heart of economic growth and productivity: "Any man of energy and initiative in this country can get what he wants out of life. But when initiative is crippled by legislation or by a tax system which denies him the right to receive a reasonable share of his earnings, then he will no longer exert himself and the country will be deprived of the energy on which its continued greatness depends."[16] Under Mellon's leadership, tax policy was redirected. For individuals, exemption levels were raised, earned income credits were instituted, and the top marginal rate was cut by some two-thirds below the World War I peak. The excess profits tax on corporations was repealed, but relatively high regular tax rates were continued, remaining above 10 percent even under the 1929 tax-cut bill. On balance, however, the corporate changes represented a massive tax cut for business, since the excess profits tax had produced considerably more revenue than the regular corporate tax during World War I (and would again in World War II).

Franklin Roosevelt and Wealth Taxes. The Depression did not immediately overturn the fiscal policy consensus of the 1920s. A 1932 tax bill substantially raised taxes. Its original version was designed by Mellon, and while Congress subsequently changed the details, there was no serious opposition to the view that taxes had to be raised to balance the budget. The Roosevelt administration initially followed this conventional path on budget and tax policy, but Roosevelt soon concluded that deficit spending would be unavoidable, given the state of the economy. Four years later, in his budget message to Congress, Roosevelt was less defensive about deficits: "The programs inaugurated during the last four years to combat the depression and to initiate many needed reforms have cost large sums of money, but the benefits obtained from them are far outweighing all their costs. We shall soon be reaping the full benefits of those programs and shall have at the same time a balanced budget that will also include provision for reduction of the public debt."[17] The president's initial hesitancy about fiscal policy carried over into tax policy. There was little administration involvement in fashioning the loophole-closing provisions of the Revenue Act of 1934. In fact, the administration objected to a number of proposals designed to eliminate or reduce favored tax treatment of corporations.

During 1935, however, President Roosevelt launched his famous attack against "an unjust concentration of wealth and economic power."[18] The direct and immediate result was passage that year of a "wealth tax." While provisions in the 1935 bill probably did not merit its hyperbolic description, the legislation did signal the beginning of increasingly contentious debates over tax policy and tax philosophy that were to continue for the rest of Roosevelt's peacetime presidency.

The 1935 tax bill included changes in both corporate and individual income taxes designed to shift tax burdens and reduce tax avoidance. The corporate tax revisions finally enacted were less far-reaching than those originally proposed by Roosevelt but did provide for increased, graduated rates and the highly controversial taxation of corporate dividends. The administration also succeeded in raising the top marginal rate for individuals (to 79 percent for incomes over $5,000,000) but was forced to accept increased estate and gift taxes instead of the new inheritance tax the president favored.

The Social Security Act of 1935 was not considered to be a profound shift in tax policy, although the long-term growth of payroll taxes has, in fact, amounted to one of the most important structural tax changes of the past half century. Further, increases in payroll taxes have undercut progressivity in individual tax liabilities. The Roosevelt administration was, by the late 1930s, perhaps the most committed of any presidential administration in the modern era to the principle of progressivity, but its policy legacy is much more ambiguous, largely because of social security.

In 1936 and 1937 Roosevelt stepped up his attacks on tax avoidance. Corporate income taxes were raised in 1936, in part through more stringent treatment of undistributed profits. There was very strenuous opposition from Republicans and their business allies, and the battle lines on tax policy sharpened as Roosevelt's program evolved. In 1937 special provisions governing personal holding companies were tightened as part of a general effort to close major loopholes. Highly publicized hearings before a special Joint Committee on Tax Evasion and Avoidance reinforced Roosevelt's case for reform, and Congress quickly enacted most of the changes Roosevelt proposed. The revenue impact of the 1937 tax bill was modest, but the legislation did express a symbolic commitment to a more progressive tax system. It was also the last occasion on which Congress would unequivocally support that commitment.

Tax legislation in 1938 and 1939 lowered and then eliminated the undistributed profits tax, one of Roosevelt's most important initiatives. Loss carryovers, which allowed firms to deduct current losses against future income, were restored to the tax code in 1939 after having been eliminated by the 1933 National Industrial Recovery Act. Congress also took the lead in fashioning new, complex, and reduced capital gains provisions for individuals in 1938 and for corporations in 1939. With the shift in initiative to Congress came a corresponding emphasis on reducing rather than redistributing tax burdens. Finally, much of the new revenue generated during the 1930s came from excise taxes. These had been periodically raised, primarily through congressional efforts.

The New Deal–inspired debates on tax policy during the 1930s highlighted questions of progressivity and equity. Roosevelt's indignation over tax avoidance by the wealthy struck a chord which has resonated ever since. Roosevelt's impact on substantive tax policy is another matter. The individual income tax, for example, remained limited in scope, despite repeated efforts to increase progressivity. In 1940 individual income taxes amounted to 1.3 percent of personal income, almost precisely the level ten years earlier.[19] On the corporate side, there was somewhat greater change. As a percentage of corporate new product, corporate income taxes rose from less than 2 percent in 1930 to 5.5 percent in 1940.[20] This increase resulted from higher rates, however, rather than from permanent changes in corporate tax policy. The most important tax policy initiative of the 1930s, then, was probably the social security payroll tax, although its long-term impact clearly was not anticipated by Roosevelt or Congress.

Income Taxes: Stage Two

Revenue demands during World War II were enormous and unprecedented. Budget receipts for the fiscal 1941–46 period topped $175 billion, dwarfing those of World War I and exceeding the total for all taxes collected during the preceding century and a half. Despite the rapid growth in revenues, the Roosevelt administration failed in its effort to finance the bulk of wartime expenditures through taxation. Budget outlays during World War II were more than double receipts, and the federal debt increased by almost $200 billion from fiscal years 1941 through 1946.

The principal sources of World War II revenues were the individual and corporate income taxes. By 1945 these taxes were generating more than three-fourths of total receipts, roughly double their combined share five years earlier. The corporate tax increases resulted from higher rates (40 percent being the top rate between 1942 and 1945), combined with a reinstated excess profits tax and a capital stock tax. Continuing disagreements over the measurement of excess profits necessitated a series of statutory adjustments, but corporate tax policy did not give rise to any unusual controversies, nor was the corporate tax system radically altered from its World War I basis.

Individual income tax policy, by comparison, changed profoundly and permanently during the war. The tax on individual incomes became, for the first time, a mass tax. Tax withholding was instituted, and steep marginal rates were applied to a significant portion of the taxpaying public. By the war's end, there was a relatively high degree of progressivity in the tax system. There was also a growing complexity, as Congress responded to taxpayer pressures for relief.

The expansion of the individual income tax was dramatic. Before the war, only about 10 percent of the labor force filed returns and roughly half of those were nontaxable. By 1945 taxable returns were being filed by nearly three-fourths of the labor force. The percentage of personal income paid in individual income taxes rose from less than 1.5 percent to approximately 11 percent.[21] From 1940 to 1944, individual income tax revenues grew from less than $900 million to almost $20 billion.

The World War II individual income tax revisions were quite different, in terms of public impact, from those enacted during World War I. For the latter, filing requirements were less stringent, and personal exemptions and the bottom income bracket were generally well above those imposed during World War II. As a result, only about 15 percent of the working population paid taxes during World War I. Moreover, while the World War I top marginal rate of 77 percent in 1919 was close to the

Table 2.2. World War II Individual Income Tax Changes

	Income Year			
	1940	1941	1942–43	1944–45
Personal Exemptions (Married Couples)	$ 2,000	$ 1,500	$ 1,200	$ 1,000
Requirement for Filing (Gross Income, Married Couple)	$ 2,000	$ 1,500	$ 1,200	$ 500[a]
Tax Rates (Taxable Income)				
First Bracket (up to) Rate	$ 4,000 4.4%[b]	$ 2,000 10%[b]	$ 2,000 19%[b]	$ 2,000 23%
Top Bracket (over) Rate	$ 5,000,000 81.1%	$ 5,000,000 81%	$ 200,000 88%	$ 200,000[c] 94%

SOURCE: *Historical Statistics*, pt. 2, pp. 1093, 1095.
[a] For each spouse.
[b] Earned income credit equal to 10 percent of earned net income allowed as a deduction.
[c] Subject to maximum effective rate of 90 percent.

1944–45 peak of 94 percent, it applied only to incomes above $1 million. The corresponding top bracket by the end of World War II applied to taxable income over $200,000, with a maximum effective rate of 90 percent. As shown in table 2.2, a series of adjustments during World War II resulted in positive tax liabilities for all but the very lowest income groups, while also applying very steep, progressive rates to a greatly expanded segment of the taxpaying public. Roosevelt never succeeded in establishing a $25,000 ceiling on after-tax income, as he advocated and the Treasury formally proposed in 1942, but he did manage to alter radically the progressivity of effective tax rates. Indeed, 1944 and 1945 stand out as "the most progressive tax years in U.S. history" according to John Witte.[22]

Roosevelt's success on other tax policy issues was more limited. Permanent tax withholding was finally enacted in 1943, although Congress forced the administration to accept a onetime forgiveness of past tax liabilities as part of the Current Tax Payment Act. Roosevelt's tax increase proposals later that year were largely ignored, and Congress passed what Roosevelt attacked as a tax relief bill over the president's veto in 1944. That the president's leverage was so weak, despite the clear-cut anti-inflation and war financing justifications for broad tax increases, suggests a developing sensitivity in Congress to the political pitfalls of a mass tax system.

The last significant accomplishment of the war years was a 1944 administration-sponsored bill which simplified filing and strengthened withholding. There was little controversy over the introduction of standard deductions and tax tables. Congress also agreed to graduated withholding, which helped to raise the withheld portion of individual income tax collections over the 50 percent mark by the end of the war.[23] The administrative complexities of a mass tax system—the number of returns filed rose from less than 15 million to almost 50 million in just five years— were reasonably well resolved. What remained were the political complexities, which have, of course, persisted.

The Stable Era of Tax Politics

The end of World War II was followed by a routine tax reduction. The Truman administration sponsored, and Congress marginally altered, reductions in individual and corporate tax rates, along with repeal of the wartime excess profits tax. The individual income tax reductions, however, were quite limited. Personal exemptions and the top and bottom taxable income brackets for individuals were unchanged, while marginal rates for these brackets were reduced only from 23 to 19 percent and from 94 to 86.45 percent, respectively. While outlays dropped precipitously— from almost $93 billion in fiscal 1945 to less than $30 billion three years later—budget receipts declined by less than 10 percent over the same period. By fiscal 1948 there was an $11.8 billion surplus, the largest surplus ever registered.

The Truman Administration

President Truman's initial support for tax cuts gave way to concerns about inflation and debt reduction. The Republican-controlled Congress that convened in 1947 acted quickly to pass large, across-the-board reductions in income taxes. The post–World War I arguments about incentives and economic growth were resurrected, but there was an additional objective for Republicans this time. The New Deal domestic policy agenda was vulnerable to spending retrenchments, and conservatives viewed tax reduction as the politically popular means to achieve that retrenchment. The first Republican-sponsored tax-cut bill passed the House and Senate and was sent to Truman on June 3, 1947. He vetoed it, with the veto barely sustained in the House. Congressional Republican leaders responded by passing a similar bill, with an effective date of January 1, 1948. Truman again vetoed, but this time the House overrode, and only a two-vote margin in the Senate sustained the president's veto.

Truman's rejection of what he criticized as the "wrong kind of tax reduction, at the wrong time"[24] emphasized economic policy. With the economy booming, there were legitimate grounds for fearing inflation. There was also the usual postwar belief that wartime debt should be reduced. For Truman, an additional objection to the Republican-sponsored tax plan was its distribution of tax reductions among income classes. Liberal Democrats in the House and Senate had attacked the initial Republican proposal as grossly unfair to lower-income groups. They were able to lessen the regressivity of cuts by the time that final action was taken by Congress, but Truman still viewed the apportionment of relief as inequitable.

With the 1948 elections drawing closer, Truman's narrow margin of veto support in Congress disappeared. This time, congressional Republicans fashioned a bill designed to put together the widest possible coalition. The personal exemption was raised, extra exemptions for the blind and the elderly were added, and income splitting on joint returns was introduced. Of particular importance, the pronounced bias in favor of upper-income groups contained in the 1947 tax bills was greatly reduced. Truman's proposal for individual tax credits of $40 that "would be particularly helpful to those in the low-income group" and would be financed by a $3.2 billion increase in corporate taxes made no progress in Congress.[25] When he vetoed a politically attractive alternative constructed by congressional leaders of both parties, the veto was overriden.

By 1949 control of Congress was back in Democratic hands, and the president attempted to pass a tax increase. He was unsuccessful. An economic recession played a role in congressional rejection, but there was the additional problem of domestic spending programs that would benefit from additional revenues. Truman's budget plans included defense increases (and, in fact, defense spending increased by over $4 billion in fiscal 1949 after three successive years of decline), but there were domestic initiates at stake also. The muted enthusiasm for the latter, together with the recession and the general congressional reluctance to reopen tax policy for another round of changes, forestalled action on major changes in tax law.

The period between World War II and the Korean War produced tax reduction but certainly nothing on a scale comparable to the post–World War I decade. Most important, the mass tax system put into place during the early 1940s was left intact. Total receipts grew less rapidly than the economy during the late 1940s, dropping from 21.3 percent of GNP in 1945 to 14.8 percent in 1950, but this percentage was still more than double the prewar level.

By the beginning of the Korean War, the Truman administration and Congress had reached a standoff of sorts. Truman had, on the whole, successfully resisted major tax cuts. Congress had prevailed against administration efforts to raise taxes in 1949, and by mid-year the president had dropped his attempt to offset the 1948 reductions. Six months after the outbreak of war in Korea, taxes were raised, but subsequent administration-sponsored increases were rejected by Congress. The result was to restore relative tax levels close to those during World War II (see table 2.3). In fiscal 1952, combined individual and corporate income taxes were 14.4 percent of GNP, their highest level since fiscal 1945.

The Eisenhower Administration

Dwight D. Eisenhower came into office pledged to cut spending, balance the budget, and reduce taxes. This initial ordering of priorities shaped budget policy throughout his tenure. The comprehensive revision of the tax code in 1954, which Eisenhower helped to engineer, had only a limited impact on total revenues. Eisenhower opposed a tax reduction bill in 1955, and the 1956 Republican platform reiterated his belief that "further reductions in taxes" were contingent on "continual balancing of the budget" and "gradual reduction of the national debt."[26] Four years later, in his fiscal 1961 budget message, Eisenhower called for the estimated $4.2 billion surplus to be used for debt reduction, leaving to his successor and Congress "the choice they should rightly have in deciding between reductions in the public debt and lightening of the tax burden, or both."[27]

Eisenhower did manage to achieve balanced budgets three times during his presidency (fiscal years 1956, 1957, and 1960). Perhaps the most remarkable feature of Eisenhower's post-Korea budgets, however, was the substantial growth in nondefense outlays and—reflecting his

Table 2.3. Budget Receipts and Gross National Product, Fiscal Years 1945-55

| Fiscal Year | Receipts as a Percentage of GNP | | |
	Individual Income Taxes	Corporate Income Taxes	Total All Receipts
1945	8.6	7.5	21.3
1946	7.6	5.6	18.5
1947	8.0	3.9	17.2
1948	7.8	3.9	16.8
1949	5.9	4.2	14.9
1950	5.9	3.9	14.8
1951	6.9	4.5	16.4
1952	8.2	6.2	19.3
1953	8.2	5.8	19.0
1954	8.0	5.7	18.9
1955	7.4	4.6	16.9

SOURCE: *Historical Tables, Budget of the United States Government, Fiscal Year 1990*, p. 28.

commitment to a balanced budget—the correspondingly high level of peacetime tax receipts. Budget receipts were 18.6 percent of GNP in fiscal 1960, compared to less than 15 percent ten years earlier. More important, individual income taxes had risen from 7.7 percent of personal income to 10.4 percent over this same period, roughly double the proportional increases registered during the 1960s and 1970s.[28]

The 1954 overhaul of the Internal Revenue Code illustrated Eisenhower's cautious approach to tax policy. The federal income tax code was entirely rewritten, with numerous technical and policy changes surviving a lengthy consultation process between the executive branch and Congress. Among the revisions were several controversial tax breaks, including dividend exclusions and credits for individuals and accelerated depreciation allowances for corporations, but most tax reduction provisions generated little or no controversy. In addition, the net revenue loss for the entire 1954 tax bill was estimated at only $1.4 billion for fiscal 1955.[29]

Moreover, the 1954 act did not change personal exemption allowances at all, despite Democratic efforts to increase them. Several Senate Democrats introduced proposals to raise the exemption to $800 in 1954 and to $1,000 thereafter. When House Democrats attempted to raise the exemption by $100, Eisenhower addressed the nation, declaring it "wrong" to excuse millions of taxpayers from all tax liabilities. "Every real American," declared Eisenhower, "is proud to carry his share of the burden."[30]

Opposition to increased exemption levels was matched by resistance to lower brackets and reduced rates. The lowest marginal rate was slightly reduced, from 22.2 to 20 percent, and the top rate cut from 92 to 91 percent, while the income brackets against which these applied were unchanged. There was no attempt during Eisenhower's tenure to follow the Mellon initiatives of the 1920s. When Sam Rayburn, who was then minority leader for the Democrats, attacked Eisenhower's 1954 tax bill as a return to the "trickle down" Republican philosophy of taxation,[31] he was ignoring some important distinctions. Eisenhower was leaving in place not only high marginal rates but also overall revenue levels that could support growing domestic spending.

The Eisenhower years produced other tax bills, but these were, for the most part, relatively minor adjustments in corporate and excise taxes. In 1958 the schedule for increases in the social security tax was revised. A ¼ percentage point increase was enacted for 1959. Additional ½ percentage point increases were scheduled for 1960, 1963, 1966, and 1969. An increase in the gasoline tax was passed the following year to rescue the Highway Trust Fund from insolvency.

The Eisenhower tax program, in sum, was governed by spending requirements. In 1959 the president explained that "under our graduated income tax system, with present rates, budget receipts should grow even faster than national income."[32] While it would be necessary to reduce and adjust taxes "in future years to help maintain and strengthen the incentives for continued economic growth," it was "essential" to postpone these reductions—and for the sixth consecutive year, to forgo promised corporate and excise tax cuts—until the budget was balanced.

Under Eisenhower, peacetime spending and receipts grew more rapidly than the economy. Individual income taxes increased sharply in relation to personal income. There was, in addition, relative stability in the tax base. Adjusted gross income was 79.2 percent of personal income in 1950. By 1960 it was 78.9 percent. Finally, despite the wide spread in marginal tax rates, there was a nearly flat tax for most of the population by the end of Eisenhower's term (see table 2.4). The balance between the tax base and marginal tax rates was not significantly changed during the Eisenhower presidency.

Table 2.4. Distribution of Marginal Tax Rates, Individual Income Tax Returns, 1961

Marginal Tax Rates	Percentage of Taxable Returns
20% - 22%	87.80
23% - 31%	10.04
32% - 72%	2.15
73% - 91%	0.01
Total	100.00

SOURCE: Congressional Budget Office, *Revising the Individual Income Tax* (Washington, D.C., 1983), p. 12.

The Kennedy-Johnson Transition

For both Truman and Eisenhower, the primary objective of tax policy was to provide revenue sufficient to balance the budget. In order to avoid deficits, it was necessary to maintain relatively high revenue levels, and this prevented major changes in tax policy. Individual tax rates changed very little under Truman and changed not at all from 1954 to 1964. Corporate tax rates were unchanged from 1951 to 1964. Even many wartime excises, which had been scheduled for postwar repeal, were repeatedly extended.

The Kennedy-Johnson era removed some of the stability from tax policy, although the particular contributions of the two administrations were really quite different. The Kennedy tax program focused on economic growth and incentives, arguing that short-term deficits could be disregarded. The Johnson tax increase was a return to the Truman and Eisenhower emphasis on deficit control (and inflation control), but without their corresponding insistence on spending restraint. Combining elements of the two, as was done during the 1970s, meant that tax cuts and spending increases could be pursued simultaneously and under the protective guise of economic stimulus.

The Kennedy Tax Cut. The Revenue Act of 1964 was by far the largest tax cut to be enacted after World War II, a distinction which it retained for another decade. What set the 1964 tax bill apart was not only its magnitude but also its justification and context. Two years after taking office, President Kennedy signaled a clear and significant departure from his predecessor's revenue philosophy: "This issue must be faced squarely. Our present choice is not between a tax cut and a balanced budget . . . [but] rather, is between chronic deficits arising out of a slow rate of economic growth, and temporary deficits stemming from a tax program designed to promote a fuller use of our resources and more rapid economic growth."[33]

Lyndon Johnson signed the Revenue Act of 1964, but John Kennedy was responsible for it. Shortly after taking office, Kennedy had sponsored investment tax credits and a variety of limited changes in tax law designed to provide immediate economic stimulus. As this legislative package moved slowly through Congress, a major reform bill was developed to address long-term growth. By mid-1962 Kennedy pledged action on basic, permanent tax reductions for individuals. When his proposals were transmitted to Congress the following January, the scope of this commitment became clear. Kennedy was pushing very large and broad-based cuts, despite an estimated deficit of nearly $20 billion for fiscal years 1963–64.[34] His proposed cuts were substantial for all income groups, with a lower and narrower set of marginal rate brackets ranging from 14 to 65 percent replacing the 20–91 percent rates then in effect. Even for high-income groups, the structural tax law increases Kennedy recommended were more than offset by the marginal rate cuts he proposed.

The Kennedy tax program explicitly acknowledged "the restraining effects of the tax system on the economy." Its basic premise was that economic growth would remain sluggish unless "the checkrein of taxes on private spending and productive incentive [is] loosened."[35] In an argument that would be resurrected twenty years later, Kennedy declared that the initial revenue losses from reductions needed to be balanced against the higher long-term yield resulting from economic expansion. Lower rates would eventually produce greater revenues than higher rates, because they would increase the incentive basis of economic growth.

It took Congress approximately one year to clear the tax cut, and during that period changes were made in both the marginal rates and the structural proposals that Kennedy had requested. Revisions of the latter were quite numerous, and their overall impact was to reduce greatly the revenue gains from structural reforms. The administration had estimated well over $3 billion in additional revenues from broadening the tax base, through, for example, limiting itemized deductions and repealing or reducing existing exclusions, deductions, and credits. Congress rejected

Table 2.5. Distribution of Tax Reductions under the Revenue Act of 1964

Adjusted Gross Income Class	Change as Percentage of Existing Liability		
	Tax Rate Changes	Tax Structure Revisions	Total Reduction
<$3,000	- 27.6	-11.4	- 39.0
$ 3,000 - $ 5,000	- 25.3	- 1.6	- 26.9
$ 5,000 - $10,000	- 21.3	+ 0.7	- 20.6
$10,000 - $20,000	- 18.0	+ 1.0	- 17.0
$20,000 - $50,000	- 17.0	+ 1.6	- 15.5
≥$50,000	- 17.0	+ 3.8	- 13.2
Total	- 20.0	+ 0.6	- 19.4

SOURCE: *Congressional Record* 110 (Feb. 25, 1964): 3570.

many of these outright and lessened the impact of most others. The result was to limit the estimated revenue gains from structural revisions to less than $300 million.[36]

The marginal rate reduction at the top end of the income scale was also slightly less after Congress finished, with the effective rate for 1965 being 70 percent instead of 65 percent and an interim level of 77 percent set for 1964. A two-stage reduction was also applied to other income groups, and although Congress accepted the 14 percent bottom rate, it increased slightly the recommended marginal rates for the more than two dozen intermediate brackets. Nevertheless, the income tax rate changes that survived were substantial, representing an overall reduction in tax liabilities for individuals of almost 20 percent. The distribution of reductions among groups was progressive, particularly with the added effect of the new minimum standard deduction for low-income taxpayers (see table 2.5). But for the large majority of taxpayers in the $5,000–$50,000 range—who accounted for approximately 60 percent of all taxable returns and 80 percent of tax liabilities under existing law—the cuts were roughly proportional.

Progressivity in the 1964 tax law changes was limited and of secondary importance. Nothing in the rhetoric or substance of the Kennedy proposals resembled Roosevelt's efforts at redistribution, and very little was heard about equity during congressional consideration. Kennedy's first accomplishment was to move tax policy into a fiscal policy framework in which economic growth was the overriding objective. His second was to establish a parallel primacy for economic growth over a balanced budget.[37]

The Kennedy tax cut has received credit from many analysts for the extraordinary economic expansion that occurred during the mid-1960s. There are, of course, dissenters who maintain that an equally plausible case can be made for other factors, especially monetary policy, in fueling and sustaining economic growth for that period.[38] It is obviously difficult to disentangle the relative contributions of tax cuts, monetary policy, or other economic stimuli, but Kennedy did establish a politically relevant precedent for large, across-the-board tax cuts on grounds of economic growth. It was this precedent that the Reagan administration successfully seized upon two decades later.

It is also important to recognize some budget policy distinctions between the Kennedy and Reagan tax cuts. The first and sharpest is that deficit estimates at the time of the Kennedy proposals proved to be much higher than actual deficits, while the Reagan deficit projections were much too optimistic. The actual 1963 and 1964 deficits, for example, totaled slightly over $10 billion, or about half the estimate in the fiscal 1964 budget. By fiscal 1965, the deficit had dropped to less than $1.5 billion, or about 0.2 percent of GNP. By comparison, the fiscal 1982–84 deficits averaged over 5 percent of GNP, although Reagan's fiscal 1982 budget revisions had projected a surplus by fiscal 1984.[39]

The early 1960s also produced limited spending growth. As a result, revenues generally kept pace with outlays, despite the tax cut (see table 2.6). It was not until fiscal 1966, when both defense and domestic spending began to increase rapidly, that outlay growth rates began to outstrip revenue growth. The receipt side of the budget grew less rapidly than the economy between fiscal years 1961 and 1966; so did spending.

Johnson's Tax Program. The economic growth and political euphoria that followed the 1964 tax cut soon gave way to deficit and inflation control pressures. Early in 1966 President Johnson acknowledged that additional revenues would be needed to finance rapidly escalating defense and domestic spending, but he was not prepared to call for a tax increase in an election year, recommending instead that scheduled excise tax cuts be delayed and tax collections speeded up. Congress quickly cleared the Tax Adjustment Act of 1966 that, among other provisions, required graduated withholding for individuals and accelerated corporate tax pay-

Table 2.6. Budget Totals, Fiscal Years 1961-66 (in billions of dollars)

Fiscal Year	Receipts		Outlays		Deficit	
	Total	Percentage of GNP	Total	Percentage of GNP	Total	Percentage of GNP
1961	$ 94.4	18.2%	$ 97.7	18.9%	- $ 3.3	- 0.6%
1962	99.7	17.9	106.8	19.2	- 7.1	- 1.3
1963	106.6	18.1	111.3	18.9	- 4.8	- 0.8
1964	112.6	17.9	118.5	18.8	- 5.9	- 0.9
1965	116.8	17.4	118.2	17.6	- 1.4	- 0.2
1966	130.8	17.7	134.5	18.2	- 3.7	- 0.5

SOURCE: *Historical Tables, Budget of the United States Government, Fiscal Year 1990*, p. 19.

ment schedules. Later in the year, Johnson recommended and Congress enacted a suspension of corporate investment tax credits, but the combined revenue increases from the two tax bills could not keep pace with the most rapid spending growth since the Korean War.

The fiscal 1966 budget was a watershed in the Johnson presidency, and not just because of Vietnam. Johnson's first budget, which went to Congress at the beginning of the 1964 presidential election year, stressed the need to control federal expenditures. In what remains the most impressive display of spending restraint of the past quarter century, outlays in fiscal 1965 were actually lower than in fiscal 1964.

By 1965, however, Johnson was ready "to grasp the opportunities of the Great Society." This meant significant increases in domestic spending. It also meant that unless defense spending dropped, Johnson could not fulfill his promise that "the ratio of federal spending to our total output will continue to decline."[40] In fiscal 1966 spending increased by almost 14 percent, and the spending-GNP ratio went up for the first time in four years. Of the $16.3 billion increase over fiscal 1964, only $7.5 billion was accounted for by defense. The remainder was for domestic programs.

The budget policy choices available to Johnson were, for him, impractical or unpalatable. Vietnam clearly precluded defense spending reductions, and the Great Society programs required more, not less, domestic spending. This left tax increases as the only way to control deficits and dampen inflationary pressures. In January 1967 Johnson finally conceded that an increase was unavoidable and recommended to Congress a 6 percent surcharge on individual and corporate tax liabilities. He did not submit a detailed request until August, however, and by that time congressional resolve to restrain domestic spending had hardened. The resulting stalemate left the tax surcharge proposal stalled in the Ways and Means Committee.

Congress did not approve the surcharge until late the following June, after a complicated and bitter fight over coupling the tax increase to spending cuts. The surcharge and a spending cutback were added as amendments on the Senate floor to a minor House-passed excise tax extension. The ensuing conference dragged on for weeks, as the administration continued to resist domestic spending cuts. During a May 3 news conference, Johnson publicly attacked Congress, declaring that "we are courting danger by this continual procrastination" and advising members not to "hold up the tax bill until you can blackmail someone into getting your own personal viewpoint over on [spending] reductions."[41] On May 20 Johnson finally conceded, accepting the $6 billion in fiscal 1969 spending cuts attached to the tax surcharge bill, and congressional action was completed in June.

The spending ceiling included in the Revenue and Expenditure Control Act of 1968 was only partially effective. Actual spending for fiscal 1969 fell about halfway between the statutory ceiling and the administration's original budget estimates. The tax surcharge, however, boosted individual and corporate income tax receipts sharply. Receipts for fiscal 1969 were 20.1 percent of GNP, the highest level since World War II, and the result was the first balanced budget in a decade.

The difficulty that Johnson had in securing passage of a tax increase which enjoyed widespread business and labor support, along with the endorsement of most economic analysts, was primarily caused by the rapid expansion of Great Society spending. Ways and Means chairman Wilbur D. Mills, for example, repeatedly tied his support for tax increases to expenditure control. According to Mills, there was first the "need, even intensified as I see it" for domestic spending cuts. John W. Byrnes, the ranking minority member on Ways and Means, echoed Mills, stating it was "impossible" to justify to the public "why the Administration was seeking a tax increase on one hand and expanding Great Society spending on the other."[42]

Spending was driving tax policy under Johnson, and domestic programs were a major part of the spending expansion. From fiscal 1965 to fiscal 1968, defense spending rose from 7.7 percent of GNP to 9.6 percent. Over that same fiscal 1965–68 period, human resources outlays increased from 5.4 percent of GNP to 7.0 percent. During the Korean War, defense spending had jumped from 32 percent to 70 percent of total spending; during Johnson's Vietnam tenure, the defense budget share went from about 43 percent to 46 percent. The Johnson presidency had established a domestic program base which over the next decade would require high revenue levels, regardless of postwar defense cuts.

The Kennedy-Johnson era also produced an important change in tax burdens which biased future policy toward deficits. Almost 90 percent of all taxpayers were clustered around the 20 percent marginal bracket in 1961. By 1969 almost two-thirds of all taxpayers were in higher brackets.[43] Individual income taxes in 1969 were 12.1 percent of personal income, by far the highest level yet encountered and almost 30 percent above the level just four years earlier. Indeed, combined federal and state and local income taxes in 1969 reached a peak in relation to personal income which would not be surpassed for another decade.[44] What had occurred, despite the 1964 tax act, was an increase in average tax rates for individuals, and this rate increase was paralleled by growth in social security taxes and in state and local income taxes.

Tax Policy in Disarray

During the Nixon, Ford, and Carter administrations, several comprehensive tax bills were enacted, along with a number of more limited pieces of tax legislation. Only one of the major bills, the Tax Reform Act of 1969, projected a net revenue gain at the time of passage. The 1975, 1976, and 1978 tax bills all reduced revenues well below existing law, with the reduction in individual tax liabilities outweighing corporate tax cuts. Additional, temporary cuts were adopted in 1971, 1975, and 1977.

Tax policy during the period was confused and confusing. After a series of tax "reform" bills, and a significant upsurge in liberal congressional strength, the tax base had declined, and marginal rates for many taxpayers had increased. Even for low-income taxpayers, reduced income tax liabilities were undercut by steeper payroll taxes. Tax expenditures—the array of exclusions, deductions, and credits that was the ostensible target of tax reformers—grew in numbers, complexity, and revenue impact.

Given the tumultuous politics of the 1970s, it may not be surprising that tax policy was erratic, especially in view of the declining influence of the White House over the substance and scheduling of tax legislation. By 1975 Congress had assumed much of the initiative on tax bills, and neither Gerald Ford nor Jimmy Carter was able to withstand congressional pressure for tax reductions. Since the Ways and Means Committee also had lost its unchallenged dominance in the House, much of the discipline in tax politics was gone. Thus, there were frantic attempts to cut taxes while spending growth accelerated and to improve equity while tax expenditures proliferated. Simply looking at individual income taxes, it appears that both the revenue productivity and the fairness of the tax code deteriorated during the 1970s. When social security taxes are added in, the decline in fairness is even more marked. The Congressional Budget Office estimates, for example, that if 1967 tax law had simply been kept in place and adjusted for inflation during the 1970s, low-income taxpayers would have paid considerably less and high-income taxpayers considerably more.[45]

The Nixon Presidency

Before leaving office, President Johnson proposed several tax hikes, including extension of the tax surcharge on individuals and corporations and higher social security taxes. In his fiscal 1970 budget message, Johnson also revived Kennedy's proposal for discretionary presidential authority to raise or lower tax rates. Richard Nixon dropped this request but did endorse the tax increases, which he and Johnson agreed were necessary to avoid deficits and to control inflation. Congress finally cleared the surtax extension and some minor revisions in tax collection requirements on August 4, 1969.

Within Congress, a parallel move was underway to effect wholesale changes in tax policy. This effort grew out of several Treasury Department studies that showed growing inequities in the tax code. Before Nixon took office and before the release of his department's formal proposal, retiring Treasury Secretary Joseph W. Barr warned of a "taxpayer's revolt" as the public became aware of tax avoidance by the wealthy. The genesis of the 1969 Tax Reform Act was very different from that of the Kennedy tax bills. Instead of economic growth, the issue was fairness, and by mid-1969 the Ways and Means Committee, under Wilbur Mills's direction, had reported out a surprisingly stiff bill which eliminated or reduced a variety of tax preferences.

The Ways and Means bill was endorsed by the House but watered down considerably by the Senate, which also added significant revenue loss provisions. Under threat of a presidential veto, the conference committee then dropped many of the Senate amendments. The final bill, while limiting the structural reforms approved by the House, successfully reconciled two different objectives. Its net effect was to increase individual and corporate tax revenues through, for example, repealing the investment credit, imposing a minimum tax on preference income, and raising capital gains levies. At the same time, higher exemptions and standard deductions reduced income tax liabilities for individuals in lower- and middle-income groups.

By 1970, as a result of these reforms, the tax base was almost identical to what it had been ten or twenty years earlier. Adjusted gross income was 79.2 percent of personal income in 1950 and 78.8 percent in 1970. In 1960 individual income taxes accounted for 10.4 percent of personal income, compared to 11 percent in 1970.[46] In 1967, the first year for which estimates are available, there were fifty tax expenditures whose cumulative revenue loss amounted to 23.8 percent of budget receipts.[47] From 1969 to 1971 this percentage rose by only 1 percentage point.

Not reflected in the revenue estimates for the Tax Reduction Act of 1969, however, was the tax cost of the 15 percent increase in basic social security benefits added to the bill by Congress. The first year's estimate for this provision was over $4 billion, which wiped out much of the revenue gain from structural reforms, but the initial increase was financed out of surplus balances in the social security trust fund, thereby postponing payroll tax increases until the following year.

Leaving the social security spending increases out of the 1969 tax act revenue calculations was technically correct and politically attractive. It was also misleading, in terms of budget policy impact and progressivity. More important, the 1969 revision was just the beginning of a series of major social security increases, on both the spending and revenue sides, that would lead to even sharper contradictions between income tax and payroll tax policies.

President Nixon signed the Tax Reform Act of 1969 on December 30, calling it "an unbalanced bill that is both good and bad. The tax reforms, on the whole, are good; the effect on the budget and on the cost of living is bad."[48] Nixon's less than ringing endorsement reflected his reservations about budgetary impact and inflation, rather than opposition to structural reforms. In January, Nixon's fiscal 1971 budget message contained several recommendations to boost revenues, including social security tax increases, excise tax extensions, and user charges for special government services. He had little success in Congress. (An excise tax extension which Congress finally approved also weakened substantially the minimum tax requirements enacted the previous year.)

The basic thrust of Nixon's tax program was continued in his initial budget for fiscal 1972, but by then budgetary and economic conditions were deteriorating. Revenue projections for fiscal years 1970–71 fell almost $20 billion below projections, and the budget moved from a small surplus in fiscal 1969 to a $23 billion deficit two years later. With the economy weakening, Nixon announced on August 15, 1971, a comprehensive economic recovery program, which included individual and corporate tax cuts. On December 9 Congress cleared the Revenue Act of 1971, which reduced tax liabilities by an estimated $25.9 billion over a three-year period. The mix between individual and business tax cuts was shifted slightly by Congress, but the major provisions conformed to Nixon's recommendations: higher personal exemptions and standard deductions for individuals; reinstatement of investment tax credits, along with a modified depreciation schedule (asset depreciation range, or ADR); and tax incentives for export companies.

There were no major tax bills from 1972 to 1974, and two of the dominant figures in tax policy, Richard Nixon and Wilbur Mills, came to the end of their political careers. The battle for spending control that Nixon launched in 1972 was lost, despite the new budgetary process that Congress instituted in 1974. Outlay growth had averaged 6.6 percent for fiscal 1969–73. Over the next two years, it averaged 16.5 percent. Social security benefits were raised by 30 percent in 1971–72, and the program was then indexed to the cost of living. In 1973 Nixon's proposals to curb tax shelters and broaden the tax base were disregarded by Congress. The following year, Congress broadened the tax-free treatment of pension plans and retirement savings, which had an enormous negative effect on long-term revenues.

The Ford Presidency

Gerald Ford had, at best, mixed success on budget policy during his tenure, and the results on tax policy were even less positive. Two months after he replaced Richard Nixon, Ford sent to Congress a 5 percent income tax surcharge proposal. Ford was faced with a growing deficit, a weakening economy, and mounting inflation. His thirty-two-point economic program highlighted the surtax, along with business tax cuts and tax relief for low- and middle-income taxpayers. None of Ford's proposals was acted upon by Congress.

In 1975 Ford recommended a onetime $16 billion tax reduction to stimulate the economy. The House boosted this reduction to almost $20 billion, and the Senate raised the total cut to over $30 billion. Even after a conference committee scaled down the Senate version to $22.8 billion, the bill was very different from the Ford proposal. It contained almost $2 billion in countercyclical spending, including bonus payments to social security recipients, changed Ford's tax rebate plan, and offset part of the revenue loss with a $2 billion curtailment of oil and gas depletion allowances. Instead of the straightforward tax cut that Ford had proposed and the Ways and Means Committee had accepted, floor action in first the House and then the Senate produced a much more complicated and controversial measure.

Ford won a symbolic victory in December, vetoing the tax cut's extension and then insisting it be linked to spending cuts. Congress could not override the veto and finally agreed to include language pledging fiscal 1977 spending cuts, although the reservations it attached were quite broad. Spending for fiscal 1977 was above Ford's $395 billion ceiling but probably lower than it would have been without the tax cut and spending cut compromise.

The tax-cut extension, however, was essentially a prelude to the Tax Reform Act of 1976. The House had passed its bill in December 1975, and the Senate Finance Committee proceeded to remove or to limit much of the reform it contained. President Ford's tax reform proposals had fared poorly in the House. By the time Senate action was completed, the Ford program had disappeared, including even its restrictions on investment expenses that had been endorsed by Senate liberals. Ford's comprehensive tax program, presented to Congress in July 1975, and his 1977 Blueprints for Basic Tax Reform contributed a number of tax law revisions that would be adopted after he left office. During his presidency, neither had an impact.

The bill reported by the Finance Committee ran to 1,536 pages, and floor action, which did force the committee to drop some of its more imaginative tax breaks, added another several hundred pages. There were more than 250 House-Senate differences to be resolved in conference, and while some especially costly Senate provisions were deleted, the long-term revenue losses resulting from corporate and individual tax cuts were substantial. The 1977 revenue loss, estimated at nearly $16 billion, was more than double that anticipated in the original House bill.

The Carter Presidency

Presidential direction of tax policy did not improve under Jimmy Carter. Starting with a bungled effort to provide immediate tax rebates, Carter's imprint on the 1977 Tax Reduction and Simplification Act was faint. An economic stimulus plan was cleared by Congress on May 16,

1977, but its major provisions were quite different from the initial Carter package.

The most important tax policy bill during the Carter years was the Revenue Act of 1978. In this case, the difference between the president's program and congressional action was profound. Carter announced his tax program on January 21, 1978. Its major features were 2 percentage point reductions in all tax brackets (dropping the 14–70 percent range to 12–68 percent), expanded tax credits to replace existing exemptions and credits, and permanent extension of the investment tax credit for corporations. On both individual and corporate tax reductions, Carter proposed partial offsets through repealing or limiting tax preferences. An estimated $23.5 billion in personal tax cuts, for example, was linked to more than $8 billion in new revenues from a long list of reforms affecting the tax treatment of capital gains, itemized deductions for certain state and local taxes, and tax preferences on fringe benefits. One of his most controversial proposals was for strict limits on the deductibility of business expenses for meals, entertainment, and travel.

The Carter tax reforms quickly encountered stiff resistance in Ways and Means, where sentiment was strong, as it was in the rest of Congress, for tax cuts rather than tax reform. In late April the committee postponed its markup in what proved to be a futile effort to put together a compromise package with the White House.

The agreement that finally emerged in July excluded Carter. Republicans and moderate Democrats on Ways and Means agreed to a plan which included reducing, not tightening, capital gains taxes and shifting tax reductions to a wider spectrum of taxpayers. This basic redirection of tax policy carried through four months of battles in the House and Senate. The conference report, which was approved by both chambers on October 15, raised the capital gains exclusion from 50 percent to 60 percent while providing for new alternative minimum tax treatment of capital gains. The resulting $2.2 billion estimated capital gains tax cut thus distributed 80 percent of its benefits to high-income (above $50,000) taxpayers.[49] Individual tax cuts were scaled down by the conference to accommodate a revenue-loss ceiling agreed to by Finance Committee chairman Russell B. Long and Treasury Secretary W. Michael Blumenthal. Except for taxpayers qualifying for the earned income credit, the individual tax cuts were roughly proportional for all income groups.[50]

In 1978 Congress also passed legislation barring the Treasury Department from issuing proposed new rules for taxing fringe benefits. A windfall profits tax approved in 1979 extended the postponement and also eased a 1976 reform which had tightened inheritance tax rules. That same year, a Carter proposal to provide tax breaks for workers whose wage increases conformed to administration guidelines ("real wage insurance") survived only briefly before being buried by Congress.

The final tax legislation of the Carter years, a series of minor tax increases incorporated into the fiscal 1981 budget reconciliation bill, was aimed primarily at the use of tax-free bonds to subsidize home mortgages. State and local governments had received authority to issue mortgage bonds in 1968 but had not begun to use them extensively until the late 1970s. Estimates that the continued lack of restrictions on their use could cost up to $12 billion in revenues by the mid-1980s led Congress to enact a phasing-out of the subsidy arrangement as part of the budget reconciliation bill. Also included were provisions to tighten treatment of capital gains taxes on foreign real estate investments and a windfall profits tax credit.

Jimmy Carter's initial hopes for tax reform were ambitious. They were also at odds with popular and congressional sentiment. Carter was able to restrain, at least to a limited extent, the size of congressionally initiated tax cuts, but he had little if any serious involvement in the substance and distribution of those cuts. Like Ford, Carter was a secondary figure in the shaping of tax policy.

Tax Policy before Reagan

During the 1970s tax reduction overwhelmed tax reform. The restraints in tax policy-making reflected in the Tax Reform Act of 1969 had disappeared a decade later. Neither the progressivity in rate reductions nor the balance between structural gains and losses that characterized the 1969 tax bill was matched by later tax-cut legislation. Moreover, budget balance had deteriorated.

The impact of statutory tax cuts on personal tax liabilities, however, was undercut by other factors, particularly inflation and social security tax increases. Inflation-induced "bracket creep," in which taxpayers were pushed into higher tax brackets without equivalent increases in real income, had become quite severe by the late 1970s. In addition, the 1977 social security tax bill, which at that time represented the largest peacetime tax increase in history, exacerbated what were already rapidly escalating payroll tax burdens. When the 1978 tax reduction bill was passed, for example, congressional estimates showed that inflation-generated tax increases and higher social security taxes would offset the income tax cuts for virtually all income groups.[51]

Table 2.7. Individual Taxes and Personal Income, 1970-81

Calendar Year	Personal Income	
	Percentage Paid in Individual Income Taxes	Percentage Paid in Individual Social Insurance Taxes
1970	11.0	3.4
1972	10.8	3.6
1974	10.8	4.1
1976	10.2	4.0
1978	10.9	4.0
1980	11.6	4.1
1981	12.0	4.3

SOURCES: Individual income tax percentages are from Congressional Budget Office, *Revising the Individual Income Tax*, p. 9. Individual social insurance percentages are calculated from income and tax figures in *Economic Report of the President, 1985* (Washington, D.C.:GPO, 1985), p. 259.

The revenue trends that developed during the Nixon, Ford, and Carter presidencies represented a marked change in individual tax burdens. The level of budget receipts in comparison to GNP had escalated, and the annual growth in budget receipts was likewise comparatively high, averaging almost 15 percent for fiscal years 1977–81. The greatest growth was in individual income taxes and social insurance taxes, with their combined share of total budget receipts growing from 67.6 percent in fiscal 1969 to 78.2 percent in fiscal 1981. In fiscal 1981 individual income taxes were 9.6 percent of GNP and social security taxes were 6.1 percent, in both instances the highest levels yet reached.

These taxes were also growing in relation to personal income (see table 2.7). Individual taxes (both income taxes and that share of social insurance taxes paid by the individual) grew more rapidly than personal income between 1970 and 1981. The social insurance tax burden alone went up by more than 25 percent. Wage base and rate increases for social security boosted the maximum tax paid by individuals from less than $375 to almost $2,000.

Progressivity in the overall federal tax system was adversely affected by this enormous expansion of payroll tax liabilities.[52] Even for the individual income tax, however, progressivity was undercut by structural tax changes that added numerous exclusions, deductions, and credits. The 1970s was an unusually fertile time for tax expenditure legislation. Data collected by John Witte show that more than half of the over 300 modifications in the tax expenditure system between 1909 and 1981 were made between 1970 and 1981.[53] And among these changes, expansions and increases outnumbered curtailments by over two to one.

In fiscal 1967, the first year for which comparative data are available, there were fifty tax expenditures with an estimated loss equal to 23.8 percent of budget receipts.[54] The revenue loss level remained stable until 1975, when it jumped to over 33 percent. By fiscal 1981 there were more than 100 tax expenditures, and their combined revenue loss of nearly $230 billion amounted to almost 40 percent of federal budget receipts.

The tax expenditure system that had developed was heavily weighted toward individual, not corporate, benefits, and the individual benefits it provided affected all income classes. The major tax expenditures for individuals that were in effect by the end of Jimmy Carter's term, for example, were extremely broad-based, although the distribution of benefits, of course, varied by the type of tax expenditure. By the late 1970s benefits were not distributed equally among all taxpayers, for example, but they were closely related to the distribution of adjusted gross income and to the amount of taxes people actually paid. Using expanded income classes and data from 1977, Witte reports that for all but the lowest (less than $5,000) and highest ($100,000 or more) income classifications, the share of taxes paid roughly equaled the share of total tax expenditure benefits. "Thus, a very plausible set of conclusions is that: (1) the highest-income taxpayers get relatively more from tax expenditures, regardless of the equity standard; (2) the poor do very well relative to the taxes they pay; and (3) the middle class is disadvantaged by the aggregate tax expenditure system from any perspective."[55] An important point here is that the "middle class," which had tax expenditure benefits roughly proportional to tax liabilities, accounted for almost three-fourths of all returns and nearly 90 percent of all taxes paid. For the vast majority of taxpayers, the effect of tax expenditures was to reduce tax liabilities in a generally proportional fashion. This meant, in turn, less progressive individual taxation during the 1970s, despite the steep marginal rates then in effect.

Of particular relevance for the Reagan presidency, a basic assumption of Jimmy Carter and of the Democratic leadership in Congress was that budget receipts would grow faster than the economy through the mid-1980s, fueled in part by inflation-generated increases. Carter's original fiscal 1981 budget, for example, projected a balance between spending (including off-budget outlays) and revenues by fiscal 1983.[56] The balance, however, would approach almost 23 percent of GNP, a revenue level that had never been reached, even during World War II. For fiscal years 1982 and 1983, the Carter budget called for receipts growth of almost 20 percent annually, with even higher rates of growth in individual income taxes and social security taxes.[57] Since Carter's four years in office already had resulted in record peacetime growth in budget receipts, the political and fiscal realism of his tax policies was questionable. With his rejection by the voters in 1980, the time was ripe for a wholesale assault on taxes.

These pressures to cut taxes, however, came at a point when the gap between spending and receipts was large. The Reagan tax-cut program did not entirely ignore this gap. Supply-side theories, which argued that tax cuts would spur economic growth that would, in turn, lead to increased revenues, were advanced to resolve the obvious difficulty in reconciling Reagan's support of tax cuts with his advocacy of a balanced budget. In fact, however, tax policy had been compartmentalized by the fiscal erraticism of the 1970s. It was now possible to pursue tax policy objectives independent of budget policy, since no one claimed responsibility for enforcing a balance between spending and revenues.

3

From Supply Side to Reform

During the Reagan years, tax policy underwent extraordinary and unexpected changes. The massive tax cuts contained in the 1981 Economic Recovery Tax Act signaled to many experts a further deterioration in the tax policy process, since the "longer the legislative debate lasted, the more the various sides offered 'sweeteners' to attract public support. . . . Opening up the proceedings to public scrutiny, moreover, led to cumulative reduction of revenues."[1] For incremental theorists, such as John Witte, the 1981 tax cut was additional evidence of a "pathology of tax politics." The procedural reforms in Congress during the 1970s and the accompanying changing balance in institutional responsibilities had led, he believed, to a "rapid deterioration of the tax base, an increasing tax expenditure system, and a dramatic increase in deficits." In effect, opening up the incremental decision-making process and making it more responsive to political demands had proved to be disastrous. According to Witte, "What should be considered is an attempt to stabilize the tax system by insulating it from politics."[2]

For Hansen, the short-term political advantages that Ronald Reagan enjoyed in 1981 had made possible "a massive redirection of taxation and economic policy." It was likely, however, that the absence of any long-term electoral realignment would mean "a return to the bipartisan pattern of compromise and incremental change which has characterized postwar tax policy."[3]

In 1982 and 1984 Congress confused the conventional wisdom slightly by passing election-year tax increases, but these were dwarfed by the continuing effects of the 1981 tax cuts and, in any case, did not disturb the individual rate reductions contained in the 1981 bill. One possibility was that a major redisciplining of the tax policy process might possibly occur in order to resolve the fiscal crisis posed by huge deficits. Otherwise, variations on the incremental theme would continue: Congress would move at a cumbersome pace, special interests would receive favored treatment, and divided government would lead to a stalemate.[4]

What ultimately occurred, of course, was enactment of the most far-reaching and, by most accounts, progressive tax reform of the post–World War II era. The 1986 Tax Reform Act eliminated billions of dollars in tax breaks, shifted tax burdens from individuals to corporations, and established a modified flat tax for individuals and corporations. From the perspective of tax policy, these were extraordinary changes, particularly since they were enacted without any electoral mandate or intense public support.[5] In addition, the 1986 Tax Reform Act was deliberately divorced from deficit problems. From the outset, Reagan insisted that tax reform had to be "revenue neutral"—neither raising nor lowering aggregate revenues compared to existing law—and he prevailed.

Passage of the 1986 Tax Reform Act demonstrated that the long-standing connection between spending and revenues had been altered. Comprehensive reform was possible, because tax policy change was not constrained by the revenue requirements of deficit reduction. In 1986 the executive branch and Congress were able to eliminate many of the inequities and excesses that had accumulated with the destabilizing of tax policy. They were able to do so, in large part, because they could ignore the enormous political gap between spending and revenue levels.

This political gap had been redefined, in a sense, by supply-side economists during the early years of the Reagan administration, who stressed repeatedly that structural tax policy was the government's "most powerful tool for influencing economic growth." The 1981 tax cuts were expected to enhance capital formation and economic growth, but nothing in the administration's early budgets or economic reports showed revenue increases erasing the deficit at current policy spending levels. The administration's 1982 economic report, for example, projected revenues at well below 20 percent of GNP through the late 1980s. Therefore, deficit reduction could only occur through continued spending cuts that kept outlay growth below economic growth. As the 1982 economic report explained, "A strategy of reducing taxes in advance of spending cuts implies that it will take some time to achieve the desired level of deficits." Over time, "enforcing a trend toward a balanced budget would impose the fiscal discipline necessary to restrain the growth of government."[6]

The transition from supply-side tax cuts to tax reform was, for the Reagan administration, a natural one, since the governing principle for tax policy was economic growth. Growth was more important than deficits, which had become worse between 1981 and 1986. It was more important than the budget impasse over spending, which had also become worse between 1981 and 1986. When it became apparent that reduced tax levels could not "discipline" spending policy, the Reagan administration deemphasized that objective.

The Reagan years thus provided a new emphasis on structural tax policy. This emphasis resulted in a widely hailed reform of tax policy. It also exacerbated, however, the problem of deficits, by shifting the composition of revenues further toward earmarked taxes (such as social security), by indexing individual income taxes against inflation, and by raising political barriers to any public advocacy of significant tax increases.

Reagan Tax Policy, 1981–85

The most important piece of tax legislation during Ronald Reagan's first term was the Economic Recovery Tax Act of 1981 (ERTA), which was signed into law on August 13. The tax bill and a related package of spending cuts, which Congress had cleared several days earlier in an omnibus reconciliation package, were the main elements of the administration's budget program. The tax plan was outlined to Congress on February 18, revised during negotiations with Congress in June and July, and finally pushed through after the president's televised appeal for public support on July 27.

Additional tax bills were passed in 1982, 1983, and 1984. The Tax Equity and Fiscal Responsibility Act of 1982 (TEFRA) reduced some of the revenue losses from the 1981 tax law. A similar approach was followed in 1984 with the Deficit Reduction Act. Major social security tax increases were enacted in 1983, in direct response to solvency problems with the social security trust funds. These measures, along with several minor tax bills passed during Reagan's first term, generated additional revenues but with two important qualifications. The revenue increases were well below the ERTA cuts, and the individual income tax provisions contained in ERTA remained in place. Reagan was able to protect both the direction and substance of his tax program, despite the unprecedented deficits that program helped produce.

The 1981 Tax Bill

By the time that the bidding process on the 1981 tax bill was completed, its cost had escalated enormously—to an estimated $750 billion in individual and corporate tax reductions for fiscal years 1981–86. This amount was much larger, by far, than any previous tax cut and greatly exceeded Reagan's original proposal. It contained, however, the heart of Reagan's tax philosophy. Individual income tax cuts were large and, of equal importance, proportional. As Reagan made clear: "Unlike some past 'tax reforms,' this is not merely a shift of wealth between different sets of taxpayers. This proposal for an equal reduction in everyone's tax rates will expand our national prosperity, enlarge national incomes, and increase opportunities for all Americans."[7] Proportional cuts in rates also meant that tax savings would increase with existing tax liabilities and therefore with income.

The business tax cuts Reagan recommended were based mainly on changes in depreciation write-offs. The new "accelerated cost recovery system" (ACRS) both simplified and speeded up the method used to deduct investments in plants and equipment. Along with two dozen other major provisions affecting business, the result was an estimated $150 billion in reductions over five years, or about 20 percent of the projected ERTA total revenue loss.

The theme of Reagan's tax plan was economic growth. Reagan repeated the incentive arguments that had been used before, most notably for the Mellon and Kennedy tax cuts. He also revived investment and productivity justifications that had accompanied past investment tax credit proposals. The magnitude of the fiscal 1981 cuts, however, suggests that Reagan was consolidating, not creating, widespread and growing support for tax relief. A Democratic-controlled Congress, after all, had produced the Revenue Act of 1978, which differed sharply from traditional Democratic tax philosophy. In August 1980 the Senate Finance Committee, then still under Democratic control, approved a $39 billion tax-cut package for individuals and businesses which was opposed by Carter but endorsed by Reagan.

Several months earlier, House and Senate Republicans had unanimously endorsed the Kemp-Roth plan, which called for three-year, 30 percent tax cuts for individuals. Congressman Jack F. Kemp and Senator William V. Roth had first introduced their plan for across-the-board cuts early in the Carter administration. Few congressional experts gave it much chance for serious consideration, much less passage, a verdict which was underscored by routine House and Senate rejection of the Kemp-Roth bill in 1978. But Ronald Reagan later adopted the Kemp-Roth proposal as a key element in his economic recovery plan during the 1980 campaign, and his overwhelming victory over Carter added enormous impetus to the taxcut movement.

What changed in the late 1970s was not just the rhetoric of tax politics. Despite legislated tax cuts, tax burdens for many individuals were increasing. In addition, the economy was doing poorly, with low growth, high inflation, and extraordinarily high interest rates. By tapping both the political support for tax relief and the widespread concern about the economy, Reagan was able to make credible an economic strategy which was highly unconventional.

By the time the House and Senate had completed their lengthy deliberations, however, Reagan's limited proposals for individual rate cuts and business depreciation increases had been refashioned into a complicated and considerably more costly bill. The program that Reagan presented to Congress in February 1981 combined a 30 percent cut in marginal tax rates (phased in over three years, with a top marginal rate of 50 percent) with business tax cuts in the form of accelerated depreciation and increased investment tax credits.

The Democratic response was outlined by the new chairman of the Ways and Means Committee, Daniel Rostenkowski, in early April. On depreciation, the Democratic plan was similar to what Reagan had proposed. It differed significantly on individual rate reductions. The Democratic proposal was limited to one year, with the marginal rate reductions especially geared to the $20,000–$50,000 income range. The total individual tax cuts, moreover, amounted to only about two-thirds of the reductions Reagan had proposed.

After two months of deadlock, the administration came out with a revised plan designed to build a coalition between congressional Republicans and conservative Democrats. Reagan stuck with his three-year cut but scaled back the first year's reduction by almost one-third. The new plan also pruned the business tax cuts Reagan had originally requested, while adding a variety of individual tax benefits aimed at wavering Democrats. What Reagan did not do was compromise on what he defined as the heart of his program—proportional, three-year cuts for individuals.

The immediate result of the president's June 4 announcement was to block an emerging compromise being worked out between Rostenkowski and the new Republican Finance Committee chairman, Robert Dole. The Rostenkowski-Dole negotiations had produced agreement on a two-year rate cut, combined with a generous list of tax-cut provisions for individuals and businesses. The congressional approach to tax cutting reflected two competing pressures. There was a good deal of concern about the total cuts and their deficit effects. There was also considerable support for numerous tax benefits. A two-year rate cut was attractive, since it provided the margin necessary to accommodate new tax benefits while holding down revenue losses.

On June 9 there was yet another administration plan. In response to an intense lobbying effort by business leaders, most of the original business tax cuts were restored, and some new ones were added. As was the case in Congress, the bidding on tax benefits was escalating, and the administration's total price tag was inflated by the president's insistence on three-year, proportional cuts.

That same day, House Democrats came out against across-the-board cuts, with Rostenkowski announcing that Ways and Means Democrats would structure a plan for targeted relief aimed at the $10,000–$50,000 income group. With the House now stalled, Dole and the Finance Committee attached a comprehensive tax bill to a House-passed debt limit measure. Reagan's three-year, across-the-board cut in income tax rates and the accelerated depreciation system for business were strongly endorsed by the committee, which also added some major new tax benefits. The most significant addition was a set of provisions offered by Senator William L. Armstrong to index individual income taxes, capital gains taxes, and estate and gift taxes to the consumer price index. While President Reagan had endorsed indexation of tax rates, the administration opposed indexing in the 1981 tax bill, in part because of its projected costs. When the Senate took up the Finance Committee bill on July 15, however, the indexing proposal was one of the first committee amendments to win approval. By a vote of 57–40, the Senate agreed to index all individual income tax brackets, including the zero bracket and standard deduction amounts, and the personal exemption, all effective in 1985.

Floor consideration, which extended over two weeks, did produce some add-ons to the Finance Committee package. The Ways and Means Committee was proceeding with its markup at the same time, and the list of new benefits expanded once more. Ways and Means agreed to an automatic round of third-year individual income tax cuts, under an "economic goals" formula, and it also proposed "expensing" (or full deduction in the year of purchase) for capital investments, combined with additional benefits for specific industries and a windfall profits exemption for the oil industry.

The Ways and Means bill was crafted to garner the widest possible support in the House, but it still failed to withstand a Reagan challenge. A substitute put together by House Republicans and conservative Democrats was adopted instead, two days after Reagan's nationally televised appeal. According to House Speaker Thomas P. O'Neill, Jr., Reagan's speech produced "a telephone blitz like this nation has never seen. It's had a devastating effect."[8] Reagan's message had been that the Republican tax bill benefited "everyone," and he even went on to list the numerous

Table 3.1. Economic Recovery Tax Act of 1981 (PL 97-34): Major Provisions

INDIVIDUAL INCOME TAXES

Tax Rate

Marginal tax rates for individuals reduced by 23 percent for 1981-83, beginning with a 5 percent reduction on Oct. 1, 1981.

Maximum Rate

The top marginal rate on individual income reduced from 70 percent to 50 percent, effective Jan. 1, 1982.

Capital Gains

The 60 percent exclusion of long-term capital gains maintained. The new 50 percent top marginal rate, however, reduced the maximum effective tax rate on capital gains to 20 percent.

Deduction for Two-Earner Married Couples

Reduction of "marriage penalty," allowing couples to deduct 5 percent of first $30,000 earnings of spouse with lower earnings in 1982. Increased to 10 percent in 1983.

Indexing

The individual income tax brackets, zero bracket amount, and personal exemption adjusted annually for inflation (measured by the Consumer Price Index), beginning with calendar year 1985.

IRA Exclusion

Eligibility for IRAs broadened to cover participants in employer-sponsored pension plans. The maximum IRA contribution increased.

CORPORATE INCOME TAXES

Accelerated Cost Recovery

Replaced depreciation rules for tangible property used in trade or business. Accelerated Cost Recovery System (ACRS) provided for faster write-off of capital expenditures under simplified and standardized rules.

Leasing

Liberalized rules allowing firms to transfer unused investment tax credits and depreciation deductions on new investments to profitable firms through leasing transactions.

Oil Tax Reductions

Reduced tax on newly discovered oil. Added exemption for independent producer stripper wells from windfall profit taxes.

Table 3.1. (cont'd)

ESTATE AND GIFT TAXES

Marital Deductions	Surviving spouse permitted to inherit unlimited amount without paying tax.
Estate and Gift Tax Credits	Increased from $47,000 to $192,800 by 1987, exempting from tax all estates of $600,000 or less.
Rate Reduction	Maximum rate reduced from 70 percent to 50 percent over 1981-85 period.
Gift Tax Exclusion	Increased from $3,000 to $10,000 per donee, effective Jan. 1, 1982.

SOURCE: Joint Committee on Taxation, *General Explanation of the Economic Recovery Tax Act of 1981* (Washington, D.C.:GPO, 1981), pp. 5-16.

beneficiaries—farmers, small business owners, working people, and so on.[9] Not included were the "rich," the "wealthy," or the "upper class," but the contrast between the Republicans' across-the-board relief and the Democrats' targeted approach was unmistakable. The public response and the subsequent House vote (238–195 in favor of the administration substitute) indicated that the appeal of redistributive tax politics was not very formidable. In fact, the Democratic argument that proportional cuts were inherently unfair—an argument which received widespread publicity from the print and broadcast media—apparently never worked very well with the public. The president's victory in the House was quickly cemented in conference. Congressional action was completed on August 4, and the president signed the Economic Recovery Tax Act of 1981 into law on August 13.

Provisions. While ERTA included some revenue-raising provisions, these were dwarfed by individual and business tax cuts Reagan had insisted on from the beginning (see table 3.1). The main individual income tax provisions were marginal rate reductions, including a one-step lowering of the top marginal rate from 70 percent to 50 percent and a three-step cutting of other marginal rates by 23 percent.

The lower marginal rates contained in ERTA represented a sharp reversal in tax policy and philosophy. Moreover, the indexing provisions insured that the real tax burden under the basic schedule could be increased only by legislation. This requirement extended to the president an effective veto on the tax side paralleling the congressional veto on indexed spending programs. Neither side could depend on inflation to achieve victories that could not be won in the legislative process. For tax policy, this was a major change from the 1970s.

For business, the most important change was the new accelerated cost recovery system. The ACRS provisions in the 1981 tax bill simplified and standardized rules governing the depreciation of tangible property, but the major innovation was a faster write-off for capital expenditures. Accelerated depreciation for real estate was generous as well, and small businesses were given the option of "expensing," or immediate deduction of specified costs for new or used machinery and equipment.

ERTA also included a variety of so-called minor tax law changes that were not consistent with its basic philosophy. Large, across-the-board cuts for both individuals and businesses were supposed to boost incentives sufficiently to eliminate the need for special treatment provisions. Nevertheless, a host of new tax benefits—for mutual savings banks, for firms rehabilitating old buildings and historic structures, for trucking firms, for oil royalty owners and independent producers, for service corporations—was added to an already impressive array of tax expenditures. And in a conceptual breakthrough of sorts, liberalized leasing rules allowed businesses that were not profitable enough to use investment tax credits and accelerated depreciation benefits to transfer them to businesses that could.

Revenue Impact. The estimated price tag of the 1981 tax bill rose as the administration and Congress sought to reach an acceptable compromise. President Reagan's fiscal 1982 budget revisions, for example, called for tax cuts totaling $645 billion for the fiscal 1981–86 period.[10] The final version of the tax bill, approved less than six months later, added more than $100 billion in projected revenue losses to the total, even though the cuts for fiscal 1981 and 1982 were actually below Reagan's original proposals.[11] Revenue losses were postponed to the "outyears" in order to dampen the immediate deficit effects, but the confluence of a severe recession in 1981 and 1982 and the tax cuts produced revenue losses and deficits that were much larger than anticipated.

The 1981 tax cuts helped to generate unusually large deficits. More difficult to assess, however, are the relative contributions to revenue losses from the tax cuts and from the recession during the fiscal 1981–83 period and, subsequently, the impact the tax cuts have had on economic recovery and economic growth. It appears that the short-term revenue losses directly associated with ERTA, for example, were less than originally estimated but still extremely large (see table 3.2).

Table 3.2. Deficits and the Economic Recovery Tax Act of 1981, Fiscal Years 1982–86 (in billions of dollars)

Fiscal Year	ERTA Revenue Losses[a]		Total Budget Deficit
	Initial Estimate	Actual Loss	
1982	− $ 37.6	− $ 35.6	− $ 127.9
1983	− 92.7	− 91.1	− 207.8
1984	− 150.0	− 136.8	− 185.3
1985	− 199.3	− 170.3	− 212.3
1986	− 267.6	− 209.8	− 221.2

SOURCE: *Budget of the United States Government*, various years.
[a] Estimates are based on the direct effect of legislative changes at a given level of economic activity.

The compelling political point about ERTA, however, was that its basic philosophy managed to withstand a barrage of controversy and criticism. The economic recovery that was well underway by the end of President Reagan's first term not only provided a major boost to his reelection effort but also gave his limited taxation approach protection against any serious legislative attack. It is in retrospect quite remarkable that Reagan was able to preserve his tax program in the face of $200+ billion deficits and to limit second-term tax law changes to a revenue-neutral standard.

Fairness. Also remarkable was the extent to which "fairness" critiques had lost currency by the end of Reagan's first term. During the 1981 debates over the president's tax plan, it was charged that his individual income tax proposals were "tax cuts for the rich," and this theme continued to be played long after the tax cuts were enacted.[12] By 1984, however, income tax data for the 1982 tax year were being cited to show precisely the opposite.[13] Between 1981 and 1982, total individual income tax revenues had declined by about 2 percent, but neither the tax revenues collected by income class nor the share of taxes paid declined in accordance with the proportional rate deductions under ERTA. Instead, tax revenues and the share of total income taxes paid by upper-income groups had increased, while revenues and tax shares for low- and middle-income groups had decreased.

This pattern continued in 1983 (see table 3.3). Nearly 70 percent of

Table 3.3. Distribution of Tax Burdens by Income Category, 1980-83

Adjusted Gross Income Class	Percentage of Total Income Taxes Paid			
	1980	1981	1982	1983
Less than $11,000	4.5	3.8	3.4	3.0
$11,000 to under $25,000	25.5	22.5	20.2	18.6
$25,000 to under $50,000	38.6	40.5	40.6	38.8
$50,000 to under $100,000	15.9	17.9	18.2	19.5
$100,000 or more	15.5	15.2	17.5	20.0
Total	100.0	99.9	99.9	99.9

SOURCE: *Internal Revenue Service Statistics of Income Bulletin* 4 (Spring 1985): 80-81.

all returns filed in 1983 had adjusted gross incomes of $25,000 or less, but this group accounted for just over one-fifth of total revenues. Four years earlier, the below-$25,000 taxpayer category had provided 30 percent of total individual income tax revenues. The middle-income category ($25,000–$50,000) was stable for the 1980–83 period in terms of its proportion of tax revenues; but for upper-income groups, the changes were quite marked and remarkably similar. The $100,000+ income category represented less than 1 percent of all returns in 1983 but produced 20 percent of total revenues; in 1980 this group had accounted for 15.5 percent of income tax revenues, and its share had actually declined slightly in 1981.

The 1981 tax cut shifted tax burdens toward upper-income taxpayers, despite the substantial rate cuts for this group. Indeed, the 1980s rate reductions and the Kennedy tax cuts had a similar impact on tax liabilities.[14] Both were proportional cuts that shifted the tax burden toward the higher tax brackets. Both increased progressivity, although neither was presented as an effort to increase fairness.

Between the Kennedy and Reagan tax cuts, tax burdens for virtually the entire population had risen. In particular, the marginal tax rates paid by the majority of taxpayers had increased. In 1979 three-fourths of all joint returns were subject to a marginal rate of 28 percent or more; in 1965 only 6 percent of joint returns were affected by rates at or above this level. By the late 1970s the stability and proportionality of middle-class tax rates had eroded. It was this phenomenon that gave the Reagan tax cuts such widespread appeal initially and also provided continuing protection against efforts to reduce or postpone the cuts.[15]

TEFRA (1982)

The 1982 tax bill, labeled the Tax Equity and Fiscal Responsibility Act (TEFRA), followed the 1981 precedent of attaching grandiose labels to revenue acts. In any case, TEFRA was a major tax increase, adding an estimated $98.3 billion in budget receipts for fiscal years 1983–85. A five-cents-per-gallon gasoline tax increase passed at the end of the year added an additional $10 billion to fiscal 1983–85 receipts. Taken together, tax increases legislated in 1982 were expected to make up well over one-quarter of the fiscal 1983–85 revenue losses projected for ERTA, and social security tax increases raised this proportion to more than one-third.[16]

The interval between final congressional action on the 1981 and 1982 tax bills was roughly one year, but the move toward a tax increase began almost as soon as ERTA passed. In September 1981 Reagan responded to increasingly negative economic and deficit projections by proposing $22 billion in tax increases, along with additional spending cuts, for fiscal years 1982–84. At this point, the president was still promising a "balanced budget by 1984," and he proposed immediate FY 1982 cuts of $16 billion to go along with $3 billion in additional revenues from eliminating "abuses and obsolete incentives in the tax code."[17] In November, as the House and Senate considered revisions in the first concurrent budget resolution for FY 1982 with its $37.65 billion deficit figure, the Senate Budget Committee adopted "sense of the Congress" language warning that future deficits of $100 billion could occur without immediate action on spending cuts and tax increases. By December, as both houses adopted a pro forma second resolution which simply reaffirmed the grossly inaccurate figures contained in the first, Office of Management and Budget (OMB) estimates were showing $420 billion in combined deficits for fiscal years 1982–84, more than double the projections made just three months earlier.

After Reagan's first year in office, the economic and budget outlook was bleak, and there was growing pressure from the administration's critics to repeal or delay the individual tax cuts scheduled for 1982 and 1983. The fiscal 1983 budget submitted by the president projected a $91.5 billion deficit, and many analysts expected it to be twice as high. The fiscal

1982 deficit was climbing to the $100 billion level, which had never been breached, putting Republicans in the predicament of defending the largest deficits in history.

Reagan was in a rather unsettling position. His economic program had not produced a quick recovery. His budget program was in a shambles. The Senate Budget Committee, for example, formally rejected the president's fiscal 1983 budget proposals by a 20–0 vote on May 5. Budget negotiations between White House chief of staff James A. Baker III and congressional leaders had collapsed at the end of April, at which point Senate Budget Committee chairman Pete V. Domenici started work independently. Within a week, committee Republicans were near agreement on a plan which included $125 billion in additional revenues for fiscal years 1983–85. A potential casualty according to this plan was the third year of the Reagan tax cuts. As Domenici stated, "I do not rule out a freeze on the third year of the scheduled tax cut if that is the final element that a compromise of this magnitude hinges upon."[18]

With the Democratic majority in the House still strongly opposed to the multiyear tax cuts and congressional Republicans increasingly nervous about the upcoming midterm elections, the prospects for a full-scale Reagan retreat appeared inevitable. Instead, there was no compromise at all on individual tax cuts. Reagan did agree to a package which curtailed a variety of exclusions, deductions, and credits for businesses and individuals. This package had been foreshadowed in Reagan's 1982 State of the Union message, when he promised to "seek no tax increases this year," while pledging also to "plug unwarranted tax loopholes and strengthen the law which requires all large corporations to pay a minimum tax."[19] The budget message that followed proposed $34 billion in additional revenues over three years from correcting "unintended loopholes," discontinuing "obsolete tax incentives," and requiring "profitable business . . . [to] contribute at least some minimum fair share to the cost of financing Government."[20] A detailed program of tax increases was subsequently produced by the administration which raised the three-year revenue increment to $86.6 billion but did so without altering the individual rate cuts or the basic accelerated cost recovery system for business.

As the size of the administration's revenue increase package grew, the split with the congressional Republican leadership began to narrow. An agreement with the Senate Budget Committee brought the projected three-year tax increases to the $95 billion level. On May 20 the Senate twice rejected Democratic efforts to repeal the third-year tax cuts.

A parallel Democratic effort to revise the Reagan tax program was also defeated in the House, although it took several weeks for the House Republican leadership to do so. The House Budget Committee's fiscal 1983 plan, which was adopted on a 17–12 party-line vote by the committee on May 13, included $147 billion in tax increases over three years, virtually guaranteeing rollbacks in the 1981 tax cuts. When the House finally agreed to a Republican substitute five weeks later, the three-year revenue target had been cut by some $50 billion, bringing it into line with the Senate's version.

The compromise FY 1983 congressional budget resolution was agreed to in conference on June 17 and adopted by both chambers on June 23, nearly six weeks after the statutory deadline. Included in the resolution were reconciliation instructions to House and Senate committees requiring $98.3 billion in additional revenues and $27.15 billion in spending reductions. On August 18 and 19 Congress completed action on two massive reconciliation bills. The Omnibus Reconciliation Act of 1982 (PL 97–253) contained the spending cuts for programs not handled by the revenue committees. The Tax Equity and Fiscal Responsibility Act (PL 97–248) contained tax increases and spending cuts for programs handled by the Finance and Ways and Means committees.

The 1982 tax bill was the product of negotiations between Reagan administration officials and Finance Committee Republicans. Senator Dole, the Finance Committee chairman, initially had hoped to build a tax bill around a $5-per-barrel oil import fee and changes in the Reagan income tax program. The oil import fee had little support in Congress, and Reagan, of course, opposed any changes in the individual tax cuts. So Dole and the Finance Committee gradually moved toward a much more complicated package of "revenue enhancers." The committee bill, adopted by an 11–9 straight party-line vote, contained some three dozen tax code changes, ranging from technical modifications, to compliance measures, to strict curtailment of the safe-harbor leasing rules adopted in 1981.

Democratic efforts to eliminate the scheduled third-year tax cut for upper-income taxpayers failed in committee and on the Senate floor. Attention then shifted to lobbying efforts by business interests, especially banks and financial institutions, to overturn the Finance Committee's business tax proposals and compliance provisions. The Senate bill that finally emerged, however, retained the primary revenue increases recommended by the committee.

In an unusual move, the Ways and Means Committee agreed to go straight to conference on the Senate tax bill, and the House narrowly sustained the committee's decision. This procedure was justified on the basis of the Senate bill's being technically an amendment to a minor House-passed tax measure. More important, the procedure allowed House Democrats to shift responsibility for an election-year tax increase to the Republicans.

The conference bill that subsequently emerged was very close to the initial Finance Committee plan.[21] With TEFRA up for floor votes less than three months before the midterm election, a major lobbying effort was mounted by the White House, which even promised personal letters of appreciation from the president to Democratic legislators concerned about having their votes for a tax increase used against them in November. After the House finally agreed to a closed rule on August 19, the tax bill quickly moved through both chambers and was signed by the president two weeks later.

Passage of TEFRA was without question a setback for Reagan. It was not, however, a full-scale retreat. The revenue increases estimated for TEFRA, while significant, essentially reduced the 1981 tax bill losses to levels not very different from Reagan's original package. TEFRA eliminated, in large part, the bidding up of business tax breaks that took place as ERTA moved toward passage.

Even more important, Reagan was able to preserve his individual income tax cuts. These cuts had not been easy to pass with the relatively favorable deficit estimates being projected during the first half of 1981. That they survived the unprecedented deficits that developed over the next twelve months was a testimony not just to Reagan's intransigence but also to the politically potent tax-cut sentiments he had tapped throughout the electorate. These sentiments turned out to be much more formidable than deficit and fairness issues combined, a result that confounded traditional positions within both parties.

The 1983 and 1984 Tax Bills

After the massive tax policy changes in 1981 and 1982, Congress agreed to ambitious deficit-reduction plans for 1983 and 1984 but then failed to pass the spending cuts and tax increases required by its budget resolutions. Once again, the individual tax cuts were successfully defended against Democratic challenges. The third-year rate reductions were implemented, and indexing schedules were maintained.

The tax bills that did pass in 1983 were largely unrelated to the partisan battles of the previous two years. Repeal of the controversial interest and dividend withholding provisions included in TEFRA came on

July 28, following months of intense pressure from banks and other financial institutions. In this instance, the administration, the House Democratic leadership, and the Senate Republican leadership were united against repeal. They succeeded in stalling floor votes, but the repeal measure finally passed by huge margins in both chambers.

Revenue losses resulting from passage of the Interest and Dividends Tax Compliance Act of 1983 were estimated at over $2 billion annually. The social security reform bill passed earlier in the year, by comparison, was expected to raise an additional $25 billion by fiscal 1989 through increased payroll taxes and a new tax on benefits for high-income recipients.[22] Solvency problems in the railroad retirement system, the only private pension plan run by the federal government, led to a similar compromise later in the year. The tax increases that were part of this rescue package were relatively minor, totaling less than $1 billion for both 1984 and 1985 but rising to the $1+ billion annual level beginning in 1986.

This assortment of 1983 legislation thus produced net increases in receipts for fiscal 1984 and future years. The revenue effects, however, were miniscule compared to the continuing impact of the ERTA cuts. In fiscal 1984, for example, estimated revenues were increased by over $3 billion, and the estimate for fiscal 1988 exceeded $20 billion.[23] The corresponding ERTA estimates, by comparison, were reductions of over $135 billion for FY 1984 and $280 billion for FY 1988.

In 1984 agreement was reached on a deficit-reduction package that was a smaller-scale version of TEFRA. The Deficit Reduction Act of 1984 (DEFRA) included several dozen provisions with an estimated revenue gain of approximately $50 billion for fiscal years 1984–87,[24] along with spending reductions of $13 billion over the same period. DEFRA's revenue provisions provided for excise tax extensions and increases and curbed a variety of tax abuses and tax shelters used by individuals and businesses. There were also direct cutbacks in existing tax benefits. For individuals, the two largest revenue increases were tied to repeal of the net interest exclusion and modification of income-averaging rules.[25] Major business tax changes included stricter rules governing leasing of equipment and cutbacks on favorable tax treatment for real estate investment. Among the several "sweeteners" in the bill were reductions in the long-term capital gains holding period from twelve months to six months, designed to appeal to conservatives, and an increase and liberalization of the earned income tax credit, which made the measure more palatable to liberals.

The procedural maze from which DEFRA emerged was a reversal of the congressional budget process. While the House followed the usual pattern of adopting a budget resolution in advance of acting on tax and spending bills, the Senate Republican leadership and the Reagan administration first agreed on tax increases and spending cuts. The first part of this package, which ultimately became DEFRA, was approved by the Senate on April 13. After approving legislation relating to other parts of the deficit-reduction agreement, the Senate adopted its budget resolution on May 18.

Reagan's endorsement of the 1984 tax increase was tied to corresponding spending cutbacks. One of the issues that prolonged the House-Senate conference on DEFRA was Senate language that imposed mandatory spending caps on domestic and defense spending through fiscal 1987. The House refused to accept binding language, and conferees finally settled on nonbinding appropriations "goals."

The deficit problem dominated budget policy debates throughout 1984. The president's fiscal 1985 budget acknowledged a $180 billion deficit but showed deficits dropping to $123 billion by fiscal 1989. The Congressional Budget Office's review of the president's budget, however, showed deficits increasing to about $250 billion by fiscal 1989.[26] This added impetus to deficit-reduction efforts across the political spectrum, but, of course, the routes differed. The balance between spending cuts and tax increases, on the one hand, and between defense and domestic spending growth, on the other, remained as divisive in 1984 as in previous years. By 1984, however, there had been some change in the House Democratic position on taxes, accepting, in effect, the individual tax cuts and indexing provisions that had been bitterly fought over for three years.

Reversing Tax Policy

The 1980 presidential election was not a referendum on tax policy, but its impact on taxes was enormous. During fiscal 1981, budget receipts as a percentage of GNP climbed over 20 percent for only the fourth time in history, but the fiscal 1981 deficit still turned out to be the largest registered up to that time. The fiscal 1982 budget that Carter submitted before leaving office and the fiscal 1982 revisions that Reagan proposed shortly thereafter showed numerous policy differences, but none was sharper than the revenue tax philosophies of the two administrations. For FY 1982–86, the Carter revenue estimates averaged $150 billion more per year than did the Reagan projections. For fiscal 1986, the gap was nearly $250 billion.

Neither spending pressures nor deficit control took precedence over tax policy for Reagan. The 1981 tax cut was largely preserved over Reagan's first term despite strong congressional opposition that emerged shortly after ERTA was signed into law and in the face of deficit levels that no one outside the administration considered politically or economically tolerable.

As shown in table 3.4, tax bills enacted during the 1982–84 period trimmed the ERTA revenue losses by about one third. Nevertheless, relative tax levels were reduced and maintained below 20 percent of GNP. Even with recovery of the economy from recession, revenue growth could not come close to erasing the deficit without a complete reversal in tax policy. That reversal was foreclosed by the results of the 1984 presidential election.

When Walter Mondale accepted the Democratic presidential nomination in 1984, he declared: "Let's tell the truth. It must be done, it must be done. Mr. Reagan will raise taxes, and so will I. He won't tell you. I just did." Mondale also revived the long-standing Democratic complaint about Reagan's tax program. According to Mondale, Reagan "gave each of his rich friends enough tax relief to buy a Rolls Royce—and then he asked your family to pay for the hubcaps." The difference in the future, Mondale stated, was that "when [Reagan] raises taxes, it won't be done fairly. He will sock it to average-income families again, and leave his rich friends alone." The Democratic platform accordingly promised to "cap the effect of the Reagan tax cuts for wealthy Americans and enhance the progressivity of our personal income tax code"; it also pledged to "partially defer indexation."[27]

By comparison, the Republican platform declared that indexing would be preserved. It went on to support "eliminating the incentive-destroying effects of graduated tax rates."[28] The differences between the platforms and the candidates were dramatic in 1984, and the election result gave Reagan the opportunity to press for equally dramatic changes in tax policy.

The Second Term: Revenue Neutral

The net effect of tax measures enacted during the first four years of the Reagan presidency was to reduce total revenues well below what they would have been under pre-1981 tax law. Structural tax policy was changed, particularly through rate reductions and indexing for individuals. Finally, the composition of receipts continued to shift toward social insurance taxes.

Table 3.4. Estimated Effects of 1981-84 Tax Legislation on Total Receipts, Fiscal Years 1984-88 (in billions of dollars)

	1984	1985	1986	1987	1988
BY STATUTE					
Economic Recovery Tax Act of 1981	-$136.8	-$168.5	-$210.8	-$250.9	-$283.0
Tax Equity and Fiscal Responsibility Act of 1982	+ 36.0	+ 40.7	+ 50.9	+ 61.8	+ 64.3
Highway Revenue Act of 1982	+ 4.2	+ 4.4	+ 4.6	+ 4.7	+ 4.8
Social Security Amendments of 1983	+ 5.7	+ 9.3	+ 9.1	+ 11.1	+ 22.9
Interest and Dividends Tax Compliance Act of 1983	- 2.6	- 2.4	- 2.1	- 1.7	- 1.8
Railroad Retirement Revenue Act of 1983	+ 0.2	+ 0.7	+ 1.1	+ 1.1	+ 1.1
Deficit Reduction Act of 1984	+ 0.9	+ 9.3	+ 15.9	+ 21.6	+ 24.6
BY SOURCE OF RECEIPTS					
Individual Income Taxes	- 105.0	- 117.0	- 140.4	- 165.5	- 190.6
Corporation Income Taxes	- 5.7	- 10.5	- 9.3	- 6.4	- 4.3
Social Insurance Taxes and Contributions	+ 11.9	+ 14.4	+ 14.3	+ 16.2	+ 29.4
Excise Taxes	+ 9.6	+ 11.3	+ 10.1	+ 10.7	+ 7.2
Estate and Gift Taxes	- 3.3	- 4.7	- 6.0	- 7.4	- 8.9
TOTAL EFFECTS	- 92.4	- 106.4	- 131.4	- 152.4	- 167.2

SOURCE: *Budget of the United States Government, Fiscal Year 1986* (Washington, D.C.:GPO, 1985), pp. 4-7--4-8.

During the second Reagan term, structure and composition continued to change rather significantly, but overall revenues were affected only marginally. For fiscal years 1986–89, the combined effect of the second-term tax legislation was to boost total revenues by an annual average of less than $15 billion, leaving in place a net tax reduction approaching $200 billion annually, along with deficits still averaging approximately $150 billion per year.

In terms of budget policy, Reagan's second term was noteworthy in that tax policy was not adjusted to balance the budget despite enormous deficits. Reagan clung to his belief that "the solution to the deficit problem must be to control the growth of the Federal Government and to give maximum opportunity for continued growth." Insisting that he would "not propose tax increases to balance the budget," Reagan successfully imposed a "revenue-neutral" standard for second-term tax policy.[29] That standard was explicitly attached to the Tax Reform Act of 1986, but it also erased any remaining doubts about the central importance Reagan assigned to tax policy. He repeatedly refused to subordinate it to deficit reduction, or to defense spending needs, or to any other budget policy goal.

Background of Tax Reform

When the 1981 tax cuts were proposed, President Reagan acknowledged the need for "other desirable . . . tax changes."[30] Some of these, such as indexing, were added to ERTA during congressional consideration. A second tax policy offensive was precluded, however, by the confluence of severe recession and large deficits. By the beginning of 1983, deficit problems were considered sufficiently serious that Reagan was persuaded to include a modest "standby tax" as part of his fiscal 1984 budget.[31]

As the economy recovered, Reagan's commitment to tax reform resurfaced. His 1984 State of the Union address rejected tax increases and called instead for a comprehensive overhaul of tax policy: "Let us go forward with an historic reform for fairness, simplicity, and incentives for growth. I am asking . . . for a plan to simplify the entire tax code so all taxpayers, big and small, are treated more fairly . . . [and to] make the tax base broader so personal tax rates could come down, not up."[32] Reagan directed the Treasury Department to come up with a detailed proposal by December 1984. The reform emphasis was repeated in the administration's budget and economic message to Congress in February 1984, and the Republican platform adopted that summer endorsed a "modified flat tax" as the centerpiece of tax reform.

On October 22, 1986, President Reagan signed the Tax Reform Act of 1986. As Reagan had promised, the tax base was broadened, while tax rates were lowered. The steeply progressive rate structure for individuals that had been maintained for decades was abandoned, and the top rate for corporations was also sharply reduced. For both individuals and corporations, numerous tax preferences were scaled back or eliminated. Tax burdens were shifted from individuals to corporations. For millions of low-income wages earners, tax liabilities were wiped out. The Tax Reform Act of 1986 was a dramatic redefinition of the substance and principles of federal income taxation.

While most conservatives had a long-standing aversion to progressive tax rates, a flat or proportional tax on incomes had never managed to achieve political credibility. In August 1982 Senator Bill Bradley and Congressman Richard A. Gephardt sought to regain some initiative on tax policy for the Democratic party with their "Fair Tax" plan. It proposed lowering individual tax rates to a maximum of 30 percent (with two additional brackets of 14 and 26 percent), while expanding the tax base through scaling back tax preferences. It also called for a parallel restructuring of corporate tax policy. Like the Kemp-Roth plan several years earlier, the "Fair Tax" was not taken very seriously. The response among congressional Democrats was at best lukewarm, and in 1984 the Democratic party platform called for a tax increase through greater progressivity.

A Republican version of the "Fair Tax" was introduced in April 1984 by Congressman Kemp and Senator Robert W. Kasten, Jr. Their "Fair and Simple Tax" included a uniform 24 percent rate for individuals, a partial exclusion for earned income targeted at lower income groups, and an expanded tax base. Like the Bradley-Gephardt proposal, the Kemp-Kasten plan extended the low rate–broad base concept to corporations.

Treasury I. The Treasury's tax plan was unveiled in November 1984, and it was much bolder than expected. Wholesale cutbacks in tax preference were linked to reduced maximum tax rates for individuals (35 percent) and corporations (33 percent). Included as well was a proposal for indexing all elements of capital income, along with interest income and income expenses. Partial integration of the corporate and individual income taxes was to be accomplished through revised tax treatment of dividend payments.

For many economists and tax experts, the Treasury proposal was appealing, since it corrected a broad range of economic distortions arising from existing tax policy. Its potential for improving simplicity and fairness, along with economic efficiency, led experts to cite it as "a milestone in tax reform."[33] Nevertheless, Treasury I (as it later became known) did not generate much political enthusiasm. The president announced, for example, that the Treasury proposal would be reviewed and revised in consultation with affected interests before any formal recommendations would be sent to Congress. The fiscal 1986 budget transmitted to Congress on February 4, 1985, did not include tax reform recommendations, noting only that "after consultations with members of Congress, the administration will submit legislation to restore fairness to the Federal income tax and to make it simpler, more neutral, and more conducive to economic growth."[34]

One major political difficulty posed by Treasury I was its shift in tax burdens from individuals to corporations. Following the president's instructions that tax reform be revenue neutral, Treasury I proposed offsetting revenue losses from individual rate cuts with higher corporate tax yields. This particular feature turned out to be an asset in the end. Several weeks before Treasury I was released, a group in Washington called Citizens for Tax Justice had issued a report detailing how more than 100 well-known and highly profitable corporations had paid little or no taxes from 1981 to 1983. This was a "fairness" issue with widespread appeal, and the report received considerable attention. Over the next eighteen months, a series of similar studies by other groups reported additional evidence of corporate tax avoidance, and this issue helped to broaden support for tax reform. The tax burden trade-off from individuals to corporations that was finally incorporated into the Tax Reform Act of 1986 paralleled the first Treasury plan.

Treasury II. The Reagan administration's official tax reform package was released May 28, 1985. Its rate structures for individuals and corporations was the same as Treasury I. Treasury II also shifted tax burdens from individuals to corporations.[35] The plans differed on how to implement a more stringent minimum tax for corporations and individuals, and Treasury II also had lower capital gains rates than had Treasury I.

The most controversial facets of Treasury II, however, were proposals to curtail tax preferences in order to increase the tax base. For individuals, these provisions included repealing the deduction for state and local taxes, limiting interest deductions for mortgages to a primary residence and capping nonmortgage interest, and narrowing the exclusion for fringe benefits (specifically employer-paid health insurance premiums). For corporations, Treasury II called for repealing investment tax credits, extending depreciation schedules, and eliminating business entertainment deductions.

Treasury II also added what would become a major selling point for tax reform—raising the personal exemption to $2,000. The value of the personal exemption ($1,080 in 1986) had eroded over the years because of inflation. The proposed doubling redressed this problem and also meant that many low-income taxpayers would have their income tax liabilities eliminated. Like the tax burden shift, the personal exemption increase helped to generate liberal support for tax reform.

As the Ways and Means and Finance committees held hearings during June and July on Treasury II, the prospects for success appeared dim. Among business groups, there were sharp divisions over the depreciation and tax credit changes, as well as over the numerous specific alterations in the tax treatment of different enterprises. Despite Reagan's attempts to develop public support for his tax program, there was little apparent interest or enthusiasm among taxpayers for tax reform. As expected, many Democrats in Congress opposed the distribution of tax savings among income groups contained in the Reagan plan, but there was especially fierce opposition to the repeal of state and local tax deductions. Congressional Republicans, while professing support for the president, were concerned about the political repercussions among business interests.

Apart from the disagreements over substantive tax policy, there was the additional problem of deficit reduction. The administration's insistence that tax reform be revenue neutral was repeatedly challenged. Liberal Democrats, for example, argued that revenues gained by restricting tax preferences should be used to reduce the deficit. The Democratic Study Group took this argument to the House Democratic caucus in October 1985, but Ways and Means was finally allowed to proceed with its markup without caucus instructions. When Ways and Means reported out a bill early in December, House Republicans found its business provisions so objectionable that they almost killed it. Only the president's personal intervention and his promise to insist on major changes in the Ways and Means bill once it reached the Senate garnered enough Republican votes to keep tax reform alive.

Gramm-Rudman-Hollings. In the Senate a recurring objection to any revenue-neutral tax reform was that it would lessen the chances for a comprehensive deficit-reduction agreement between the administration and Congress. Paradoxically, the collapse of efforts to reduce the deficit during 1985 made clear the president's absolute opposition to a tax increase. With that option foreclosed, the Gramm-Rudman-Hollings bill that passed later in the year effectively compartmentalized tax reform and allowed the revenue-neutral requirement to succeed.

In the spring of 1985 House and Senate conferees were unable to reach agreement on a fiscal 1986 budget resolution, and the Senate Republican leadership decided to use the impasse to raise the stakes. It put forth a deficit-reduction package which linked together the most controversial parts of the budget—entitlements, defense, and taxes. The Senate Republican plan called for a partial freeze on defense spending, a three-year, $60 billion tax increase, and limits on scheduled increases for social security and other retirement programs.

During July, President Reagan met with House and Senate leaders to negotiate a budget agreement. The first blow to the Senate Republican plan was a decision by Reagan and House Speaker O'Neill to scrap the proposed cutbacks on social security and defense. The second was Reagan's refusal to support a tax increase. Another Senate effort to balance spending cuts with tax increases (a fee on imported oil and a delay in the scheduled indexing of tax brackets) was formally rejected by Reagan on July 29.

At this point, the Senate and House agreed to a budget resolution which accommodated full cost-of-living adjustments (COLAs) in retirement programs, excluded any tax increase, and froze real spending for defense. Since virtually everyone in Congress recognized that this budget plan would not significantly lower the deficit, Gramm-Rudman-Hollings was seen as a means to force agreements in the future. It was rushed to passage without committee hearings or markups. Since its final version provided for automatic spending cuts to achieve deficit ceilings, the Reagan administration could enforce its "no tax increase" requirement without abandoning deficit reduction entirely. The price of that victory was that 50 percent of any automatic spending cuts would have to come from defense. Thus, for the second time, Reagan showed he was willing to subordinate defense spending to tax policy.

Gramm-Rudman-Hollings did not completely remove the deficit issue as an obstacle to tax reform, but it did make enforcement of revenue neutrality easier. The Senate Finance Committee, which decided in January not to work from the bill that had just passed the House, started with a revenue-neutral markup draft prepared by its chairman, Robert W. Packwood. Packwood subsequently insisted that proposed amendments be revenue neutral (that is, that any new tax preferences be offset by specific tax increases), both during committee deliberations and during floor debate.

The Final Stage. The twin threats to tax reform—deficit reduction and tax preferences—came into play during early 1986. The first complications arose in February as the administration submitted its fiscal 1987 budget and a key provision in Gramm-Rudman-Hollings was invalidated by a three-judge federal court. The Reagan budget for fiscal 1987 ostensibly met the statutory deficit ceiling of $144 billion, but its economic assumptions and defense spending estimates were immediately challenged as unrealistic. Two days later, the automatic spending cut procedure under Gramm-Rudman-Hollings was held unconstitutional. The result was renewed skepticism that any meaningful compromise on deficit control between Congress and the administration would be reached. In March half the Senate signed a letter to President Reagan asking that tax reform be delayed until a deficit-reduction accord was put into effect. On April 10 the Senate adopted, by a 72–24 vote, a sense-of-the-Senate resolution that tax reform legislation should not be considered until Congress and the administration agreed to a deficit-reduction plan. Instead, the Finance Committee and administration representatives proceeded to work on an alternative to the House-passed bill.

Like its counterpart in the House, the Finance Committee successfully resisted pressures to link tax reform with deficit reduction. In both instances, the committee chairman was indispensable. Congressman Rostenkowski had pushed the Ways and Means bill through the House in spite of criticism from liberal Democrats and wavering support from Republicans. Senator Packwood faced opposition from members of both parties who repeatedly tried to derail tax reform.

Through several weeks of Finance Committee markup, Packwood was challenged particularly by the difficulty of controlling tax preferences. Many committee members were reluctant to give up tax breaks for economic interests in their states, and the reinstatement of one after another led to a widening revenue shortfall. By mid-April the committee was holding a package of tax law changes that violated the five-year revenue-neutral standard by an estimated $30 billion. On April 18 markup was suspended.

The conceptual and political breakthrough came shortly thereafter. Packwood decided to cut through the impasse on tax preferences by proposing rates much lower than had previously been thought feasible in exchange for doing away with tax breaks. The most dramatic proposal, drafted by the staff of the Joint Committee on Taxation, included just two individual tax rates (15 percent and 25 percent). It also called for repeal of most large deductions and exclusions. The Finance Committee ultimately settled on a slightly higher top rate (27 percent) and a less ambitious pruning of tax preferences, but the lower rate–broader base trade-off was the key to unanimous committee approval of Packwood's plan. Within just twenty-eight hours, the committee agreed to a massive change in income tax policy and to a shift in tax burdens of more than $100 billion from individuals to corporations.

Senate consideration of the Finance Committee bill took most of June. The revenue-neutral requirement was enforced from the outset, and a procedural challenge to the requirement was rejected by a 54–39 vote on June 24.[36] In addition, the Finance Committee's proposal withstood attempts to restore popular tax deductions for Individual Retirement Accounts (IRAs) and state sales taxes. A Democratic amendment to create a third rate bracket of 35 percent for upper-income taxpayers was also rejected.

On June 24 the Senate approved its tax reform measure with only three dissenting votes. The House-Senate conference, which lasted until mid-August, turned out to be somewhat less arduous than anticipated because of the broad appeal of the dramatically lower rates contained in the Senate bill. It was this key point that allowed Packwood and Rostenkowski, who privately negotiated most of the compromise, to overcome important differences over business taxes and tax preferences between the House and Senate. At one point, staff estimates showed a $21.2 billion shortfall over five years from the Senate bill, which helped to lessen Senate opposition to higher business taxes. In the end, the top brackets in the Senate bill were increased by 1 percentage point—to 28 percent for individuals and to 34 percent for corporations—while approximately $120 billion in tax burdens was shifted from individuals to corporations. The sales tax deduction was eliminated, and partial IRA deductions for low- and middle-income taxpayers were approved. While these issues received the greatest attention, there were literally hundreds of transition rules and related technical points that had to be worked out during conference. The result was a 2,000-page conference report which was filed on September 18.

While the House and Senate approved the conference report by wide margins, there were objections from Republicans in both chambers to the increased taxes on business. The bill's impact on the economy was its most problematic feature. Of the president's original objectives, simplification had been severely compromised, if not abandoned. By contrast, fairness had been improved by the strengthening of minimum tax rules, the curtailing of tax preferences, and the raising of personal exemption and standard deduction levels. The third objective—incentives for growth— was difficult to assess. Lower individual and corporate rates meant that incentives had been increased. Since lower rates had been purchased with major changes in business taxation, however, some opponents charged that the economy would suffer. In his final speech before the Senate voted, Packwood acknowledged that no one could tell "for sure" whether the tax bill would "help the economy or hurt the economy." He continued: "But taxes are about more than money, they are about more than economics. They are about fairness—and this bill is fair."[37]

Redirecting Tax Policy

The policy changes incorporated into the Tax Reform Act of 1986 were far-reaching. The steeply progressive rate structure that had dominated individual income tax policy for half a century was abandoned. The long-term proliferation of tax references was halted, and their costs were reduced by lower tax rates for individuals and corporations. The law also established a new distinction between active and passive income, the goal of which was to curtail the use of certain business activities for tax shelter purposes. Finally, the taxpaying population was reduced by raising significantly personal exemption and standard deduction amounts.

From the mid-1930s through 1980, the top bracket rate for individuals ranged from 70 percent to 94 percent.[38] Over that period, the taxable income threshold at which the top rate applied dropped from $5 million to $200,000. The 1986 tax law established a 28 percent top bracket, effective in 1988, applied to taxable income at a considerably lower level—$29,750 for 1988 with an adjustment for inflation each year thereafter.[39] The political attractiveness of lower individual rates is suggested by the chronology in table 3.5. As the administration, the House, and finally the Senate developed their separate versions of tax reform, the real breakthrough came with the unexpectedly sharp rate cuts contained in the Senate's proposals. The corporate rate changes finally enacted, by comparison, were almost exactly what the administration had proposed initially. Finally, the appeal of lower rates was sufficient to overcome efforts to preserve the favored treatment of capital gains income. The 1986 tax act followed the Senate's lead in removing the deduction for long-term capital gains income and in treating capital gains like ordinary income. The resulting 28 percent top rate on capital gains was higher than prior law. It was also considerably above the levels recommended by the administration and by the House.

For high-income taxpayers, the lowering of the top rate was linked to a phasing-out of the 15 percent rate, effectively applying a flat tax to all

Table 3.5. Comparisons of Tax Rates, Existing Law through Tax Reform Act of 1986

	Existing Law	Treasury II May 1985	House Bill Dec. 1985	Senate Bill June 1986	TRA 1986 Oct. 1986
Individual	11–50% (14 brackets)	15, 25, 35%	15, 25, 35, & 38%	15 & 27%[a]	15 & 28%[a]
Corporate	15–46%	15–33%	15–36%	15–33%	15–34%
Capital Gains	20% top effective rate	17.5% top effective rate	22% top effective rate	Same as regular income	Same as regular income

SOURCE: *Congressional Quarterly Almanac, 1986* (Washington, D.C.: Congressional Quarterly, 1987), pp. 492–93.
[a] Lower rate phased out for high-income taxpayers through surcharge.

taxable income.[40] For low-income taxpayers, the increase in the personal exemption (from $1,080 to $2,000 in 1989) and standard deduction (from $3,670 to $5,000 for a joint return) was expected to eliminate all income tax liability for an estimated six million taxpayers, leading House Speaker O'Neill to call the Tax Reform Act "the best anti-poverty bill in this House for at least half a dozen years."[41]

The second major component of the 1986 tax bill—broadening of the tax base for individuals and corporations—featured a number of significant revisions in tax preferences. For individuals, the lower rates under tax reform were only partly offset by base-broadening provisions. For corporations, however, lower rates were more than compensated for by reductions in tax preferences. In fiscal year 1991, when scheduled phasing-in of the 1986 tax cut will be almost complete, individual income taxes are estimated at approximately $22 billion less and corporate income taxes about $27 billion more than under prior law.[42]

Several of the costliest tax preferences were repealed outright by the Tax Reform Act of 1986 (see table 3.6). Repeal of the capital gains deduction and investment tax credit are projected to reduce revenue losses in fiscal year 1991 by nearly $100 billion. Smaller but still substantial

Table 3.6. Revenue Losses from Major Tax Expenditures, Fiscal Year 1991: Comparison of Tax Reform Act of 1986 and Prior Law (in billions of dollars)

	Projected Revenue Losses FY 1991	
	Prior Law	TRA 1986
Tax Expenditures Repealed by TRA		
Capital gains deduction	$56.1	0.0
Investment tax credit	38.6	$ 1.6[a]
Two-earner married couple deduction	9.4	0.0
Tax Expenditures Modified by TRA		
Net exclusion from income of pension contributions and earnings	71.7	53.6[b]
Deductibility of mortgage interest on owner-occupied homes	43.6	35.8[b]
Deductibility of state and local income and sales taxes	36.1	18.4
Accelerated depreciation of equipment	23.9	16.5
Exemption of income on private purpose tax-exempt bonds	19.6	10.2
Exclusion of IRA contributions and interest earnings	19.2	9.0
Accelerated depreciation of nonresidential structures	12.9	6.9
Nonmortgage consumer interest deductions	14.7	0.9[c]

SOURCE: Congressional Budget Office, *The Effects of Tax Reform on Tax Expenditures* (Washington, D.C., 1988), pp. ix-x.
[a] Reflects unused credits from previous years.
[b] Also includes additional (and relatively minor) changes from the Omnibus Budget Reconciliation Act of 1987.
[c] Results from deductions during calendar year 1990.

reductions in revenue losses are also expected from a variety of tax preference modifications, such as revised depreciation rules and restrictions on the number and value of residences eligible for the home mortgage interest deduction. A number of large tax preference items survived the 1986 tax law reforms intact, the largest of these being the exclusion of employer-paid fringe benefits (such as health insurance).

The Tax Reform Act of 1986 also set important constraints on overall revenue policy. Its indexing provisions preclude inflation-driven, automatic increases. Raising income tax rates has always had a degree of political difficulty, which is why the boosts have typically occurred during wartime. The lower rates now in place were also "purchased" by the curtailing of tax preferences. The individual and corporate rate structures could be raised, but such an increase might simply revive the long-term growth in tax expenditures that was halted in 1986.

Deficit Reduction Revisited

Once the tax reform effort was completed, there was renewed pressure on Reagan to deal with the deficit by accepting a tax increase as part of a deficit-reduction plan. During 1986 and most of 1987, this pressure had very little effect. Selected excise taxes were included as part of the Consolidated Budget Reconciliation Act of 1985 (which was finally passed during March 1986). The Omnibus Budget Reconciliation Act of 1986 included accelerated collection of excise and social insurance taxes along with increased user fees, compliance measures, and limitations on foreign tax credits. The Superfund Reauthorization Act of 1986 also levied a variety of excise taxes, along with a general corporate tax, to fund toxic waste cleanup programs. The Continuing Resolution for 1987 included additional funding for the Internal Revenue Service to improve tax compliance. Taken together, these measures were expected to increase total receipts by almost $35 billion over the period from 1987 to 1990.[43] Almost half this amount, however, was accounted for by excise taxes, customs duties, and miscellaneous receipts.

In October 1987 the stock market crash led to yet another effort to resolve the deficit issue. The interpretations were many and varied as analysts tried to explain why such an extraordinary and unexpected market decline had occurred, but the chief suspect was the deficit. What soon became the conventional wisdom on this point was somewhat perplexing, since the fiscal 1987 deficit that had just been totaled represented a drop of more than $70 billion from the previous year. In fact, the $150 billion fiscal 1987 deficit was the smallest in five years.

Table 3.7. Revenue Effects of Major Legislation Enacted during the Reagan Presidency, Fiscal Years 1987-91 (in billions of dollars)

	Estimated Direct Effect for Fiscal Year				
	1987	1988	1989	1990	1991
First-Term Tax Legislation					
ERTA 1981	- $241.7	- $260.8	- $285.5	- $315.7	- $350.2
All Other	+ 95.2	+ 111.5	+ 118.7	+ 116.0	+ 122.9
Net Change	- 146.5	- 149.3	- 166.8	- 199.7	- 227.3
Second-Term Tax Legislation					
TRA 1986	+ 21.5	- 4.5	- 17.2	- 13.5	- 9.5
All Other	+ 7.6	+ 20.2	+ 25.6	+ 26.7	+ 25.6
Net Change	+ 29.1	+ 15.7	+ 8.4	+ 13.2	+ 16.1
Total Revenue Effect	- 117.4	- 133.6	- 158.4	- 186.5	- 211.2

SOURCE: *Budget of the United States Government, Fiscal Year 1989*, (Washington, D.C.: GPO, 1988), p. 4-4.

Nevertheless, the political pressures to do something were overwhelming, and the result was a month-long "budget summit" during which congressional leaders and administration officials finally agreed on a fiscal plan which reduced the deficit by an estimated $76 billion for fiscal years 1988 and 1989. The agreement was implemented through a reconciliation bill which combined spending cuts with $23 billion in additional revenues. The Omnibus Budget Reconciliation Act of 1987 was a partial concession by the administration on tax policy, with more than two dozen provisions raising corporate and individual taxes. The bill did not affect, however, income tax rates or indexing or the major structural features of the Tax Reform Act of 1986. Instead, it extended, and in some instances raised, several excise and payroll taxes, revised accounting and compliance standards, and reduced corporate and individual deductions. The largest revenue-raising measures were extension of the telephone excise tax ($3.6 billion over two years), repeal of installment sales accounting ($4.4 billion over two years), and technical corrections to reduce deductions for estate sales of securities to employee stock ownership plans ($2.8 billion over two years).

While the 1987 budget summit solved some immediate political problems, its tangible results were mixed. The fiscal 1989 budget transmitted to Congress shortly thereafter incorporated the agreed-upon tax increases for fiscal years 1988 and 1989 and also included some very minor additional increases (totaling $0.7 billion) for fiscal 1989. The budget also showed that, despite these increases, revenues would actually decline slightly as a percentage of GNP from 1987 (19.4 percent) to 1989 (19.2 percent). For individuals, moreover, the decline would be considerably greater, with individual income tax revenues falling from 8.7 percent of GNP in fiscal 1987 to 8.2 percent in fiscal 1989.

Over the entire second term, Reagan was able to preserve the essential elements of his tax program, despite the persistent criticism about deficits. The tax increases enacted during 1987 and 1988 more than offset the short-term revenue losses resulting from the Tax Reform Act of 1986, but they affected the deficit only marginally (see table 3.7). Altogether, estimated net tax reductions from the entire Reagan program reduced receipts levels by an average of approximately 3 percent of GNP for fiscal years 1987–91.

Tax Policy and Budget Policy

During the Reagan era, income tax policy was radically changed. Indexing was applied to marginal rate brackets and to personal exemptions and standard deductions. The steeply progressive marginal rate structure that had been in place for decades was replaced by a modified flat tax. The tax base was, against all expectations, broadened through cutbacks in tax preferences.

Without question, these were major accomplishments, although they drew upon precedents. Tax indexing, for example, had never been enacted at the federal level, but Congress through the 1970s had periodically reduced taxes to offset, at least in part, losses in real, after-tax income. The progressive rate structure, likewise, had been kept largely intact, but its impact had been undercut by the steady accretion of tax preferences. Prior tax reforms had previously advanced economic efficiency (as in 1964) and equity (as in 1969).

The Reagan tax reforms, however, were unprecedented in their scope. As a result, structural tax policy was greatly improved, especially in terms of equity and economic efficiency. The impact on budget policy was similarly unprecedented but considerably less positive.

The Reagan tax cuts were not aimed exclusively at economic recovery. They were also used to press for "smaller government," in the form of reduced domestic spending levels. Whether this was fully developed as a spending-control strategy at the time of the 1981 tax cuts is arguable, but the evidence from later years is fairly conclusive. The revenue-neutral requirement Reagan imposed on the 1986 tax bill and his agreement on Gramm-Rudman-Hollings, for example, meant that spending would have to be lowered to meet revenues (either by design or by sequestration) in order to eliminate deficits.

Of course, Gramm-Rudman-Hollings can be repealed or ignored, and future tax increases could be used to attack the deficit. Additional political obstacles to tax increases, however, have been created by the changing composition of revenues. As percentages of GNP, social security and corporate income taxes rose substantially during the 1980s, while individual income taxes declined. Erasing all or part of the current GNP differential between spending and revenues through a tax increase, therefore, will require deliberate, disproportionate increases in individual income taxes.

Thirty years ago, for example, general budget receipts (not including social insurance taxes) and general government outlays were roughly balanced at about 16 percent of GNP. By FY 1989, general budget outlays had risen to over 17 percent of GNP, while general budget receipts had declined to 14 percent of GNP. While the level of total budget receipts as a percentage of GNP in FY 1989 was slightly higher than it had been three decades earlier, the portion available to support general outlays was much lower. Current social security surpluses are masking the size of the deficit. They also disguise the magnitude of the tax increases necessary to eliminate the deficit.

The long-term development of tax policy, then, shows the importance of budgetary considerations. If taxation is subordinated to spending and balanced-budget requirements, incrementalism is almost guaranteed, regardless of which party controls the presidency. If tax policy is removed from these constraints, major changes are possible. These changes can be positive or negative in terms of structural tax policy. In the context of budget policy, the results are likely to be dismal, since policymakers have no protection against the incessant political pressures to boost spending and lower taxes.

The 1986 tax reform reinforces this last point. While many factors affected its passage, one of the most important was the revenue-neutral requirement Reagan imposed, which provided a revenue margin which created large groups of potential "winners" from tax reform. Shifting tax liabilities from individual to corporate taxpayers helped to finance the dramatic marginal rate cuts. For most individual taxpayers, the marginal rate reductions greatly outweighed the base-broadening increases.

These trade-offs would have been impossible if the 1986 tax bill had carried the burden of reducing significantly the $200+ billion deficits. Tax reform would then have meant increased tax liabilities for virtually everyone, and reform of this type has been extremely rare. Indeed, the only prominent examples have occurred during wartime fiscal emergencies. A peacetime tax reform which raises revenue levels to any significant degree is going to require a parallel emergency justification, and deficit concerns have not been equal to that task.

The traditional determinants of appropriate revenue levels—spending commitments and deficit reduction—have been subordinated if not abandoned. As a result, structural tax policy has been improved. The relationship between tax policy and the rest of the budget, however, has been considerably weakened.

II

Defense Budgets and Spending Control

4

Presidential Defense Policy

At the end of World War II, the United States was the dominant military and economic power in the world. Within a short period of time, it became clear that one corollary of this status was the maintenance of a permanent and massive military establishment. For over two decades, defense spending was the largest component of the federal budget, requiring a substantial and unprecedented peacetime commitment of economic resources. Nevertheless, defense budgets generated much less conflict than they have in recent years. Moreover, despite a political environment in which public opinion and congressional opinion were highly supportive of defense spending, presidents during this period imposed tight ceilings on defense budgets.

The era of presidential defense budgets was characterized by distinctive executive and congressional budget processes. Within the executive branch, defense spending decisions were made within a framework of high-level political and economic considerations, including nondefense spending needs, fiscal policy objectives, and international threats and commitments.[1] The principal restraint on military spending was exercised by the president, and the predominant concern was the economic impact of large, permanent defense budgets. For defense, top-down budgeting was essential in order to reconcile national security needs with what the economy and the budget could bear.

In Congress, by contrast, budgetary incrementalism marked defense decision making.[2] Defense budgeting was an "inside game," dominated by armed services committees and defense appropriations subcommittees that made only minor changes in the Department of Defense's budget requests.[3] In addition, Congress reviewed the president's defense budget independent of decisions on other spending bills.

The division of institutional responsibilities and differentiation between institutional processes was made possible by a policy consensus. Congress was willing to accord the president considerable deference, because there was widespread agreement that external threats precluded defense cuts of any magnitude.[4] Congress could also handle the defense budget in a bottom-up, decentralized manner, because the necessary integration of defense with other budget policy requirements had already been conducted by the president.

Finally, the budget policy effect of this approach to defense was somewhat surprising. The defense budget share gradually declined in the years between Korea and Vietnam. The relative size of the entire spending budget was stable. Real defense spending fluctuated within a narrow range. Thus, presidential defense budgeting allowed for modest, gradual trade-offs from defense to nondefense programs, but it prevented these trade-offs from becoming highly politicized. In a parallel fashion, the relatively closed (by current standards) decision-making process in Congress provided an institutional constraint on the politicization of defense issues.

Establishing the National Security Presidency

Just as World War II changed forever the politics of taxation, it also profoundly altered national security policy. Even after demobilization, the defense budget was enormous by prewar standards. This change in budget policy institutionalized the national security component of presidential leadership.

Between the two world wars, the United States maintained a modest military establishment. Even as the international situation in the late 1930s grew more and more ominous, the defense buildup in the United States moved forward very slowly. Whether President Roosevelt could have provided more assertive and effective leadership at that time is arguable, since he faced very strong isolationist critics in Congress.[5] The president had enormous difficulty convincing Congress and the public that the threat to American security was sufficiently serious to necessitate a massive and immediate rearmament program.[6]

The domestic policy agenda of the New Deal dominated the Roosevelt presidency for most of its first two terms. Roosevelt was either unwilling or unable, given the political situation he faced, to develop the national security side of the presidency with the same energy and imagination he devoted to its domestic responsibilities.[7] In his 1939 State of the Union message, the president warned Congress that "all about us wage undeclared wars—military and economic. . . . All about us are threats of new aggression." The defense budget submitted to Congress, however, hardly lived up to "the real necessity for expanding our national de-

Table 4.1. National Defense Outlays, Fiscal Years 1920-39 (in millions of dollars)

Fiscal Year	Total Dollars	Percentage of Federal Outlays
1920	$3,997	62.9%
1921	2,581	51.0
1922	929	28.3
1923	680	21.7
1924	647	22.4
1925	591	20.5
1926	586	20.3
1927	578	20.4
1928	656	22.4
1929	696	22.3
1930	734	22.1
1931	733	20.5
1932	703	15.1
1933	648	14.0
1934	540	8.1
1935	711	10.9
1936	914	10.8
1937	937	12.1
1938	1,030	15.2
1939	1,075	12.1

SOURCE: *Historical Statistics*, pt. 2, p. 1115.

fense."[8] Instead, the fiscal 1940 budget proposals included $1.3 billion for defense, an increase of just over $300 million compared to the year earlier.

From the end of the World War I demobilization through the 1930s, defense budget growth was minimal. For the 1920s, when the overall budget was stable, the defense share stayed at about 20 percent (see table 4.1). As overall spending began to grow rapidly under the New Deal, defense did not keep pace. By fiscal 1934 defense had dropped to less than 10 percent of total outlays. Even with a series of increases that started the following year, the defense allocation remained well below pre–New Deal levels.

Military manpower levels also grew very slowly during this period. Active duty military personnel in 1935 totaled just over 250,000, approximately the same as in 1925. As late as 1940, only 460,000 active duty personnel were available. Combined strength for the army, navy, and Marine Corps jumped to 1.8 million the following year, but this force level was less than 20 percent of the levels reached during 1943–45.[9]

There were a number of important defense-related actions by Roosevelt that were not reflected in spending or manpower levels. In 1938 Roosevelt initiated the expansion of defense plant capacity, setting among other goals an initial production target of 10,000 combat planes annually. Two years later, the annual target was raised to 50,000. In 1939 Roosevelt consolidated strategic and production control under his direction, moving the Joint Board of the Army and Navy and the Munitions Board into the newly established Executive Office of the President.[10]

As U.S. arms production was being accelerated, Roosevelt arranged for secret French and British munitions purchases.[11] Following the German invasion of Poland in 1939, Roosevelt convened a special session of Congress for the purpose of revising the embargo provisions of the 1935 and 1937 Neutrality Acts. After several weeks of bitter debate, the Senate finally agreed to a "cash and carry" system for selling war munitions and materials, and the House went along a few days later. The next year Roosevelt signaled the beginning of all-out assistance to Britain, executing the destroyers-for-bases agreement and promoting successfully the passage of lend-lease legislation. It was also Roosevelt's leadership that was responsible for securing approval of military draft legislation in 1940 and 1941. The Selective Service Act of 1940, enacted in an election year, contained a twelve-month service limitation. The president's strong appeal for an extension the following year nearly failed. Even after the president agreed to an eighteen-month extension rather than the unlimited one he originally requested, the House supported him by only a single vote, 203–202.

Despite these accomplishments, Roosevelt's foreign policy leadership in 1939 and 1940 has been criticized by one of his most sympathetic biographers as little more than "pinpricks and protests."[12] The 1940 Republican platform attacked Roosevelt for "unpreparedness and for the consequent danger of involvement in war." Of course, the Republican platform four years earlier had hardly sounded a call to arms. The party's defense plank in 1936 stated, "We favor an army and navy, including air forces, adequate for our National Defense." The Democratic platform that year was equally tepid, pledging "to observe a true neutrality in the disputes of others; to be prepared, resolutely to resist aggression against ourselves."[13]

Given the isolationist beliefs in Congress and the country, these statements were not at all remarkable. It is also understandable that Roosevelt felt the need for caution even as he sought to expand the defense effort. In 1940 he identified defense as his first priority: "The only important increase in any part of the Budget is the estimate for national defense."[14] Still, Roosevelt maintained that most of the defense budget was routine. The fiscal 1941 defense estimate was "needed to develop and maintain our normal defense preparations." The only "extraordinary" funds being requested were defense supplementals of $272 million for fiscal 1940 and $302 million for fiscal 1941.[15]

It is interesting to compare Roosevelt's performance with the portrait of presidential leadership supplied by the Supreme Court in the 1936 *Curtiss-Wright* case. Even as the Court was trying to cripple Roosevelt's domestic presidency, it declared that the "President alone has the power to speak or listen as a representative of the nation." In the field of international relations, the Court stated, presidential power was "very delicate, plenary, and exclusive." Lest there be any confusion, the Court distinguished between domestic and foreign affairs:

> It is quite apparent that, if in the maintenance of our international relations, embarrassment . . . is to be avoided and success for our aims achieved, congressional legislation . . . must often accord to the President a degree of discretion and freedom from statutory restriction which would not be admissible were domestic affairs alone involved. Moreover, he, not Congress, has the better opportunity of knowing the conditions which prevail in foreign countries, and especially is this true in time of war. He has his confidential sources of information. He has his agents.[16]

This robust view of the president's national security powers is fully consistent with the most expansive definitions of the modern presidency, but it had limited relevance during Roosevelt's first two terms. Roosevelt finally secured his domestic policy agenda against constitutional challenges in 1937, but he was not able to extend national security leadership in a parallel fashion until almost the eve of direct American involvement in World War II. The Supreme Court in *Curtiss-Wright* was describing an executive office which did not yet exist during peacetime. World War II and Roosevelt's direction of strategic policy on an unprecedented global scale added a national security dimension to the presidency that postwar American commitments quickly institutionalized. Those commitments also necessitated continued defense expenditures at levels that made presidential direction inevitable.

The 1930s provide a useful perspective from which to view subsequent periods of executive-congressional relations in the area of national security policy. The degree of discretion accorded presidents Truman and Eisenhower, along with the accompanying efforts to foster bipartisanship in Congress, no doubt reflected a reaction against congressional performance during Roosevelt's first two terms. At the same time, the competition between defense needs and domestic programs that emerged during the 1930s was a precursor of the post-Vietnam trend in budget policy. The antidefense and noninvolvement sentiments that were so strongly represented in Congress during the 1970s were not unique. Samuel Huntington quotes a professional soldier, Major J. H. Burns, writing about American attitudes toward the military just before World War II: "So these workers in words, ideas, and thoughts, the articulate part of the American folk, were mainly alike in their aversion—to use a mild term—to the Army. Strange, wasn't it, how this heterogeneous list of writers, speakers, idealists, religionists, philosophers, pseudo-philosophers—practically all the vocal parts of our population—had one powerful emotion in common? They disliked the professional soldier."[17]

What Huntington characterized as an "epitaph for the old system of civil-military relations," in which the "world of scholars, writers, and liberals had nothing but scorn for the professional military man,"[18] did not appear quite so final in the wake of Vietnam. It is important to recognize that defense budgets frequently are the focus for conflicts about the military, about U.S. foreign policy, and about the respective powers of the president and Congress. As the Roosevelt experience suggests, domestic politics can frustrate defense planning in the face of even the most blatant threats to U.S. security. With the more problematic threats of recent decades, it is not surprising that the tensions between defense and domestic politics have reemerged. The parallels between the 1930s and 1970s are far from exact, of course, but it is simply incorrect to treat recent antidefense moods as historical aberrations peculiarly rooted in Vietnam or other misadventures.

Defense and the Economy

From the end of World War II until Vietnam, the defense budgetary process was dominated by the president's assessment of national security objectives and military funding requirements. Defense was by far the dominant component of the spending side of the budget, accounting for approximately one-half of the total outlays between 1945 and 1965. Nevertheless, the defense budget did not serve as a means for congressional challenges to presidential power, nor was it part of congressional debates on priorities.

Instead, Congress usually went along with the strategic doctrines, force-level recommendations, and major weapons systems proposed by the president.[19] Congress was also generally willing to allow the president considerable discretion in the use of funds, even to the extent of acquiescing to presidential impoundments of appropriations about which there were policy disagreements.[20] In addition, Congress had neither the staff nor the expertise to compete with the executive branch's civilian and military bureaucracies. The Legislative Reorganization Act of 1946 was the first step toward institutionalizing the use of professional staff for all standing committees, but it was not until the 1970s that committee and subcommittee staffs began to approach current levels.

By recent standards, congressional review of the defense budget was straightforward. Annual authorizations were not extensively required.[21] Appropriations classifications were broad.[22] Controls on shifting or carrying over funds were loose, and large, undesignated contingency funds were common.[23] Moreover, those committees that conducted routine oversight for the Department of Defense were supportive. As a recent study commented, "A generation ago the Senate and House Armed Services Committees were enthusiastic and deferential supporters of the Pentagon, operating more as advocates than as watchdogs of defense policy and spending."[24] The appropriations defense subcommittees, which had by far the greater influence over the Department of Defense budget during this period, usually confined themselves to very modest changes in the president's defense estimates. Huntington points out that congressional challenges to presidential recommendations most often took the form of "an increase in the funds allocated to one particular service or program." By comparison, congressional cuts generally indicated agreement with presidential military policy, not dissents from that policy.[25]

For the Truman, Eisenhower, and Kennedy administrations, executive dominance of the defense budgetary process was the norm. In Congress, there was a widespread agreement on according defense spending a privileged position. The principal check on defense spending was exercised by the president, and it was based upon the economic burden of defense spending.

The Truman Reversal

The budgets submitted by President Truman before the Korean War were, in his words, an attempt to define "a proper relationship between our security requirements and our economic and financial resources." This effort meant steep reductions in the requests of the military services, with Truman explaining his fiscal 1950 objective as a "position of relative military readiness" which could be maintained "in the foreseeable future at approximately the level recommended in this budget."[26] Truman maintained this stance throughout 1949, despite the Communist takeover in China and the successful Soviet atomic bomb test. His fiscal 1951 defense budget was $1.2 billion below the previous year's figure, emphasizing again "a balanced structure which can be maintained over a period of years without an undue use of national resources."[27]

The prevailing view in Congress, despite sharp disagreements over air force funding, was similar to Truman's. When the chairman of the House Appropriations Subcommittee on Defense, George H. Mahon, reported to his colleagues on the fiscal 1950 appropriations bill, he stressed that proposed funding was less than one-half the $30 billion semireadiness estimate and one-fourth the complete readiness estimate prepared by the Joint Chiefs of Staff. Still, Mahon described himself as "shocked and disturbed" over the "vast funds we are spending and preparing to spend for national defense." He explained that defense budgets had to be controlled tightly, because "nothing would please a potential enemy better than to have us bankrupt our country and destroy our economy by maintaining over a period of years complete readiness."[28]

The Senate Appropriations Committee echoed this concern. Its report on the House-passed fiscal 1950 defense appropriations bill called for over $1 billion in cuts, warning that "a nation which exhausts itself in enervating overpreparation . . . may well fall prey to a cunning and patient enemy who fully realizes the debilitating influences of a war-geared economy over a long period of time."[29] The Senate agreed to the recommended cuts, and when the House insisted on restoring funds for the air force as part of the conference agreement, Truman announced that he would not spend the additional money.[30]

Truman's efforts to stabilize military spending were part of a broader policy of limiting and balancing the budget. Postwar fears of inflation, for example, lent urgency to Truman's calls for balanced budgets, and he backed those up with repeated vetoes of tax-reduction bills in 1947 and 1948. In addition, the containment policy that began to take shape over the same period required substantial outlays for economic and military aid, which reduced further the budgetary margin available for direct expenditures to support U.S. forces.

Demobilization after World War II had been rapid and steep. In just over two years, national defense outlays dropped by more than $70 billion, while active duty military personnel were reduced by over 10 million. In fiscal 1948 both defense spending ($9.1 billion) and manpower

Table 4.2. National Defense and International Affairs Outlays, Fiscal Years 1946-61 (in billions of dollars)

Fiscal Year	National Defense	International Affairs	Total	As Percentage of Budget
1946	$42.7	$1.9	$44.6	80.7%
1947	12.8	5.8	18.6	53.9
1948	9.1	4.6	13.7	46.0
1949	13.1	6.0	19.1	49.2
1950	13.7	4.7	18.4	43.2
1951	23.6	3.6	27.2	59.8
1956	42.5	2.4	44.9	63.6
1961	49.6	3.2	52.8	54.0

SOURCE: *Historical Tables, Budget of the United States Government, Fiscal Year 1990*, pp. 39-41.

levels (1.4 million) fell to their lowest levels of the entire postwar era. Even when combined with military and economic aid (functionally classified as international affairs), defense and associated national security spending in the late 1940s was significantly lower than during the post-Korea period (see table 4.2).

Since tight military expenditure control coincided with the centralization of defense budgeting in the newly created Department of Defense, interservice disputes over funding were intense. The navy and air force, for example, quickly locked into a battle over supercarriers versus a seventy-group air force.[31] It was this type of budget allocation issue that tended to carry over into Congress, where spokesmen for the services then sought to enact specific increases for the contested programs. The amounts involved, however, were limited. Congress was no more willing than the Truman administration to fund semireadiness military budgets, much less complete readiness ones. Instead, both sides agreed to comparatively stable, low military budgets backed up by the American monopoly of atomic weapons.

The ending of that monopoly in 1949 led to the first comprehensive review of U.S. national security policy and strategic requirements. Truman appointed Paul Nitze, the director of the Policy Planning Staff of the State Department, to head an interdepartmental task force, whose report, designated "NSC-68," was submitted in the spring of 1950. It called for greatly increased defense spending to neutralize the Soviet ground threat in Europe and to counter the growing Soviet strategic threat. The cost estimates for NSC-68 were later calculated at about $40 billion annually, compared to a defense budget submitted by President Truman for fiscal 1951 of roughly one-third that level.[32]

The enormous gap between the administration's strategic planning requirements and its budget policies created serious political difficulties for Truman. It was not politically feasible to triple peacetime defense budgets, but it was also dangerous to ignore the growing criticism of military unpreparedness. A so-called year of maximum peril, initially identified as 1954, would see the Soviets strong enough to attack the U.S. directly.[33] The American rearmament effort therefore had to be dramatic and immediate.

The outbreak of war in Korea became the catalyst for a broad military buildup in the U.S. Shortly before Congress approved the regular fiscal 1951 defense appropriation, Truman warned that larger forces would be needed "for a long time to come."[34] On September 22 Congress passed a supplemental appropriation of $11.7 billion for the Department of Defense and $4 billion for military aid. On January 2, 1951, Congress completed action on a second supplemental appropriation, adding nearly $17 billion for the Department of Defense along with about $3 billion for expanded atomic energy and military stockpiling programs.

Within a year, defense outlays almost doubled, from $13.7 billion in fiscal 1950 to $23.6 billion in fiscal 1951. In fiscal 1953 defense spending reached its Korean War peak of $52.8 billion, nearly two-thirds of the fiscal 1945 World War II high. This rapid buildup was not devoted exclusively to the Korean conflict. Included as well were conventional and strategic force expansions along the lines advocated in NSC-68. U.S. army divisions were sent to Europe. Air force production lines were greatly expanded, and new air bases were constructed in the U.S. and abroad. Atomic energy programs were boosted dramatically. The entire defense production base was broadened and modernized.

In fiscal 1950, for example, national defense outlays for major capital investment totaled $2.0 billion, or less than 15 percent of defense spending (see table 4.3). For fiscal 1953 capital investment programs of $20.6 billion accounted for just under 40 percent of the defense budget, reflecting a marked acceleration in procurement, military construction, and atomic energy defense programs. The Truman defense reversal, then, was a comprehensive effort to correct perceived deficiencies in U.S. forces.

Table 4.3. National Defense Outlays for Major Direct Physical Capital Investment, Fiscal Years 1946-54 (in billions of dollars)

Fiscal Year	Procure-ment	Military Construction	Atomic Energy	Total	Percentage of Total Defense Outlays
1946	$19.1	$1.0	--[a]	$20.1	47.1%
1947	3.0	0.4	--[a]	3.5	27.3
1948	2.0	0.4	$0.3	2.7	29.7
1949	1.7	0.1	0.5	2.3	17.5
1950	1.5	0.1	0.4	2.0	14.6
1951	4.3	0.4	0.7	5.5	23.3
1952	11.0	1.7	1.4	14.2	30.8
1953	17.1	1.9	1.5	20.6	39.0
1954	16.0	1.7	1.6	19.3	39.1

SOURCE: *Historical Tables, Budget of the United States Government, Fiscal Year 1990*, pp. 39-40, 161-62.
[a] Less than $100 million.

When Truman announced in September 1950 that there would be "substantial increases in the United States forces to be stationed in Western Europe in the interests of the defense of that area," he was committing the United States to a costly long-term conventional force buildup.[35] And it was cost that led the Eisenhower administration to revise but not abandon the strategic doctrines that had evolved after NSC-68.

The New Look

In the penultimate budget he transmitted to Congress, President Eisenhower called the defense program changes then under way "one of the greatest transitions in history." Eisenhower was referring specifically to "the change of emphasis from conventional-type to missile-type warfare," a change which his administration had helped to engineer.[36] One of the major reasons for this change was a renewed concern over the economic and budgetary effects of defense spending. Eisenhower and his budget advisers were convinced that the budget had to be balanced without raising taxes and that this required significant reductions in defense. Heavy reliance was therefore placed upon substituting technology for manpower, since nuclear forces were (and still are) considerably cheaper than conventional forces. The substitution required new strategic and tactical doctrines that were fairly controversial, but Eisenhower was quite successful in implementing his "New Look" for defense.

Efforts to revise defense budget policy began almost immediately after Eisenhower took office. The fiscal 1954 defense estimates that his predecessor had sent to Congress were keyed to force-level peaks by the end of the fiscal year. According to Truman, defense expenditures "should begin to decline in the fiscal year 1955 and should continue to decline until they reach the level required to keep our armed forces in a state of readiness." How rapid that decline might be was unclear, but eventual stabilization was forecast "in the neighborhood of 35 to 40 billion dollars annually."[37] His final budget was a stark reminder of just how much Truman's defense policy had changed. Defense accounted for almost 60 percent of this $78.6 billion budget, compared to roughly half that level for the fiscal 1947–50 period. In actual dollars, the $35–40 billion long-term projections were about three times the fiscal 1947–50 average.

Eisenhower moved quickly to reduce Truman's defense estimates and to reorient the focus of U.S. preparedness efforts. A report approved by the National Security Council on April 29, 1953, called for up to $5 billion in fiscal 1954 cuts and for a leveling off of defense spending at $35 billion in fiscal 1956.[38] In a nationwide radio address on May 19, 1953, the president explained that his defense program would need to be sustained for "a long—an indefinite—period of time."[39] His warnings about an "unbearable security burden"[40] were reminiscent of Truman's in the late 1940s, but Eisenhower went on to reject planning scenarios based on the "year of maximum peril." Defense needs, declared Eisenhower, could not "be based solely on the theory that we can point to a D-day of desperate danger, somewhere in the near future, to which all plans can be geared."[41]

What Eisenhower called "a new concept for planning and financing our national security program" was heavily dependent upon airpower, especially strategic airpower.[42] Its centerpiece was the deterrent concept of massive retaliation, in which the United States would reserve the option of responding "instantly" and "massively" to Communist aggression.[43] The United States would thus exploit the greatly improved strategic capabilities the Truman administration had provided. The Strategic Air Command (SAC) had a large, long-range bomber fleet in place, with a new generation of advanced bombers well along in the research and development stage. Stocks of atomic weapons had been greatly enlarged, and the

United States had already tested (on November 1, 1952) the world's first hydrogen bomb.

The massive retaliation doctrine generated considerable controversy and criticism throughout Eisenhower's tenure,[44] but its budgetary appeal was found in the enormous economic advantage that nuclear weapons enjoyed over conventional forces. In Europe, for example, Warsaw Pact forces were much stronger than NATO's, and the conventional force buildups necessary to achieve parity were considered too costly by Eisenhower's budget planners. Addressing a closed session of the North Atlantic Council in Paris on April 23, 1954, Secretary of State John Foster Dulles admitted that "current NATO force programs fall short of providing the conventional forces . . . required to defend the NATO area against a full-scale Soviet bloc attack." The United States could accept this shortfall "on the premise that atomic weapons in substantial quantities would be available for the support of its presently programmed forces." Further, stated Dulles, "the ability to use atomic weapons as 'conventional weapons' was essential."[45]

For Eisenhower, costs were only part of the defense problem. During a National Security Council meeting on October 7, 1953, Eisenhower reportedly observed that "he doubted if we could get this so-called adequate defense over a sustained period without drastically changing our whole way of life." When Secretary of Defense Charles E. Wilson rejoined that "it was perfectly possible . . . to spend more money on defense . . . without radically changing the American way of life," Eisenhower emphasized the importance of the time element: "You could get the American people to make these sacrifices voluntarily for a year or two or for three years but no eloquence would sell this proposition . . . for the indefinite future."[46]

In terms of budget policy, the New Look was a return to the pre-Korean defense spending ceilings, albeit at a much higher level. The initial plans to balance the budget in fiscal 1955 assumed expenditure reductions of $11.5 billion in fiscal years 1954 and 1955, with over 80 percent of the proposed cuts in national security programs and well over half specifically in the Department of Defense. By fiscal 1956, it was hoped that "expenditure levels can be progressively reduced . . . to approximately $35 billion."[47] While these reductions were not achieved, defense spending was stabilized well below its Korean War peaks. From FY 1955 through FY 1961, defense spending grew at an average annual rate of less than 3 percent; in real terms, defense outlays dropped by more than 7 percent over this period.[48]

Table 4.4. Eisenhower Defense Budgets, Recommended and Enacted Budget Authority, Fiscal Years 1955-61 (in billions of dollars)

| Fiscal Year | New Obligational Authority[a] | | |
	Recommended	Enacted	Change
1955	$ 34.8	$ 33.7	- $ 1.1
1956	36.7	35.9	- 0.8
1957	39.7	41.3	+ 1.6
1958	43.6	40.4	- 3.2
1959	44.3	45.5	+ 1.2
1960	45.2	44.8	- 0.4
1961	45.3	46.0	+ 0.7
Total	289.6	287.6	- 2.0

Source: *Budget of the United States Government*, fiscal years 1955-63.
[a] New obligational authority was the term used during this period to designate new budget authority becoming available in a given fiscal year for the purpose of making commitments.

The Eisenhower defense program was noteworthy in several key areas. First, the budgets that Eisenhower submitted to Congress were changed very little. The post-Korea budget authority levels that Eisenhower proposed, for example, were generally indistinguishable from the appropriations enacted by Congress (see table 4.4). In several instances, Congress increased rather than cut proposed budget authority. The net change for six years was less than 1 percent.

Second, defense budget changes were geared toward airpower and missiles. In fiscal 1950 the air force had the smallest of the service budgets (see table 4.5). By the end of the decade, its budget nearly equaled the combined army and navy budgets. On the procurement side, reported net expenditures for missiles grew from $631 million in fiscal 1955 to $3.8 billion in fiscal 1960.[49] Over this five-year period, missile outlays climbed from less than 5 percent of net procurement expenditures to over 26 percent.[50]

The buildup of strategic forces was spurred by evidence of a changing U.S.-Soviet power balance. By 1956 the Soviet stockpile of nuclear weapons, advanced bombers, and intermediate-range ballistic missiles was

Table 4.5. Service Budgets, Fiscal Years 1950-60 (in billions of dollars)

Fiscal Year	Gross Expenditures		
	Army	Navy	Air Force
1950	$ 4.0	$ 4.1	$ 3.6
1951	7.5	5.6	6.3
1952	15.6	10.2	12.7
1953	16.2	11.9	15.1
1954	12.9	11.3	15.7
1955	8.9	9.7	16.4
1956	8.7	9.7	16.7
1957	9.1	10.4	18.4
1958	9.0	10.9	18.4
1959	9.5	11.7	19.1
1960	9.4	11.6	19.1

SOURCE: *Budget of the United States Government*, fiscal years 1952-62.

growing rapidly. On October 4, 1957, the Soviets successfully launched the first artificial earth satellite and followed it with an 1,100-pound satellite one month later. The rocket boosters used in these launches demonstrated unexpected Soviet progress in developing long-range ballistic missile systems, and President Eisenhower conceded in his 1958 State of the Union message that "we are probably somewhat behind the Soviets in some areas of long-range ballistic missile development."[51] Bipartisan congressional demands for defense spending increases were reinforced by a series of reports that called for comprehensive improvements in U.S. preparedness. The Gaither Commission Report (issued by a presidentially appointed committee) coincided with the Sputnik launches and was followed up by reports from a Rockefeller Brothers Fund defense panel and from the Senate Armed Services Preparedness Subcommittee headed by Senator Lyndon B. Johnson. The recommendations in each case ranged from strategic to limited war capabilities, and there was agreement that immediate and significant defense budget increases were necessary.

Eisenhower's fiscal 1959 budget called for a comparatively modest defense supplemental appropriation of $1.3 billion for fiscal 1958 and for $39.6 billion in appropriations for fiscal 1959. This proposal was above the $38 billion ceiling the administration had earlier hoped to maintain but well below the levels proposed by the defense study panels. In addition, the Eisenhower budget concentrated most of the increase in ballistic missile and other strategic programs and proposed offsetting military manpower reductions, thereby ignoring the recommendations to upgrade limited war forces.

Congressional action on a series of defense spending bills—the fiscal 1958 supplemental appropriation, along with the fiscal 1959 defense and military construction appropriations—made only minor changes in program allocations and in the requested budget totals. Congress did not accept the manpower reductions contained in the president's defense plan, but it did not directly challenge his decisions about the balance between strategic and conventional force increases. These decisions, however, were beginning to stimulate increased criticism from those who believed that conventional forces were being slighted.

Military manpower had declined from a Korean War peak of 3.6 million to 2.9 million in 1955 and to 2.5 million in 1960, with the army's strength being reduced by nearly half. Noting that an even smaller share of procurement programs would now be directed toward conventional or limited war forces, some prominent congressional Democrats charged that Eisenhower's defense budgets were inadequate to support the balanced forces that the country required.

A second line of criticism, which became highly publicized during John F. Kennedy's presidential campaign, focused on the alleged inadequacy of United States strategic weapons. The "missile gap" critics charged that Soviet strategic capabilities were outpacing those of the United States and were endangering U.S. retaliatory forces. Eisenhower administration spokesmen forcefully rebutted these charges, and the president continued to impose a "directed verdict" or budget ceiling on the military services. To some extent, the congressional debates on the Eisenhower defense program reflected interservice competition for funds that had been intensified by the president's budget ceilings. The balanced forces proponents in Congress, for example, tended to be army and navy partisans, while the air force's advocates were fond of the missile gap critique.

Both sides, however, shared the belief that defense budgets were too low. In 1959 and again in 1960, Democrats took the lead in congressional efforts to increase Eisenhower's defense estimates. In 1960, when Congress overwhelmingly approved a defense appropriations bill nearly $800 million above the administration's $41 billion request, Kennedy and several other Democrats refused to support it as inadequate. Kennedy's campaign later in the year continued the debate, and his election insured that defense budgets would increase at least over the short term. The Democratic platform had described the U.S. military position as filled with gaps—"missile gap, space gap, limited-war gap"—and pledged not only to erase them but also to insure continued support for "essential programs now slowed down, terminated, suspended, or neglected for lack of budgetary support."[52]

When John Kennedy took office, defense spending accounted for approximately half the budget and almost 10 percent of GNP. Kennedy, along with most moderate and liberal Democrats, was not committed to reducing these levels. In fact, the "flexible response" initiatives that the Kennedy administration quickly formulated to replace massive deterrence required higher spending for both strategic and conventional forces. In the early 1960s there was nothing in the Democratic party comparable to the antidefense bloc that would emerge during Vietnam.

Flexible Response and Domestic Needs

The Kennedy presidency supplied new doctrines for U.S. defense policy, and it pushed initially for higher levels of defense spending. Pronouncements about "flexible response," for example, reflected Kennedy's belief that greater balance was needed among strategic, conventional, and limited-war forces. Flexible response also was supposed to make available to the president more options within each of these force categories. Both elements of flexible response, along with the Soviet-American disputes over Berlin in 1961 and Cuba in 1962, combined to push defense spending above levels recommended by the Eisenhower administration, but the changes in defense budgeting were perhaps less dramatic than Kennedy and his military advisers were willing to admit. There is even some evidence that the first round of defense increases was in part a politically acceptable way to stimulate the economy.[53]

President Kennedy followed up quickly on his election campaign attacks against Republican defense policy by proposing a series of defense budget increases. On March 28, 1961, the president requested nearly $3 billion in accelerated funding, primarily for Polaris-armed submarines and for upgraded limited-war forces. He also began what turned into a continuing dispute with Congress by calling for offsetting reductions of $750 million in the B-70 manned-bomber program and in other strategic bomber programs. On May 25, before he was to meet with Soviet premier Nikita Khrushchev in Vienna, Kennedy asked Congress to add $225 million to the army and Marine Corps budgets. Two months later, responding to Soviet threats against the allied presence in Berlin, Kennedy requested $3.5 billion for additional manpower, along with weapons and equipment procurement.

Congress responded quickly and affirmatively to each of these requests. A fiscal 1961 defense supplemental appropriation was approved on March 31. A new requirement for prior authorization of aircraft, missile, and naval vessel procurement was met by early June. On August 10 Congress completed action on the fiscal 1962 defense appropriations bill, which was approximately $6 billion above the Eisenhower estimates for fiscal 1962.

Kennedy's fiscal 1963 and fiscal 1964 budgets continued to stress the need for defense increases. His fiscal 1963 budget message asserted that "expenditures for the military functions of the Department of Defense are estimated at about $9 billion higher [for FY 1962–1963], and new obligational authority at $12 to $15 billion more, than would have been required to carry forward the program as it stood a year ago." Programs for which Kennedy sought additional funding ranged across the spectrum of defense forces. The fiscal 1963 budget called for strategic force buildups, principally Minuteman missiles and Polaris submarines, that could "survive and respond overwhelmingly after a massive nuclear attack." These strategic weapons were to be complemented by conventional force improvements, including an increase in the regular army from fourteen to sixteen divisions and expanded airlift and sealift capabilities for deployment of limited-war forces. Another Kennedy priority, which proved increasingly controversial as the U.S. commitment in Vietnam expanded, involved increased "special forces" to help U.S. allies cope with "the threat of Communist-sponsored insurrection and subversion."[54]

The Cuban missile crisis during October 1962 provided additional support for the U.S. defense buildup. It also erased whatever doubts still remained that the "missile gap" charges in 1959 and 1960 had been false.[55] The Kennedy administration's fiscal 1964 budget, submitted to Congress three months after the successful confrontation with the Soviets, announced that "there is no discount price for defense. The free world must be prepared at all times to face the perils of global nuclear war, limited conventional conflict, and covert guerrilla activities."[56] While this declaration seemed to indicate that defense budgets would continue to increase indefinitely, there were contrary signs that defense spending would be curbed.

By 1963 criticism in Congress was beginning to build over the decisions on strategic and other weapons systems being made by the administration. Kennedy's secretary of defense, Robert S. McNamara, had imposed an unusually high degree of centralized control over weapons procurement by the military services. The "planning-programming budgeting" system developed by McNamara's civilian staff and first used for the fiscal 1963 defense budget was designed to provide systematic comparisons of the costs and benefits of alternative programs and systems. In practice, it reduced greatly the authority that the separate services had enjoyed on procurement decisions. It also led to a series of controversies with the services, as McNamara opposed the new manned bombers, the nuclear surface fleet, and the separate fighter aircraft that had been strongly recommended by his military advisers.

Coupled with McNamara's efforts to limit the discretionary authority of the separate services was his advocacy of strategic balance between the United States and the Soviet Union. Efforts to distinguish the Kennedy administration's strategic doctrines from Eisenhower's produced at first a confused switching between counterforce and countercity deterrence. The secretary of defense's 1963 defense posture statement and later elaborations then began to spell out a doctrine of mutual deterrence that, by 1964, had evolved into mutual assured destruction.[57] A basic assumption of McNamara's deterrent theory was that strategic buildups by one side would inevitably be countered by the other. As a result, McNamara opposed new strategic systems, such as the antiballistic missile system (ABM), being pushed by the military to insure superiority rather than balance.

As in the 1950s, the complaints of the military services were received sympathetically by their partisans on the congressional military committees, and with similar results. Overall budget levels were not seriously challenged, efforts to force weapons systems on the administration were rebuffed, and congressional participation in defense policy-making remained limited.

Lacking any strategic justifications for a new cycle of procurement increases, the Department of Defense revived the Eisenhower objective of limiting and stabilizing defense budgets. Two months after John Kennedy was assassinated, Lyndon Johnson presented the fiscal 1965 budget to Congress, and it called for a reduction of $800 million in defense outlays. According to Johnson, the defense increases from 1961 to 1964 had created "the most formidable defense establishment the world has ever known." Strategic retaliatory forces, which were slated for a $3.1 billion reduction below FY 1962 budget authority levels, were described as

Table 4.6. Defense Outlays, Fiscal Years 1955-65 (in billions of dollars)

Fiscal Year	Constant (FY 1982) Dollars	Percentage of Total Outlays	Percentage of GNP
1955	$211.0	62.4%	11.1%
1956	198.5	60.2	10.2
1957	203.5	59.3	10.3
1958	198.3	56.8	10.4
1959	196.0	53.2	10.2
1960	192.1	52.2	9.5
1961	195.2	50.8	9.6
1962	202.2	49.0	9.4
1963	197.1	48.0	9.1
1964	198.8	46.2	8.7
1965	181.4	42.8	7.5

SOURCE: *Historical Tables, Budget of the United States Government, Fiscal Year 1990*, pp. 47-48, 124-26.

"vastly superior to the Soviet nuclear force."[58] No increases were sought for general-purpose forces or for the airlift and sealift forces that had been major priorities in previous years.

Actual defense spending in fiscal 1965 showed an even sharper decline than Johnson had estimated, dropping nearly $4 billion below fiscal 1964 spending. Moreover, the real level of defense spending in fiscal 1965 was the lowest since the Korean War, as were the defense budget share and GNP percentages (see table 4.6). The defense boosts over the fiscal 1961–64 period were substantial, but they did not reverse ongoing budget trends. In addition, the major weapons systems behind the 1961–64 procurement increases had been started during the Eisenhower presidency. With McNamara committed to strategic balance, a similarly ambitious package of new weapons systems was considered unnecessary.

By 1963 the Kennedy defense plan was being shaped by some of the same budgetary constraints that had been so sharply criticized during the late 1950s. At the same time, there was an important difference between the Eisenhower and Kennedy budgetary strategies. For Eisenhower, the defense budget's economic impact was the overriding concern. For Kennedy and Johnson, an emerging issue was defense spending versus social program spending. In part, this difference merely reflected the lessening economic significance of the defense budget. Defense outlays as a percentage of GNP had declined from more than 11 percent in 1955 to 7.5 percent ten years later. By the mid-1960s, however, defense was still absorbing nearly half of the total budget, which meant that the margin available to support other programs was still narrow. The fiscal 1965 and 1966 budgets attempted to widen that margin, but the budget policy shift was interrupted by Vietnam.

Defense Budgeting before Vietnam

For almost the entire period from the end of World War II to the U.S. escalation in Vietnam, defense spending was the largest component of the federal budget. Its claim on total economic resources was substantial, with defense spending averaging close to 10 percent of GNP annually for fiscal years 1946–65. Nevertheless, partisan splits over the defense budget were not severe, nor were differences between the president and Congress bitter and protracted. Before Vietnam, there was a clear political consensus concerning the high priority assigned to defense spending.

The roots of this consensus were based in specific defense realities. Military threats against the United States were perceived as serious. The defense requirements arising from those threats were, by most accounts, considerably greater than the funds that could be devoted to defense. As a consequence, the president was given a good deal of discretion in fashioning a defense program which would fit within available budgetary resources.

Congressional deference toward presidential defense budgeting was not absolute. There were disagreements over defense totals and interservice allocations, and Congress expected periodic justifications of the strategic implications of presidential defense programs. Within Congress, however, the circle of serious participation in annual defense budgeting was fairly small. In a sense, the hierarchical arrangement accepted within Congress mirrored the hierarchy between Congress and the president.

It is important to recognize, however, that the institutional relations pertaining to defense were not unique. The budget process in general assigned great weight to the president's recommendations. Congress was expected to modify presidential estimates within a fairly narrow range, and, here again, active participation on budget matters within Congress was confined to specialized committees.

The limited politicization of defense budgeting was part of a budget process in which conflict was usually moderate. This relative harmony did not mean, however, that defense was unconstrained by other budget policy goals. During the late 1940s, for example, Truman was attempting to balance defense against domestic spending requirements. Eisenhower's defense budgets were explicitly governed by his beliefs about what the economy could sustain and what the public would be willing to support over the long term. Under Kennedy and Johnson, an initial expansion of defense spending was followed by an attempt to expand the domestic side of the budget.

Competition between defense spending and domestic programs was not absent. What the era of presidential defense policy provided, however, was a presidential responsibility to manage the competition. This arrangement did not entirely eliminate volatility in defense funding, although Eisenhower came close to doing so, nor did it necessarily satisfy the military. It did keep budget policy debates from overwhelming presidential-congressional relations, and it did fasten responsibility and accountability on the president. Moreover, the legitimate demands of defense and non-defense programs were reconciled within budgets that grew slowly and that were close to balance.

5

Politicized Defense Policy

The Vietnam War has had a lasting impact on presidential-congressional relations, an important manifestation of which has been the politicization of defense budgeting. The politicization of defense goes beyond dissensus over the size and allocation of the military budget. It extends to political, procedural, and institutional shifts that have heightened the instability of defense budgeting and weakened the relation between defense and spending control.

The political environment for defense has become more challenging. Partisan and ideological splits on defense within Congress have deepened, and an antidefense bloc exists for which there is no pre-Vietnam counterpart.[1] Public opinion on defense spending has become highly unstable, switching between positive and negative assessments every few years.[2]

The procedural alterations in defense budgeting have been significant. Congress now utilizes a three-stage process for defense consisting of (1) congressional budget resolution targets for total budget authority and outlays in the national defense function; (2) defense authorization requirements covering most of the annual defense budget; and (3) annual defense appropriations bills. The circle of participation in defense budgeting has expanded to include twenty-one House and Senate committees with formal jurisdiction over some aspect of defense policy. In addition, participation by House and State members in debating, amending, and challenging defense-related bills has become widespread.[3]

The institutional relations between Congress and the executive branch have become more confrontational and less structured. Congressional deference to the president on national security matters has clearly diminished, and this change directly affects defense budgeting. Instead of the relatively clear-cut division of roles and responsibilities that once prevailed, Congress now duplicates much of the president's work. Lacking the centralization and hierarchy of the executive branch, however, Congress often finds it difficult to make clear-cut and binding decisions.

The policy results of politicization have been criticized by many defense experts, including prominent members of Congress.[4] First, the sheer level of defense spending has acquired a symbolic value, both for defense proponents and defense critics, which often overshadows truly important issues of military preparedness and military policy. Second, the proliferation of congressional reviews of defense matters has encouraged more and more intervention into internal defense management (micromanagement). Defense budget debates, as a result, veer from the purely fiscal to the substantively trivial.

In addition, the rate of growth in defense budgets has been sharply discontinuous, reflecting its sensitivity to outside pressures that are themselves problematical. A recent study of changes in U.S. defense spending, for example, identified fluctuations in public opinion and uncertain estimates of Soviet military spending as having had dramatic effects. These and other external factors, the study concluded, "can lead to dramatic changes in the expenditure decision [even] within the confines of a stable policy-making process."[5]

Incrementalism in defense budget decision making, in sum, has been supplanted by efforts to integrate defense into a comprehensive, coordinated congressional budget process. Unfortunately, the comprehensiveness of this process is undercut by the shrinking share of spending controlled by the annual appropriations process, and its coordination is diminished by the lack of centralized control over spending. Thus, the president is faced with a highly unpredictable political environment on defense along with procedural obstacles to long-term defense planning. Simply put, the president can no longer be confident that his efforts to restrain the defense budget will be matched by a congressional willingness to restrain spending elsewhere. Nor can he assume that modest requests will lead to stable growth. Duplicative top-down budgeting has not improved the substantive quality of the defense budget. It has, however, made it much more difficult to control spending and deficits.

The Vietnam Transition

The direct costs of the war in Vietnam were substantial. Between 1965 and 1969 the defense budget increased by more than $30 billion, with Vietnam-related expenditures accounting for virtually all of this increase.[6] For the first few years, however, Vietnam had a comparatively positive impact on the defense budgetary process in Congress. While antiwar sentiments in Congress grew along with the U.S. commitment from 1965 to 1967, by far the dominant congressional criticism at this time was that the war was not being prosecuted forcefully enough and that non-Vietnam defense needs were being slighted.

Phase One

The decision by President Johnson to commit large numbers of U.S. forces to the defense of South Vietnam during 1965 blocked plans to cut and stabilize the defense budget. In the fiscal 1965 budget, for example, defense outlays had been cut by over 7 percent. The fiscal 1966 budget, submitted to Congress shortly after Johnson's overwhelming reelection victory, projected a further redirection of spending policy toward domestic programs.[7] On March 8, 1965, however, Marine units landed at Da Nang to supplement the more than 23,000 U.S. military advisers already stationed in South Vietnam. By year's end, troop levels were climbing toward 200,000. Within three years, more than half a million U.S. troops were in Vietnam.

The first funding request designated specifically for Vietnam was a fiscal 1965 supplement of $700 million for the "Southeast Asia Emergency Fund." This legislation was cleared by Congress on May 6, less than three days after it was submitted by the president. The president later submitted a request for an additional $1.7 billion to support the Vietnam buildup. This item was included in the fiscal 1966 defense appropriations bill approved unanimously by the House on September 17 and by the Senate on a voice vote four days later. There was, during 1965, no widespread opposition in either party to Johnson's Vietnam policy. Criticism among Democrats and Republicans was chiefly aimed at defense budget ceilings that were considered dangerously low.

The pattern of underestimated costs and follow-up supplementals continued the next year, with only a modest increase in antiwar congressional sentiment. The administration's fiscal 1967 defense budget, which was well below $60 billion, was criticized by the military committees as inadequate for non-Vietnam defense needs. The fiscal 1967 authorization was raised by Congress $500 million above the administration's request, and the fiscal 1967 appropriation bill added $400 million, including funding for ABM deployment, nuclear-powered guided-missile frigates, and manned bomber development. Moreover, the House pushed for language mandating that the additional funding be spent and prohibiting Secretary of Defense McNamara from eliminating any major weapons system without prior reporting to Congress. Although these directives were weakened during conference, they demonstrated the strong support the military continued to command in Congress.

The fiscal 1968 budget brought defense funding well above the $70 billion level and included nearly $3 billion in non-Vietnam defense increases. The defense authorization and appropriations bills finally approved by Congress were similar to the administration's totals, although Congress again added funding for weapons systems being pushed by the services and cut systems being advocated by McNamara. The fiscal 1968 defense spending bills and a fiscal 1967 defense supplement generated some antiwar opposition in Congress, but the protest was still quite limited. An effort in the House to include authorization language tied to the fiscal 1967 supplemental that would have prohibited bombing North Vietnam attracted only eighteen votes. Only eleven House members and three senators voted against the subsequent appropriation.

During January 1968 Clark Clifford succeeded McNamara as secretary of defense, a change that was initially viewed as insuring a more forceful prosecution of the war and a more harmonious relationship between the Department of Defense and Congress over weapons systems. Instead, the year 1968 turned out to be a watershed for Vietnam and for the rest of the defense budget. A massive spring offensive by the North Vietnamese severely weakened support for the war in the United States and forced the Johnson administration to search for ways to de-escalate the American commitment and to reach a negotiated settlement.

The intensifying criticism of Vietnam policy also served to legitimate more general antidefense critiques, among both the American public and members of Congress. By the late 1960s a sharp reversal in public attitudes toward military spending was under way, but it was not yet clear that the political balance on defense budgets had shifted. Congressional military advocates, such as Senate Armed Services Committee chairman Richard Russell, argued that defense budget increases would be needed to maintain adequate military strength even as the war wound down.[8] Richard Nixon's successful presidential campaign featured an attack on the concept of parity with the Soviet Union, and the Republican platform declared that "we have frittered away superior military capabilities, enabling the Soviets to narrow their defense gap, in some areas to outstrip us, and to move to cancel our lead entirely by the early Seventies."[9]

Nevertheless, the convergence of negative perceptions about Vietnam, about military waste and mismanagement, and about the leadership and competence of the armed services meant that the military's budget was no longer privileged. Instead of pressing the president to accept more weapons systems, as it had during the mid-1960s, Congress was now looking to cut defense budgets. It was also tying defense cuts to increased

Table 5.1. Defense Outlays, Fiscal Years 1966–76 (in billions of dollars)

Fiscal Year	Constant (FY 1982) Dollars	Percentage of Total Outlays	Percentage of GNP
1966	$197.9	43.2%	7.9%
1967	235.1	45.4	9.0
1968	254.8	46.0	9.6
1969	243.4	44.9	8.9
1970	225.6	41.8	8.3
1971	202.7	37.5	7.5
1972	190.9	34.3	6.9
1973	175.1	31.2	6.0
1974	163.3	29.5	5.6
1975	159.8	26.0	5.7
1976	153.6	24.1	5.3

SOURCE: *Historical Tables, Budget of the United States Government, Fiscal Year 1990*, pp. 48–50, 126–28.

social spending. Defense was moving into the same budget policy squeeze that was developing just before Vietnam, but by 1969 it was in a much more vulnerable position.

Phase Two

Official U.S. involvement in South Vietnam ended with the signing of the Paris peace accords in February 1973, but the political impact of Vietnam continued well beyond that point. In terms of budget policy, this impact was manifested in sharp congressional cuts in presidential defense budgets. The cuts were especially severe in the investment areas of procurement and research and development.[10]

By the mid-1970s social welfare spending had replaced defense as the driving force behind budget growth. Over the fiscal 1969–76 period, defense outlays rose slightly—from $82.5 billion to $89.6 billion—while overall spending almost doubled. As a result, the defense share of the budget was cut almost in half (see table 5.1). The corresponding decline in the defense share of GNP was about 40 percent, bringing defense to its lowest level since fiscal 1950.[11] Of particular importance, real spending for defense dropped by more than one-third, again to a level that predated the Korean buildup.[12]

Each of the defense budgets submitted by Richard Nixon was attacked at both the authorization and appropriations stages. The annual defense authorization bills produced lengthy debates over a number of weapons systems that had previously enjoyed very strong congressional support, including the ABM, Trident submarine, and B-1 bomber programs. In another reversal of its pre-Vietnam orientation, Congress repeatedly urged the administration to step up military personnel reductions. From fiscal 1970 to fiscal 1975, regular defense appropriations bills passed by Congress averaged nearly $4 billion per year below the administration's requests.[13] Cuts of this magnitude were unprecedented, although they were considerably lower than those being advocated by some of the more vocal defense critics in the House and Senate.

Priorities Debates

Although congressional review of the annual military budget targeted a variety of strategic and conventional weapons systems, Congress usually chose to delay or to stretch out, rather than to terminate, the weapons research and procurement programs proposed by the Nixon administration. One result of these congressional actions, coupled with the increased manpower costs of the all-volunteer force, was to alter significantly the shape of the defense budget. Despite a greater than one-third decline in the number of military personnel between fiscal 1969 and fiscal 1976, outlays for manpower rose by more than 20 percent. By comparison, the two largest investment categories—procurement and research, development, testing, and evaluation (RDT&E)—dropped by about one-fifth.[14] In fiscal 1976 combined spending for procurement and RDT&E was less than $25 billion, or just over one-fourth of the defense budget (see table 5.2). Before Vietnam, their combined share was about 40 percent.

The defense budget obviously did not fare well during the early 1970s, but the Nixon administration managed to minimize the damage, at least for a time. In part, expenditures were tightened through Department of Defense reforms aimed at improving procurement practices, reducing support costs, and expanding the capabilities of existing forces. Strategic and force doctrines were gradually adjusted to accommodate budgetary constraints. The "Nixon Doctrine," outlined in a series of speeches during 1969 and 1970, pledged that the United States would fulfill its treaty commitments but stressed that other countries would need to supply the

Table 5.2. Procurement and RDT&E Outlays, Fiscal Years 1969-76 (in billions of dollars)

Fiscal Year	Procurement Outlays	RDT&E Outlays	Percentage of Defense Budget
1969	$24.0	$7.5	38%
1970	21.6	7.2	35
1971	18.9	7.3	33
1972	17.1	7.9	32
1973	15.6	8.2	31
1974	15.2	8.6	30
1975	16.0	8.9	29
1976	16.0	8.9	28

SOURCE: *Historical Tables, Budget of the United States Government, Fiscal Year 1990*, pp. 54-55.

manpower for their defense.[15] Improvements in the accuracy and power of strategic missiles allowed the administration to place increased emphasis on nuclear weapons in its contingency planning, particularly for the defense of Western Europe.[16] A degree of political protection for these initiatives was supplied by Nixon's decision to resume arms control talks with the Soviets and to commit the administration to replacing the draft with an all-volunteer force.

As the American commitment in Vietnam wound down, however, attacks on the defense budget escalated. The sharpest of these was the alternative defense budget that the 1972 Democratic presidential nominee, Senator George S. McGovern, presented during his primary and general election campaigns. The McGovern defense plan called for major cuts in almost every force category with the goal of reducing total defense spending by some $30 billion (or more than one-third) by fiscal 1975.[17]

In order to broaden the political appeal of massive defense cuts, McGovern and his supporters used the rhetoric of budget priorities. The budget priorities argument posited that defense had to compete directly with domestic programs. The 1972 Democratic platform clearly outlined this approach:

But military defense cannot be treated in isolation from other vital national concerns. Spending for military purposes is greater by far than federal spending for education, housing, environmental protection, unemployment insurance or welfare. Unneeded dollars for the military at once add to the tax burden and preempt funds from programs of direct and immediate benefit to our people. Moreover, too much that is now spent on defense not only adds nothing to our strength but makes us less secure by stimulating other countries to respond.[18]

The 1972 Republican platform, by contrast, assailed what it called the "slash-now, beg-later approach" of the "New Democratic Left."[19] Nixon's campaign attacks on McGovern's defense policies were harsh and unrelenting, and he used the McGovern candidacy to portray the entire Democratic party as antidefense and isolationist.

With the debate framed this way and with Nixon's landslide victory over McGovern, the Democratic-controlled Ninety-third Congress that opened in January 1973 was unable to mount a coherent challenge to Nixon's defense or domestic policies. Nixon followed up his election triumph with a fiscal 1974 budget calling for a spending ceiling and domestic program reductions and terminations. He also stepped up the impounding of domestic program appropriations and, during 1973, vetoed five spending bills, none of which was overridden.

Nixon's post-Vietnam budget program was designed to produce public battles with Congress, and until the Watergate investigations began to destroy his political standing, Nixon was reasonably successful in these confrontations. The budget reform effort that commenced early in 1973, for example, was a response to criticisms that Nixon had been directing toward the congressional budget process.[20]

As the Nixon presidency deteriorated in the latter half of 1973, his congressional opponents saw the opportunity to wrest control over budget policy away from the executive branch. What had begun as an effort to strengthen congressional spending control was refashioned into the "policy-neutral" 1974 Congressional Budget and Impoundment Control Act.[21] One of its prime features was a provision for congressional budget resolutions setting congressional fiscal policy and spending priorities. These resolutions would be used to allocate spending totals among spending categories. As explained by one of the proponents of alternative congressional budgets, the functional spending levels would "allow meaningful debates on national priorities at the beginning of each Congress."[22]

For defense, the new budget process was an obvious threat. First, defense had to compete against politically popular domestic programs. Second, defense was at a disadvantage in this fiscal competition, because it was more easily controllable than domestic entitlements, many of which had been indexed. If defense was to overcome these handicaps, a serious presidential commitment to make the public case was essential. Further, that commitment had to come from a president with political leverage in Congress. Gerald Ford had succeeded Nixon on August 9, 1974, and the Nixon pardon one month later hardly helped his standing with the public or Congress. By the end of the year, Ford had suffered four veto overrides by Congress, the worst veto record in nearly three decades. In addition, the Ninety-fourth Congress that Ford faced the following January was even more heavily Democratic than its predecessor, with Democrats having an almost 150-vote margin in the House and a three-to-two edge in the Senate.

Ford's first budget, for fiscal 1976, was also the first to be considered under the new congressional budget process. The first concurrent budget resolution for fiscal 1976 differed greatly from Ford's budget, and one of the clearest differences was on defense. Ford had requested $107.7 billion in budget authority for the defense function. Congress reduced this by $7 billion in its first budget resolution, and the fiscal 1976 defense appropriations bill was cut by approximately the same amount.[23]

The fiscal 1976 budget demonstrated what "priority setting" could mean for the defense budget.[24] Defense and foreign aid were cut well below presidential requests, while spending for most domestic functions was set well above the president's budget (see table 5.3). One of the biggest policy-based differences was in function 500 (education, employment, training, and social services), one of the few social welfare categories with a high degree of year-to-year controllability. Congress raised expenditures for this category 40 percent above Ford's budget authority and outlay levels in its first resolution.[25] The second resolution for fiscal 1976 further increased the spending levels for function 500 to $21.3 billion in budget authority and $20.9 billion in spending.

At the same time that Congress was making the spending trade-offs that many architects of budget reform had envisioned, it was also demanding much more detailed and lengthier reviews of the defense budget.[26] Hearings were longer, more witnesses were called, the number of committees and subcommittees reviewing the defense budget increased, and floor debates on defense authorizations and appropriations became more and more time-consuming.[27] Floor amendments to annual defense bills also proliferated.[28]

There was also more aggressive congressional intervention in the internal operations of the Department of Defense. This intervention di-

Table 5.3. Comparison of Fiscal 1976 Budget Authority Levels (in billions of dollars)

	President's Budget	Congressional FCBR	Change
Functions Cut by Congress			
National Defense	$107.7	$100.7	- $ 7.0
International Affairs	12.6	4.9	- 7.7
Allowances	8.3	1.4	- 6.9
Total Change			- 21.6
Functions Increased by Congress			
Natural Resources, Environment and Energy	12.2	13.8	+ 1.6
Commerce and Transportation	6.6	11.3	+ 4.7
Community and Regional Development	5.2	11.0	+ 5.8
Education, Employment, Training and Social Services	13.7	19.0	+ 5.3
Health	31.0	33.1	+ 2.1
Income Security	135.3	140.9	+ 5.6
Veterans Benefits and Services	16.2	18.0	+ 1.8
All Other Functions	57.2	57.6	+ 0.4
Total Change			+ 27.3

SOURCE: *Congressional Quarterly Almanac, 1975* (Washington, D.C.: Congressional Quarterly, 1976), p. 121.

rectly affected the format of the defense budget. Between FY 1965 and FY 1975, for example, the number of line items in the defense budget rose from 155 to 720, making it more difficult for the Department of Defense to reallocate funds among major programs. Requirements that funds be spent as specified ("special interest items") grew in number from zero to 436 over this same period. Policy directives in annual authorization and appropriations bills ("action items") more than tripled in number in just one decade.[29]

Congressional criticism of the Pentagon's use of discretionary authority to shift funds within appropriations accounts ("reprogramming") had predated Vietnam.[30] In response, reporting requirements had been tightened and, in certain cases, prior approval by the appropriations committees had been mandated. Nevertheless, the high volume of reprogramming actions continued during the 1960s, and much broader congressional controls were then applied to the defense budget. As a result, the number of reprogramming actions and their dollar value declined severely during the mid-1970s.[31]

The war in Vietnam and the domestic programs that were part of Lyndon Johnson's Great Society program had combined to weaken severely the post–World War II consensus on defense. The former legitimated antidefense politics, while the latter created budgetary trade-offs for defense cuts that were appealing to a wide spectrum of legislators. The abruptness and severity of these trade-offs were unprecedented. By the mid-1970s each of the important defense budget indicators—real spending, GNP share, and total budget share—was significantly below pre-Vietnam levels. Between fiscal 1960 and fiscal 1975, the defense budget share had been cut in half, the defense GNP share had dropped by 40 percent, and real defense spending had declined by one-sixth.

In 1976 the Ford administration stepped up its efforts to reverse these downward trends in defense spending, submitting a fiscal 1977 budget calling for $7 billion in real growth for defense.[32] Ford's defense program received an immediate boost from two studies released early in the year. In January 1976 the Senate Armed Services Committee made public a study by the Congressional Research Service (CRS) which analyzed the quantitative balance of forces between the United States and the Soviet Union and assessed the severity of asymmetries between the two countries. The quantitative comparisons were highly unfavorable for the United States in strategic and tactical nuclear forces, ground forces, and naval forces. The interpretation of these force comparisons, moreover, was unexpectedly grim. Shortcomings in U.S. forces were characterized as very severe, and the study further noted that "U.S. budgetary projections paint a bleak picture when related to pressing U.S. problems, even though absolute outlays are very large."[33]

The CRS study was followed closely by release of a Central Intelligence Agency (CIA) comparison of U.S. and Soviet defense programs for the period 1965–75. Although the CIA emphasized that differences in mission, structure, and other major characteristics made comparisons difficult, its findings were nonetheless disquieting. The CIA reported that in 1971 Soviet military spending had begun to exceed U.S. spending; by 1975 the Soviet advantage was estimated to have grown to 40 percent. This disparity applied to operational forces and also to research and development of major weapons systems. For strategic offensive and defensive forces, the estimated Soviet advantage was nine to one.[34]

Mounting concern about Soviet military strength was also found in public opinion surveys. A Gallup national survey in January 1976 found that 63 percent of the public expected that Soviet power in the world would increase during the year, while only 18 percent expected it to decline. This was the most favorable assessment of Soviet power in sixteen years, and it stood in contrast to a plurality sentiment—44 to 42 percent—that U.S. power would decline.[35] At the same time, public opinion was becoming much more supportive of U.S. defense spending.

With this shift in public opinion, the Ford administration's defense spending proposals fared better in Congress, where reductions were modest in comparison to its cuts just one year earlier (see table 5.4). After eight consecutive years of declining real growth, defense spending registered an increase in fiscal 1977. The amount by which it grew was almost imperceptible (less than 0.5 percent), but the symbolic change turned out to be quite important.

Although Congress generally endorsed Ford's recommendations for strengthening conventional forces, it continued to challenge new weapons systems. In most cases, Congress did not cancel or terminate programs. Instead, it forced reductions, stretch-outs, and delays as weapons systems moved along the research and development track and on to procurement.

Congressional enthusiasm for controlling defense spending diminished, however, when domestic base closings were at issue. For years the Department of Defense had maintained that significant savings could be obtained by closing unnecessary bases.[36] The Ford administration, which had made base closings a central part of its defense spending plan, was forced to veto the initial 1976 defense authorization because of the stringent checks Congress included on the Defense Department's authority to close or to scale down domestic military facilities. The authorizations bill that followed granted somewhat more discretion to the Pentagon but still

Table 5.4. Presidential versus Congressional Defense Spending Targets, Fiscal Years 1976-77 (in billions of dollars)

Fiscal Year	President's Budget	Congressional FCBR	Actual
1976			
Budget Authority	$107.7	$100.7	$ 97.3
Outlays	94.0	90.7	89.6
1977			
Budget Authority	114.9	112.5	110.1
Outlays	101.1	100.8	97.2

SOURCES: *Budget of the United States Government*, various years; House and Senate Budget Committee reports, various years.

imposed requirements for notification, justification, consultation, and even environmental impact statements that obviously were intended to discourage base closings.

The defense decline came to a halt during the Ford presidency. In 1976 Congress endorsed Ford's argument that real defense spending had to increase. At the same time, antidefense sentiments remained formidable. This ambivalence on defense was underscored by the 1976 Democratic platform. It criticized the Nixon-Ford administrations for what it termed an "undue emphasis on the overall size of the defense budget" and called for reducing "present defense spending by about $5-billion to $7-billion." This reduction was to be accomplished by "cutbacks on duplication and waste," along with the "proper management, [and] the proper kind of investment . . . , and with the proper choice of military programs."[37] The only weapon system singled out for possible challenge was the B-1 bomber, and here the platform wording was ambiguous.[38] When Jimmy Carter tried to carry this reduction out after his election, he eventually found himself moving closer and closer to the defense spending program that his opponent had set forth before leaving office.

The Carter Program
By the late 1970s defense experts and the public had grown increasingly pessimistic about U.S. military preparedness and particularly

about the military balance between the United States and the Soviet Union.[39] Between 1977 and 1980 the percentage of the general population stating that "too little" was being spent on defense doubled, reaching nearly 60 percent. In its second budget resolution for FY 1980, Congress mirrored this remarkable turnaround, adopting higher defense spending levels than the Carter administration had requested.[40]

While Jimmy Carter attempted to lead this budding post-Vietnam consensus, his efforts were overwhelmed by events and perceptions. Carter's reelection year budget projected a $60 billion defense budget authority increase for the fiscal 1980–83 period, which translated into annual increases averaging approximately 13 percent.[41] The 1980 Democratic platform boasted of having reversed "the threatened decline in America's world position" and castigated the Nixon-Ford administration for "a steady decline of 33 percent in real U.S. military spending between 1968 and 1976."[42] Nevertheless, Ronald Reagan was able to exploit the "soft on defense" label against Carter and the Democratic party generally, at least partly because of the confusion over defense budget policy during Carter's tenure.

The Carter presidency can be divided into two reasonably distinct segments. For fiscal years 1978 and 1979, Carter's budget program comprised healthy increases for most domestic programs and comparatively modest ones for defense. In fiscal 1980 Carter proposed 3 percent real growth for defense, while total budget outlays were almost flat in real terms. For fiscal 1981 the Carter budget recommended a 3.5 percent real increase in defense outlays and a 1 percent real decline in nondefense spending.

Round One (FY 1978–79)

In fiscal 1978 budget revisions transmitted to Congress, Carter abandoned the defense-cut proposals in his party's 1976 platform, settling for a proposed cut of $0.4 billion from the $112.3 billion defense outlay figure that the Ford administration had submitted. Carter also boosted Ford's total budget by $20 billion, raising the functional outlay targets in almost every domestic category. In May, when Congress adopted its first budget resolution for fiscal 1978, its defense and domestic spending targets mirrored the Carter revisions.

This surface agreement masked a good deal of chaos over defense totals and weapons programs. When the House Budget Committee was preparing its spring budget resolution, it first lowered the defense spending targets contained in the Carter fiscal 1978 revisions. When the resolution reached the House floor, the administration lobbied for amendments in line with its defense figures. The House went along but then proceeded to boost spending for numerous domestic programs. The result was a budget resolution which failed to win House approval by a decisive 84–320 vote.

A budget resolution was eventually adopted which deleted the defense increases along with most of the other spending increases that had doomed the effort to rewrite a budget resolution on the floor. House Democratic leaders were more than willing to blame the White House and its representatives for their troubles. House Speaker O'Neill castigated the secretary of defense for "not knowing the procedures of Congress." House Budget Committee chairman Robert M. Giaimo declared: "This is the United States Congress where the Democratic majority is going to write the legislation. It is not the Georgia legislature."[43]

Just what the White House was responsible for was equally problematical at the level of defense policy. The 1977 defense appropriations bill, for example, had been enacted under Gerald Ford and included funding for three B-1 bombers. Carter had attacked the B-1 program during his campaign, and when Congress signaled that it might continue B-1 funding during FY 1978, Carter announced that he would cancel production. Carter then submitted a request to Congress to rescind (or cancel) $462 million in fiscal 1977 B-1 funding, and this proposal finally received grudging congressional approval in 1978. Almost simultaneous with the B-1 cancellation was Carter's announced termination of Minuteman III missile production. This time, however, Congress did not approve the rescission proposal, and program funding was made available automatically in October.

A third rescission fight, concerning a nuclear aircraft carrier, also surfaced in 1977. Carter opposed construction of a Nimitz-class carrier, proposing instead smaller and less costly carriers. Congress first authorized compromise funding for both types of carriers, with a final decision to be made in fiscal 1979. It then proceeded to approve an appropriations bill deleting the large carrier, having already rescinded prior-year appropriations. When the Congress again authorized a nuclear carrier in 1978, Carter's veto was sustained in the House. In 1979 Congress ultimately prevailed, as the administration agreed to a $2.1 billion nuclear carrier.

Strained relations between the White House and Congress over defense policy eased somewhat during 1978. Carter continued to pursue what he characterized as "prudent real growth" in defense spending. This prudence was defined by contrast to the Ford program. The defense

Table 5.5. Carter Administration's Fiscal 1979 Budget Program: Budget Totals and Defense Spending (in billions of dollars)

Fiscal Year	Budget Authority		Outlays	
	Total	Defense	Total	Defense
1977	$465.2	$110.4	$401.9	$ 97.5
1978 (est.)	502.9	117.8	462.2	107.6
1979 (est.)	568.2	128.4	500.2	117.8
Increase				
1977-79	22.1%	16.3%	24.5%	20.8%

Source: *Budget of the United States Government, Fiscal Year 1979* (Washington, D.C.:GPO, 1978), pp. 443, 454, 456, 468.

budget recommendations for fiscal 1979 were, it was emphasized, "considerably more moderate than those proposed . . . by the previous administration."[44] The manner in which this was done, moreover, was calculated to defuse liberal Democratic opposition. Over the fiscal 1977–79 period, proposed increases in defense spending were not at the expense of other spending programs (see table 5.5). The change from previous years was that defense cuts were not being used to finance domestic program increases.

The Carter compromise succeeded. Carter's defense figures were upheld. He prevailed on the B-1 and nuclear carrier issues. Moreover, his overall budget program appeared to be on track. The fiscal 1979 deficit, originally projected at $60 billion, fell to less than half that amount.

Round Two (FY 1980–81)

A much stronger commitment to the defense budget emerged early in 1979. The only parts of the fiscal 1980 Carter budget slated for real increases were defense, retirement and health care, and interest on the debt. The 3 percent real growth target for defense, along with increases in these other areas, meant negative real growth in many domestic programs. Liberal Democratic opposition was immediate and fierce, and it was translated once again into a battle over defense and discretionary social welfare funding.

The spring budget resolution impasse was only a preliminary round. By late fall the administration had lost the initiative on defense policy. The Senate gave the clearest indication yet of its defense turnaround, endorsing planned increases in weapons systems for the early 1980s and agreeing to overall real growth rates in defense for future years at or above projected fiscal 1980 levels. The Strategic Arms Limitation Treaty (SALT II) that the Carter administration had signed on June 18, 1979, had already been subjected to nearly two years of mounting criticism, and it soon became evident that Senate approval would be difficult even with accelerated defense budget increases. On September 18 the Senate voted by a 55–42 margin to support annual 5 percent real increases in the defense budget for fiscal years 1981 and 1982. The Carter administration opposed the commitment, holding instead to the 3 percent figure it had initially proposed.

On September 19 the House rejected its Budget Committee's proposed second budget resolution. One among many explanations for the defeat centered on defense spending. A Democratic member of the Armed Services Committee, Samuel S. Stratton, offered an amendment to the resolution raising its defense figures to the levels endorsed by the Carter administration. Stratton's amendment was defeated, after which he complained that "in the past two or three years, the Armed Services Committee has always made an effort to restore the administration's defense figure after the Budget Committee cut it. This year we couldn't even get the administration to come in and support their own figure."[45] The House took another week to fashion a resolution which would pass, and the ensuing conference went on for twenty-three days.

When the second budget resolution was finally adopted on November 28, defense budget authority and outlay levels were well above those set in the first resolution. On November 4, however, Iran had seized U.S. embassy personnel in Tehran, and latent public and congressional complaints about U.S. military weakness were catalyzed. On December 12 President Carter tried to regain some initiative, pledging a 5.6 percent real increase in defense for fiscal 1981 and similarly large rates of growth through 1985.

A number of senators interpreted Carter's promises as a desperate effort to prop up SALT II, which was having a very difficult time in the Senate. On December 15 nineteen uncommitted senators, led by Democratic defense expert Sam Nunn, requested specific assurances from Carter about future defense plans. Less than two weeks later, on December 27, the Soviet Union invaded Afghanistan, dooming the SALT II treaty and underscoring the image of U.S. military impotence that the Carter administration was finding impossible to shake.

The situation grew worse in 1980. At the urging of congressional Democratic leaders, the administration quickly modified its initial fiscal 1981 budget. Among the more prominent changes submitted to Congress were increases of approximately $3 billion in defense budget authority and $4 billion in defense outlays. The Senate Budget Committee then proceeded to adopt defense targets considerably above those included in the revised request. The Senate went along with the Budget Committee, overwhelmingly rejecting amendments to transfer portions of the defense increase to domestic programs.

The House had, as usual, approved defense allocations well below those adopted by the Senate. After the conference had agreed to defense figures only marginally lower than those in the Senate's budget resolution, the House rejected the conference report. After two weeks, a settlement was reached which again established defense budget authority and outlay targets at levels approximating those proposed by the Senate. At a point when public opinion regarding defense spending had become highly supportive and even the Democratic-controlled House was responding to the public transformation, the Carter administration lagged behind.

Carter's problem with defense was compounded by apparent indecisiveness. The initial fiscal 1981 budget had stressed a buildup of strategic and conventional forces as "essential" to counter "large increases in Soviet defense capability." The president's defense budget, it was stated, "exceeds that objective."[46] Two months later, the president's requests had to be increased in response to congressional pressure.

The Carter Buildup

Real defense spending rose each year under Jimmy Carter, and by the end of his presidency the composition of the defense budget was shifting toward the investment accounts (such as weapons procurement) that had been especially hard hit by post-Vietnam reductions.[47] In 1978 and 1979 the Carter administration also persuaded the NATO countries to accept annual 3 percent real growth defense targets for their own forces. A limited program of strategic modernization along with a more broadly based effort to upgrade U.S. conventional forces was already in place by the time the major political shocks from Iran and Afghanistan occurred.

The administration's own assessments of the adequacy of the U.S. buildup, however, were tentative. In his fiscal 1980 report to Congress,

Secretary of Defense Harold Brown reviewed U.S. strategic force structure and concluded:

> Whether these strategic force capabilities, and current programs for their improvement, are at the appropriate level . . . is not an easy issue to resolve. Despite SALT, the competition from the Soviet Union in strategic forces remains strong. The assessment is also made difficult by substantial differences over what measures to use . . . ; what Soviet measures and attitudes may be; and what, as a consequence, constitutes sufficiency to deter the Soviets under various situations.[48]

Brown and others in the administration were caught in a budgetary squeeze. Acknowledging that "relative defense spending, annual or cumulative, is the best single crude measure of relative military capabilities," Brown also noted that the Soviet defense effort exceeded that of the United States by "as much as 45 percent, or as little as 25 percent."[49] By this standard, the Carter administration's defense program could never come close to matching the Soviet effort. The problem, moreover, did not rest with force planning but with funding.

While real defense spending was increasing, the rates of increase lagged behind those for nondefense spending (see table 5.6). Left unresolved was the critical problem of the defense spending base, which had been cut drastically in real terms after Vietnam. Average real spending for defense was nearly $195 billion annually for fiscal years 1960–65. The average for fiscal years 1977–81 was almost 20 percent lower, and even the fiscal 1981 peak was below pre-Vietnam levels.

The pace of change was similarly glacial in addressing problems with investment underfunding. Despite large reductions in military personnel after Vietnam, the percentage of the defense budget devoted to manpower costs had risen steadily, while spending for procurement and research and development had declined dramatically. By the time the Carter administration took office, outlays for investment accounts were at least 20 percent lower, as a percentage of the defense budget, than they had been before (or during) Vietnam. When the administration left office, the investment share had climbed only marginally.

The Carter years illustrated the shortcomings of annual budget priority debates, at least for defense. Twin pressures to reduce deficits and to support domestic programs made it difficult to adjust defense spending sharply upward. By 1980 there was a consensus that defense budgets were seriously inadequate. The difficulty was that neither the administration

Table 5.6. Real Spending, Defense and Nondefense, Fiscal Years 1977-81 (in billions of dollars)

	Constant Dollars (FY 1982)	
Fiscal Year	Defense	Nondefense
1977	$154.3	$468.3
1978	155.0	497.1
1979	159.1	501.1
1980	164.0	535.1
1981	171.4	555.2
Average Annual Increase	2.8%	4.6%

SOURCE: *Historical Tables, Budget of the United States Government, Fiscal Year 1990*, pp. 128-29.

nor Congress was willing to sacrifice other budget policy goals to remedy this inadequacy.

The Reagan Defense Budgets

Beginning with the fiscal 1983 budget, Congress began to cut the Reagan administration's defense requests by increasingly large amounts. In fiscal year 1987 alone, the budget authority enacted by Congress was more than $30 billion below the president's budget. The Reagan defense program was then significantly reduced for fiscal years 1988 and 1989 under a budget accord reached with Congress after the October 1987 stock market crash. For fiscal years 1988–92, reductions from this initial plan were estimated at $177 billion.[50]

The discrepancy between what Ronald Reagan wanted for defense and what he was able to achieve was also quite large in the context of his initial budget planning. Reagan's fiscal 1982 budget revisions projected defense outlays at 37.6 percent of the total budget by fiscal 1986, with the defense-GNP index climbing to approximately 7 percent by that time.[51] Neither of these goals was achieved. Defense outlays peaked, in terms of budget share, at 28 percent in fiscal 1987, while the defense-GNP level averaged slightly over 6 percent for the fiscal 1982–89 period.[52]

Perspectives on the Reagan Buildup

Nevertheless, the defense budget increases that Reagan did achieve moved real defense spending to unprecedented peacetime levels. Perhaps the single most telling point about the Reagan defense program is illustrated in figure 5.1. By the mid-1980s real defense outlays had climbed to the $230–$250 billion range, close to a 50 percent increase over fiscal 1981 defense spending and also the highest peacetime level yet recorded. Real defense spending under Reagan was roughly equal to peak levels during the Korean and Vietnam wars.

The magnitude of the U.S. buildup was also enough to erase the gap between U.S. and Soviet military spending. According to the Department of Defense, the annual disparity had finally been eliminated in 1987, although cumulative U.S. expenditures for the preceding decade were still much lower than those of the Soviets:

> Over the last decade, the magnitude of the Soviet military effort greatly exceeded that of the United States. Based on a dollar cost comparison of cumulative US and USSR military programs for the past 10 years, the total Soviet military effort was almost 20 percent greater than that of the United States. In 1987, as a result of the continued growth of US outlays, primarily for procurement, the annual difference in the cost of the military programs was virtually eliminated.[53]

Budget Changes from Carter. Another important point of comparison is provided by the Carter defense program. Particularly during the early years of the Reagan presidency, Carter administration budgets sometimes were used to demonstrate the supposedly incremental nature of the president's program. Outlay differences were, in fact, relatively modest for the first few years. For the fiscal 1982–84 period, for example, defense outlays proposed by Reagan totaled approximately $645 billion, or about 5 percent higher than Carter's projections.[54]

These outlay differences did not fully reflect the sharp contrasts between the Carter and Reagan programs in budget authority, real growth rates, and the allocation of real growth within the defense budget. For the fiscal 1982–86 period, budget authority projections under the initial Reagan defense plan were much higher than Carter's. In addition, Reagan's figures were based on lower inflation rates, so that actual differences in real growth turned out to be extremely large.[55]

Finally, the Reagan defense plan was more heavily tilted toward investment accounts. Carter's secretary of defense, Harold Brown, emphasized in his fiscal 1982 report the significance of investment spending

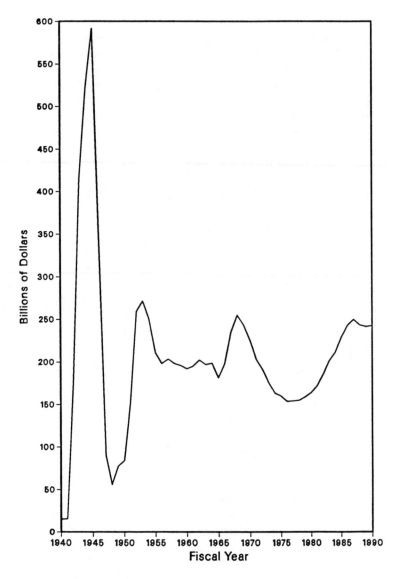

Figure 5.1. Defense outlays, fiscal years 1940-90 (in billions of FY 1982 constant dollars). Source: Compiled by author.

trends for comparisons of *"future* capabilities—the quantity and quality of military forces" supported by the United States and the Soviet Union. The investment categories specifically mentioned by Brown—procurement, research and development, and military construction—were recommended for slightly higher rates of growth than the defense budget as a whole. Between fiscal 1980 and fiscal 1982, investment spending was to increase from 36 percent to 38 percent of total Department of Defense spending.[56] Brown's successor, Caspar W. Weinberger, immediately boosted the fiscal 1982 investment share to 42 percent and targeted the fiscal 1983 investment categories for over 46 percent of the total defense program.[57]

The goal of the Reagan program was to boost spending quickly in all areas of the defense budget and also to incorporate high rates of growth in investment budget authority that would drive the budget in future years. For fiscal years 1981–85, outlay growth for investment was over 90 percent, more than double the growth in readiness accounts, and the budget authority differential was even greater.

The defense budget is also analyzed by breaking it down into mission categories, such as strategic forces and general-purpose forces. Here also, the Reagan program was distinctive. Carter's fiscal 1982 defense plan included across-the-board increases for all mission categories but did not radically alter prior budget authority allocations. Strategic force budget authority, for example, was estimated at 7.6 percent for fiscal 1982, compared to 7.8 percent for fiscal 1980.[58] Within the Reagan program, strategic force funding was slated to grow much more rapidly than most other mission categories. According to the administration, its five-year expansion represented "the greatest addition of modern, strengthened strategic forces planned and funded by any United States President."[59]

Weapons Systems. At the level of particular weapons systems, there were surprisingly few policy changes after Reagan took office. Perhaps the most noteworthy was the decision to resurrect the B-1 strategic bomber program that Carter had canceled. Development of a new version, the B-1B, was immediately requested. Full procurement funding was later approved by Congress, and the full complement of B-1Bs was deployed by 1988.[60]

For most major weapons systems, the new defense program meant accelerated development and procurement schedules and much higher planned force levels (see table 5.7). With a few highly publicized exceptions, Reagan's defense program ratified the conventional and strategic weapons system decisions made by the Carter administration. It was

Table 5.7. Selected Weapons System Procurement Increases, Fiscal 1983 Reagan
Defense Program (in billions of dollars)

Weapons Program	FY 1981 Actual		FY 1983 Proposal	
	Quantity	Amount	Quantity	Amount
M-1 Tank	569	$1.5	776	$2.0
Bradley Fighting Vehicle	400	0.7	600	0.9
AH-64 Attack Heli- copter	--	0.06	48	1.0
Stinger Missile	1,415	0.1	3,816	0.3
Patriot Air Defense System	130	0.5	376	0.9
Aircraft Carrier	--	0.1	2	6.8
AV-8B (Harrier Tactical Fighter)	--	0.1	18	0.9
MX Missile	--	--	9	1.5
Trident Submarine	1	1.1	2	2.8
B-1B Bomber	--	--	7	4.0
Pershing II Missile	--	--	91	0.5
GLCM (Ground-Launched Cruise Missile)	11	0.2	120	0.5
C-5 Aircraft	--	--	2	0.9
KC-10 Aircraft	6	0.3	8	0.8

SOURCE: *Annual Report to the Congress, Fiscal Year 1983, Caspar W. Weinberger, Secretary of Defense* (Washington, D.C.: GPO, 1982), pp. III-3--III-91.

much more willing, however, to fund those programs at levels requested by the military.

A similar pattern emerged with naval force planning. Carter's five-year shipbuilding program had been fairly ambitious, with over eighty ships scheduled for construction during the fiscal 1982–86 period (see table 5.8). Reagan's naval planning assigned a central role to large-deck, nuclear-powered aircraft carriers, while Carter had argued for smaller and less costly carriers. In addition, Reagan's defense planners were committed to fifteen navy carrier groups, a much higher level than Carter had ever been willing to support. The Reagan defense plan also included new destroyers to help support the higher carrier force levels. The most striking departure, however, was again one of scale. The fiscal 1983–87 plans

Table 5.8. Five-Year Shipbuilding Programs, Carter versus Reagan

Type of Ship	Carter FY 1982–86 Total	Reagan FY 1983–87 Total
Ballistic Missile Submarine (Trident)	6	6
Attack Submarine (SSN-688)	6	17
Nuclear Aircraft Carrier (CVN)	0	2
Guided Missile Cruiser (CG-47)	16	17
Guided Missile Destroyer (DDG-51)	1	4
Guided Missile Frigate (FFG-7)	1	12
Oiler (T-AO)	7	18
Mine Countermeasure Ship (MCM, MSH)	13	24
Destroyer	0	3
Other New Construction/ Acquisition	35	30
Conversions	14	16
Total	99	149

SOURCES: *Department of Defense Annual Report, Fiscal Year 1982* (Washington, D.C.: GPO, 1981), p. 171; *Annual Report to the Congress, Fiscal Year 1983, Caspar W. Weinberger, Secretary of Defense*, p. III-36.

submitted by the Department of Defense increased the shipbuilding program by 50 percent, with an even more marked disparity for the costlier types of ships. The shipbuilding budgets requested by Reagan and approved by Congress were therefore much higher than Carter's—about 60 percent higher for the fiscal 1982–85 period, according to the Congressional Budget Office.[61]

By the time the Reagan administration left office, the initial goal of a 600-ship navy had been largely achieved.[62] This increase did not fulfill the objectives for all types of ships, nor did it insure that modernization would be sustained at required replacement levels during the 1990s. It did, however, establish a new benchmark for U.S. naval forces.

Budgets and Strategy. The various programs to modernize and to improve U.S. military forces during the Reagan years did not constitute a basic redefinition or redirection of military strategy. The Strategic Defense Initiative that President Reagan unveiled in 1983 had profound long-term implications, of course, but it did not revise in any way the fundamentals of the Reagan program. Instead, the enormous and rapid defense budget expansion during Reagan's first term allowed the administration to spread increases broadly.

With respect to force structure, for example, there was an immediate emphasis on raising planned force levels across the board. For the navy, this meant additional carrier task forces, amphibious forces, and antisubmarine warfare forces. For the army, it meant additional divisions and additional special forces. For the air force, the number of fighter wings was increased, while airlift capabilities were expanded.

Funding for readiness and sustainability was also boosted substantially.[63] This item was perhaps the least controversial element of Reagan's overall program, since it addressed a problem which defense specialists in both parties had long acknowledged. With the defense budget constraints of the 1970s, readiness and sustainability had deteriorated in areas ranging from spare parts to flying time to ship-steaming days. Carter's fiscal 1982 budget had included funding to support greater training readiness levels and reduced maintenance backlogs.[64] These initiatives were continued under Reagan's military program.

The most prominent element of the Reagan defense budget expansion, however, was modernization, which meant expanded procurement of virtually every category of planned weapons systems, along with stepped-up efforts in research and development of new systems. It is important to recognize, however, that this emphasis was largely confined to the first term. As congressional cuts eventually brought real growth to a halt, the administration reluctantly adjusted its modernization initiatives downward. It did so, however, slowly and grudgingly.

The first Reagan budget to incorporate downward adjustments into defense planning was the fiscal 1989 submission by Secretary of Defense Frank C. Carlucci, who had replaced Weinberger in November 1987. The Pentagon's new plan highlighted force structure reductions and weapons system cancellations, as the means for accommodating scaled-back budgets. As Carlucci stated, "Resource constraints have forced us to accept increased risks to our security and a smaller force structure as we strive to preserve required levels of readiness and sustainability."[65]

Again excepting the Strategic Defense Initiative, the Reagan presidency did not produce a dramatic reformulation of defense policy and strategy. Even its equating of the size and growth of defense budgets with military power was not entirely new. The 3-percent real growth policy that took shape over the course of the Carter presidency was really a foreshadowing of the fiscal symbolism approach to defense budgeting. In effect, a long-term budget goal was established, with the intention of then effecting discrete objectives to improve U.S. military capabilities. An important aspect of this goal was long-term real growth that would signal to allies and foes the seriousness of the U.S. commitment.

With Reagan and Weinberger, the symbolism became more pronounced. It was reinforced by hard-line rhetoric about the use of force and the central importance of military power, but the importance of the sheer size of the defense budget was stressed time and time again. As Weinberger declared early in the first term, detailed discussions of individual programs were important, but it was essential to recognize "the broad and fundamental reasons for the increase in the defense budget as a whole, so that Congress can properly weigh the needs of the defense of the nation against the many other demands on the Federal Budget."[66]

The Congressional Response

The differences between the Reagan administration and Congress over defense budgets took a variety of forms. There were extended battles over several major weapons systems, most notably the MX missile and the Strategic Defense Initiative. Over the years, conflicts over the mix between conventional and strategic forces became more heated. Defense spending bills were also delayed by congressional efforts to add arms control interpretations and restrictions.

The overriding difference between Reagan and Congress, however, was tied to overall budget policy. From the outset, Reagan was intent on funding an unprecedented peacetime defense expansion while reducing overall spending growth and relative tax levels. After the first major package of domestic spending cuts was adopted in the 1981 Omnibus Budget Reconciliation Act, Congress rejected further attempts to fund defense increases with substantial domestic cuts.

Upon taking office, Reagan immediately requested upward adjustments in the fiscal 1981 and fiscal 1982 defense budgets. These adjustments were in line with defense spending targets Congress had previously adopted, and Congress incorporated them into its fiscal 1982 budget resolution. Indeed, when the House Budget Committee reported out a budget resolution with defense outlays set nearly $7 billion below Rea-

Table 5.9. National Defense Function, Budget Authority and Outlays, Fiscal Years 1982-89 (in billions of dollars)

Fiscal Year	Reagan Budget	Actual[a]
Budget Authority		
1982	$226.3	$216.5
1983	263.0	245.0
1984	280.5	265.2
1985	313.4	294.7
1986	322.2	289.1
1987	320.3	287.4
1988[b]	312.0	292.0
1989 (est.)[b]	332.4	298.8
Budget Outlays		
1982	188.8	185.3
1983	221.1	209.9
1984	245.3	227.4
1985	272.0	252.7
1986	285.7	273.4
1987	282.2	282.0
1988[b]	297.5	290.4
1989 (est.)[b]	312.0	298.3

SOURCE: Requests are based on the president's budgets for the years shown. Actual figures are from *Historical Tables, Budget of the United States Government, Fiscal Year 1990*, pp. 43-44, 97-98.

[a] The use of actual budget authority and outlay figures provides a reasonably accurate comparison, since supplemental funding enacted late in a fiscal year is included. The budget resolutions and initial appropriations bills would not reflect these adjustments.

[b] These figures are based on the two-year budget for 1988 and 1989 originally submitted in 1987. The 1986 Defense Authorization Act included this requirement.

gan's budget, the House Democratic leadership actively supported a floor amendment restoring the entire difference in order to "stand together" on defense policy.[67] Actual budget authority enacted for fiscal year 1982, however, was still almost $10 billion below the budget request.

Reagan's first complete budget was for fiscal 1983, and at this point the congressional cuts became much sharper (see table 5.9). For fiscal years 1983–86, enacted budget authority for the national defense function averaged $20 billion annually below the Reagan budgets. Outlay differentials for these years were, on the average, approximately $15 billion lower. Nevertheless, real growth in defense spending for the fiscal 1982–86 period was over 30 percent. The Reagan budget increases were so large that even unprecedented congressional reductions still allowed for rapid growth. Moreover, since Congress was accepting the concept of budgeted real growth, inflation overestimates helped to boost outlay and budget authority levels adopted by Congress.[68]

By the beginning of Reagan's second term, the consensus on budgeting for real increases had weakened. Public opinion on defense spending had shifted once again, with the percentage of the public supporting defense increases having dropped from over 70 percent in 1980 to less than 15 percent in 1985.[69] Congress was becoming increasingly concerned about soaring deficits. The Reagan administration was not willing to trade tax increases for defense increases, just as Congress was unwilling to trade domestic cuts for defense increases. Quite to the contrary, Congress was beginning to return to its earlier pattern of attempting to use defense cuts to fund domestic program increases. In 1984 the budget process had bogged down under this pressure, forcing enactment of a massive continuing resolution. The following year, the appropriations committees tried to boost domestic spending above levels set in the budget resolution, while reducing defense. This attempt set off a battle with the Senate Budget Committee, and the result was another protracted delay in the appropriations process and another large continuing resolution.

It was the prospect of future trade-offs from defense to domestic programs that helped make the Gramm-Rudman-Hollings bill acceptable to an otherwise unenthusiastic White House. The 1985 version that was signed into law on December 12 required that one-half of any automatic spending cuts needed to meet statutory deficit targets be applied to defense accounts, with the other half from nonexempt domestic programs. Gramm-Rudman-Hollings was applied to the fiscal 1986 budget, and the result was a reduction in defense budget authority after years of increases (see table 5.10). The decline continued in fiscal 1987, and it was disproportionately sharp in procurement accounts. While other defense appro-

Table 5.10. Budget Authority by Appropriations Category, Fiscal Years 1985-87 (in billions of dollars)

| | Fiscal Year | | |
Appropriations Category	1985	1986	1987
Military Personnel	$ 67.8	$ 67.8	$ 74.0
Operations and Maintenance	77.8	74.9	79.6
Procurement	96.8	92.5	80.2
Research, Development, Test, and Evaluation	31.3	33.6	35.6
Atomic Energy	7.3	7.3	7.5
All Other	13.6	13.0	10.4
Total	294.7	289.1	287.4

SOURCE: *Historical Tables, Budget of the United States Government, Fiscal Year 1990*, p. 97.

priations categories increased or remained stable over the fiscal 1985–87 period, procurement budget authority dropped from $96.8 billion to $80.2 billion.

At the program level, Congress used the slowdown in defense funding to cut back sharply appropriations requests for some of Reagan's more controversial strategic systems. The fiscal 1986 defense appropriations bill, for example, cut the Strategic Defense Initiative funding requested by Reagan by 25 percent, while the fiscal 1986 defense authorization bill capped deployment levels for the MX at one-half of Reagan's recommendations. Congress also blocked Reagan's plans for antisatellite missile systems (ASAT), limiting testing in 1984 and enacting a permanent ban on full-scale testing in 1985.

The consequences of annual defense budget debates during the Reagan years were often confusing, because conflicts between the administration and Congress were fought and refought several times each year. There was first the effort to reach an accord on congressional budget resolution allocations for defense. There was an overlapping series of disputes over the defense authorization bills. Finally, there were prolonged difficulties in Congress with appropriating defense funds at the levels specified in the budget resolutions.

In 1984, for example, it finally took a negotiated agreement between the White House, the Democratic House leadership, and the Republican Senate leadership to set the congressional budget resolution numbers for defense. This agreement was not reached until September 20, less than two weeks before the beginning of the fiscal year.

The following year, the House and Senate were unable to reach agreement on budget resolution figures for defense until August. The House went to conference arguing for no growth at all in defense over fiscal 1985, while the Senate was supporting no real growth over fiscal 1985. The conference accepted the Senate's position, and both chambers endorsed it. House Democrats then blocked action on the defense authorization bill, which conformed to the $302.5 billion budget authority level set in the budget resolution, until the House Democratic leadership agreed to press for the House's original $292.5 billion in the defense appropriations bill. Action on the appropriations bill was sufficiently delayed, as were other appropriations, so that a continuing resolution became necessary. At this point, the House-Senate appropriations difference was split almost exactly in half ($297.6 billion).

The "real zero growth" versus "zero real growth" argument resurfaced in 1986. This time further complications were introduced, since actual defense spending for fiscal 1986 had been reduced by almost $14 billion through automatic Gramm-Rudman-Hollings cuts. The issue was whether the "base" for fiscal 1987 should be agreed-upon levels for fiscal 1986 or actual spending levels. In the end, Congress adopted budget authority levels that fell between the two, with final appropriations incorporating several gimmicks to keep outlays within required limits.[70]

In 1987 the administration requested only 3 percent real growth for fiscal 1988 defense outlays. The Senate then put forth a two-tier defense plan, with the higher defense target contingent upon the administration's acceptance of a tax increase. This arrangement was agreed to by the House, but the entire plan was then scrapped after the October stock market crash. In the month that followed, the White House and Congress agreed to a $292 billion fiscal 1988 budget and a $299.5 fiscal 1989 budget for defense. What this meant, among other things, was four years of declining real growth in budget authority. This decline was occurring, however, in the context of real defense spending levels that were still extremely high by peacetime standards.

The Necessity for Choice
The year-to-year battles over defense spending numbers often obscured significant disputes over policy. For most of the Reagan presidency,

Congress used defense bills to change procurement management practices and to prod the administration on arms control or foreign policy. In 1986 it also enacted the Goldwater-Nichols Reorganization Act, which shifted authority from the civilian service secretaries to the chairman of the Joint Chiefs of Staff and to operational commanders.

These and related efforts to reform the Pentagon were predictably tied to an ongoing debate about the proper role of Congress in defense budgeting. Even within Congress, defense experts such as Senator Nunn decried the "535 individual program managers [in Congress] that are micromanaging the department [of Defense] at an alarming rate."[71] While "micromanagement" was the most widespread criticism, there was concern as well about the impact of the complicated and chaotic defense budgeting process in Congress on military funding and planning.

The chaos, however, was hardly new or unexpected. The political symbolism of defense spending and domestic budget priorities had made budget resolutions convenient targets for ideological battles since the mid-1970s. Because defense was the only major authorization coming up each year in Congress, it provided a splendid opportunity for numerous members to press their views on weapons systems, procurement reforms, arms control, and foreign policy. With the defense appropriations bill comprising the bulk of controllable spending in each year's budget, incentives were multiplied for fighting over relatively small amounts.

The three-layer defense budgeting process, the almost complete overlap between annual authorizations and appropriations, and the increased stringency of line-item budgeting created problems for the Reagan administration and undoubtedly will continue to frustrate defense planners in the future. These problems were partially overcome, however, by the scope and breadth of the Reagan defense buildup. Despite its annual battles with Congress, the Reagan administration was able to pursue simultaneously every significant component of its defense program, from larger force structure to modernization to readiness and sustainability. By Reagan's second term, budget constraints were forcing modification, particularly in modernization, but even this trend was more pronounced in short-term procurement than long-term research and development. The leveling off and subsequent decline in real defense spending obviously forced the administration to make choices it would have preferred to avoid. At the same time, the stakes involved were considerably smaller than during the preceding decade, because the expansion had been so broad.

One of the sharpest critiques of Reagan's budget strategy was that it resulted in precisely the volatility that defense planners find wasteful. The argument is that lower levels of real growth sustained over the entire tenure of the administration would have been preferable from the standpoint of defense planning. The question is whether Congress would have gone along with this stable growth plan. Once deficit control and domestic spending issues began to erode the defense consensus, it seems unlikely that Congress would have lived up to a long-term growth agreement. Indeed, Congress accepted 3 percent real increases for fiscal years 1987 and 1988 when it decided to halt real growth in fiscal 1986, but it abandoned these targets as other budget policy issues came to the fore. In particular, the deficit-control argument was used against defense, despite the fact that the deficit reduction during fiscal 1987 ($70+ billion) was the largest annual drop in history.

The Reagan years redefined what had become the single most important defense question—the size of the defense budget. By using size as the measure of military strength at a time when concerns about U.S. forces were widespread, the Reagan defense planners were able to mount a massive buildup without any significant alteration in U.S. commitments or strategy. The defense numbers were meaningful when translated into programs, but for much of the Reagan presidency the numbers themselves dominated annual defense debates, reducing congressional interventions to trimming at the margins. For all of the congressional appropriations reductions, authorization amendments, and investigative scrutiny, Reagan's impact on the defense budget was massive.

Defense Policy and Budget Control

In theory, defense spending should be among the more stable components of peacetime budgets. The commitments and external threats that underlie national security policy change slowly. The force structures designed to carry out that policy are therefore likely to evolve at a similar pace. The military policy and the planning process that define defense budgeting are directed toward enhancing continuity and certainty. In fact, however, stable defense budgets are not the norm.

For the past two decades, it has been difficult to shape and to maintain a lasting consensus, embracing the executive branch and Congress, on the appropriate allocation for defense. Instead, sharp declines in real defense spending took place through the mid-1970s, followed by a very modest upturn until the Reagan administration pushed through a series of very steep, real increases. In just over a decade, real defense outlays went from a post-Korean peacetime low of just over $150 billion to a peacetime peak of nearly $250 billion. At that point, however, the consensus started to weaken in Congress, and real declines began once again.

The composition of the spending budget has evolved in such a way that efforts to control spending and reduce deficits are largely restricted to defense and discretionary domestic programs. The resulting competition between them greatly intensifies the volatility of both. Defense does not always lose, as the Reagan years demonstrated, but it is difficult to plan and to implement effective defense and domestic policies when they are being forced to compete for scarce budget resources.

The congressional budget process has made defense budgeting a confused and confusing year-round exercise. The diffusion of committee control and expertise in Congress, the enormous demands for information by oversight committees, and the seemingly endless debates over nonsubstantive defense budget levels have contributed to an unwieldy and oft-times incoherent decision-making process. The chorus of complaints over congressional micromanagement of defense, moreover, is usually linked to charges that Congress has no time, ability, or inclination to analyze defense policy seriously.

These are not, however, the root problems in defense budgeting. Defense will always be disadvantaged in long-term budget competition, because it confers no tangible benefits and depends upon perceptions of threat. Expecting stability in public opinion under these conditions is unrealistic, unless there is a political leadership consensus which shapes the public's response. There was such a consensus for nearly two decades after World War II, but it was shattered by Vietnam.

Shattered as well as a budget process based upon a workable division of responsibilities. It seems rather obvious that the president is uniquely situated to integrate defense planning and defense budgets. Congress can conduct valuable policy oversight, but it cannot be expected to plan or to implement defense strategy.

The president must also be responsible for controlling the size of the defense budget. This task cannot be done, and never has been done, in isolation from other budget policy needs. Top-down budgeting, which the president can enforce, provides the framework for coordinating defense and nondefense spending with revenues and deficit levels.

The incentives for the president to constrain defense, however, disappear when Congress pursues trade-offs from defense to domestic programs while also allowing deficits to grow. This situation occurred during the 1970s. What followed was a Reagan defense program that was pursued with a similar disregard for budget totals and deficits.

A congressional budget process characterized by incremental decision making may have had flaws, but it produced better fiscal results than the comprehensive, coordinated, and participatory system now in place. The simple and inescapable fact is that two decades of "coequal" defense budgeting by the president and Congress have led to the highest real defense budgets ever registered during peacetime and the worst deficit record in history.

The budget process has not created the more serious problems and uncertainties in defense budgeting. Partisan and ideological disagreements over national security policy have precluded the forging of a political consensus which could, in turn, shape long-term defense planning. The current congressional budget process does, however, exacerbate defense budgeting problems. The annual budget priorities debates, for example, inject a heavy dose of politicization by focusing on defense and non-defense spending totals that are largely divorced from substantive policy. In a forum devoted to making symbolic points, defense totals are set that facilitate subsequent attacks on specific weapons systems. Thus, the debates over totals are defended as being abstracted from line items, but they have no meaning apart from line items.

The budget process in Congress makes virtually impossible any binding commitments to gradual, real growth over an extended period. Under these conditions, defense proponents, especially in the executive branch, are well advised to seize upon public and congressional opinion swings to get as much as they can as quickly as they can. There is a price to be paid for this approach, as the defense spending volatility and deficit record of the Reagan years demonstrate, but it is a price that the budget process makes virtually inescapable.

III

**The Budget Politics of
Domestic Policy**

6

The New Politics of Social
Welfare Policy

Before the New Deal, there was no federal social welfare policy. The
federal government had provided small grants to the states for education
and health but had assumed no responsibility for assisting the aged, the
unemployed, or the poor.[1] The Social Security Act of 1935 signaled the
beginning of what has become a dominant federal presence in designing
and funding social welfare policy. The federalization of social welfare has
meant, in budgeting terms, complex spending-control problems. The social welfare share of the budget is by far the largest component of current
and projected outlays, even after more than a decade of consolidation and
retrenchment. It also represents a new type of budget politics which has, in
Wildavsky's view, "squeezed the old budget process."[2]

The new politics of social welfare comprises interrelated legal, procedural, political, and ethical factors. Most social welfare programs, and
especially the largest ones, are entitlements. The payment of benefits
(entitlements) is required to those who meet eligibility requirements set by
law. The legal rights of beneficiaries, which have been firmly established
by the courts, have made authorizations for entitlements a "binding obligation . . . of the Federal Government."[3] As a result, appropriations to
provide budget authority are nondiscretionary, and indeed many entitlements are funded through permanent appropriations.[4]

Most social welfare spending is on a different budgetary track. For
entitlements, there is no meaningful control through the appropriations
process, which makes possible "disproportionate influence by authorizing
committees that may be dominated by program proponents." This potential policy monopoly by program advocates, however, requires political
and ethical supports.[5] The political supports come from large and well-
organized beneficiary groups. The ethical supports reflect societal beliefs
about which groups deserve assistance.[6] Social welfare programs, even
those that enjoy entitlement status, are not all equal.

This last point is underscored by the recent divergence between social welfare programs for the poor and the nonpoor. From the mid-1930s through the mid-1960s, growth for both categories of programs was moderate. The Great Society then triggered an expansion which significantly boosted public assistance and income security program outlays for the next decade. At that point, the explosive costs associated with this expansion led to consolidation and retrenchment, but retrenchment was aimed primarily at the less costly public assistance component of federal social welfare policy. As Wildavsky has concluded, the efforts to strengthen spending controls for entitlements have usually meant "preventing entitlements from rising too fast, not abolishing or severely diminishing them. Since the largest entitlements, especially the family of programs under social security, are the most sacrosanct, their growth overwhelms efforts to control their poorer cousins."[7]

The tension between social welfare policy and budgetary control demonstrates a complicated political calculus, one that does not conform well to the argument that policymakers use "their activities and votes to claim credit with constituents and clientele groups for actions taken in their interests."[8] The credit-claiming thesis applied to social welfare programs would posit steadily rising real benefits, since the pressures to distribute benefits are concentrated and tangible, while the potential gains from controlling spending are diffuse. The latter is especially true when deficits, rather than taxes, are used to finance programs.

Instead of steadily rising real benefits, there have been indexation formulas applied to large programs and real benefits cuts for smaller ones. In R. Kent Weaver's view, politicians are usually "torn between conflicting motives: for example, between perceptions of what is good policy and desire to claim credit for a popular action or avoid blame for an unpopular action." The indexing of benefits for large, politically potent social welfare programs has elements of each of these motives, but Weaver's conclusion is that "blame-oriented objectives and strategies—when the political environment gives rise to them—are an especially powerful influence on policymakers' behavior."[9]

The comparatively aggressive attack on the costs of public assistance programs is usually explained by the more problematic politics associated with these programs, but there is also a policy explanation. Public assistance programs raise serious issues about family stability, work incentives, and individual responsibility. The almost ceaseless tinkering with public assistance over the past several decades reflects the elusiveness of definitive policy solutions.

The budgetary politics of social welfare policy defies what Wildavsky

terms "a full explanation-cum-prediction of the trajectory of entitlements . . . [which] would be equivalent to comprehending most of American national public policy." What we do know is that entitlements, while
not inviolable, are not the same as ordinary programs. Their evolution
clarifies the reason why social welfare programs generally, entitlements
more specifically, and social security and medicare most especially sit
"uneasily with the concepts of resource allocation and budgetary control."[10]

Establishing the Base

During the 1930s federal social welfare policy developed along two
different tracks. The first was emergency relief, designed to provide immediate assistance in the form of jobs and food. With the economic recovery
spurred by World War II, the necessity for temporary relief largely disappeared, as did most of the New Deal's emergency programs.

The Social Security System, 1935–45

The permanent track was defined by the Social Security Act of 1935
(PL 74-271). It combined what have remained the two contrasting approaches to social welfare: income security and public assistance. An
insurance approach was used for the social security system, with a self-
financing payroll tax, trust fund, and automatic benefits for retirees. It
was also applied to the unemployment compensation program set up
under the 1935 act.[11]

The other income programs contained in the Social Security Act were
assistance-based. The old-age assistance (OAA) program authorized federal matching grants to the states to help finance monthly cash benefits to
the aged indigent. Need was to be established through a means test, and
coverage extended to all of the elderly, not just to those covered by the
new old-age insurance program. Similar to old-age assistance was aid to
the blind (AB), which also used federal matching grants to help finance
state cash assistance programs for indigent blind adults. The aid-to-
dependent-children (ADC) program likewise used a means test to determine eligibility. The recipient population in this instance consisted of
needy children, adequate financial support for whom was otherwise unavailable because of the death, incapacity, or absence of a parent (usually
the father).[12]

As shown in table 6.1, the initial set of federal programs maintained
state involvement in decision making as well as administration for all but
the old-age insurance program. The requirements associated with federal

Table 6.1. Major Components of the 1935 Social Security Act (PL 74-271)

I. Old-Age Insurance (OAI)

Recipient Population	Retired workers in covered employment
Financing	Federal payroll tax, trust fund
Administration	Federal
Eligibility	Automatic
Benefit Level	Based on preemployment earnings

II. Unemployment Insurance

Recipient Population	Unemployed workers in covered employment
Financing	State payroll tax on employers (credited against 3 percent federal payroll tax), trust fund
Administration	State
Eligibility	Determined by state
Benefit Level	Determined by state

III. Old-Age Assistance (OAA)

Recipient Population	Indigent aged, 65 or older
Financing	Federal matching grants, 50 percent of benefit (maximum federal grant of $15 per month per recipient)
Administration	State
Eligibility	Determined by state (means test)
Benefit Level	Determined by state

IV. Aid to the Blind (AB)

Recipient Population	Indigent blind adults
Financing	Federal matching grants, 50 percent of benefit (maximum federal grant of $15 per month per recipient)
Administration	State
Eligibility	Determined by state (means test)
Benefit Level	Determined by state

V. Aid to Dependent Children (ADC)

Recipient Population	Indigent children
Financing	Federal matching grants, one-third of benefit (maximum of $6 per month for first child, $4 each additional child)
Administration	State
Eligibility	Determined by state (means test)
Benefit Level	Determined by state

SOURCE: Compiled by author.

matching grants were loose, allowing the states considerable discretion in defining eligibility and benefit levels. There was no nationwide standard for defining either need or adequate benefits. The 1935 framework has had a long-term impact on social welfare policy. Its distinction between income security and public assistance has given the social security system strong protection against political attack. The assistance programs, by comparison, have been much more controversial.

The New Deal Strategy. Franklin Roosevelt announced to Congress on June 8, 1934, that he would recommend a permanent federal social insurance system the following year. Later that month, Roosevelt appointed a Committee on Economic Security to develop specific programs to serve the aged, the unemployed, and the indigent. On January 17, 1935, Roosevelt transmitted the committee's recommendations to Congress. Over the next eight months, Congress changed numerous details, adding aid to the blind, for example, while dropping government-sponsored retirement insurance for those not covered by the proposed social security system.

The legislation that was signed into law on August 14, 1935, however, incorporated the basic framework that Roosevelt's committee had proposed. Social security was exclusively federal, but its financing was based on payroll taxes paid partly by workers. Assistance programs were modest in scope and benefits, and their implementation accorded considerable discretion to the states.

Of particular importance, the 1935 Social Security Act did not include a national health insurance component. The Committee on Economic Security had endorsed compulsory national health insurance but had not included a specific program proposal in its report. Roosevelt explained that "groups representing the medical profession are cooperating with the Federal Government in the further study of the subject, and definite progress is being made."[13] The implication was that a program might be proposed in the future, but, in fact, Roosevelt never recommended to Congress even a limited national health insurance system.

The Roosevelt plan's self-imposed moderation was a tactical concession to conservatives in both parties who were intensely opposed to the concept of a federalized welfare system. It was also designed to limit immediate costs. The old-age insurance trust fund, for example, was to begin collecting payroll taxes in 1937, but benefits were not scheduled to be distributed until 1942. This original target was later moved to 1940, but average monthly benefits from 1940 to 1945 were less than $25 per month.[14] Benefit levels for public assistance programs were also comparatively low, with the maximum federal reimbursement to the states for aged, indigent individuals set at $15 per month.

The popular alternatives to Roosevelt's proposals underscored the emphasis on costs. The Townsend Plan (named after Dr. Francis Townsend, a physician and social reform advocate) had attracted considerable support among the elderly. It called for a $200 per month pension for those sixty years of age or older, with financing through a form of sales tax. The Lundeen bill (introduced by Ernest Lundeen, a Farmer-Labor party member from Minnesota) was a comprehensive, exclusively federal social insurance scheme which offered high benefits to be financed through income, inheritance, and gift taxes levied on upper-income groups. In the Senate, the principal counterpart to these proposals was Senator Huey P. Long's "share-the-wealth" scheme, which included generous pensions for the elderly and the unemployed financed by a tax on personal property and other assets.

The New Deal's social welfare initiatives also faced constitutional challenges. The Supreme Court, however, upheld the constitutionality of both the old-age insurance system and the unemployment insurance system in three cases decided on May 24, 1937.[15] With the corollary easing of the Supreme Court's hostility to other elements of the New Deal domestic agenda in 1937, the Roosevelt administration was freed from direct constitutional attack, but it still faced formidable political and budgetary pressures.

The New Deal Framework. As a consequence Roosevelt subsequently pushed for only modest legislative changes. In 1937 a federal old-age retirement system was established to cover railroad workers, and a federal unemployment insurance program for railroad workers was created the next year. In 1939 extended coverage and benefits were incorporated into the social security system.

The 1939 Social Security Act Amendments provided for a major structural change in social security coverage. Under the original act, monthly benefits were available to an eligible worker on retirement at age sixty-five. The 1939 amendments authorized benefits for dependents and for survivors of a covered worker. What had been the old-age insurance trust fund (OAI) became the old-age and survivors insurance trust fund (OASI). The start-up date for benefits was also moved from 1942 to 1940, eligibility was changed to "quarters" worked in covered employment, and monthly benefit levels were redefined based on average monthly wages over a working career. The other components of the original social security system were left largely intact through World War II, although the

1939 amendments also raised the federal share for the three public assistance programs.

Federal public assistance spending grew throughout the New Deal's tenure, and by the end of World War II, annual outlays in the three principal programs were over $400 million. By far the largest of these was old-age assistance, which by 1945 accounted for approximately two-thirds of the 3.1 million individuals receiving federally assisted benefits. Nevertheless, the federal government had not federalized public assistance. The states continued to control important program decisions, and the states (and local governments) continued to supply more than one-half of public assistance expenditures.[16]

Over the next two decades, the federal-state balance with respect both to programmatic decisions and funding moved gradually toward greater federal control. The basic issue of federal responsibility was rarely confronted directly, but it came up repeatedly in debates over federal matching shares and federally imposed national standards. In a number of cases, Congress used additional funds to encourage states to expand their programs. Most of these changes, in turn, were enacted as part of periodic extensions of the social security program.

The Pre-Johnson Changes

Amendments to the 1935 Social Security Act, both major and minor, were enacted frequently between the end of World War II and the Johnson presidency. For social security, the result was to increase by more than 60 percent the proportion of the workforce in covered employment, while raising benefits significantly and adding long-term disability insurance (DI) for workers below retirement age. For public assistance programs, two new coverages were enacted—aid to the permanently and totally disabled (APTD) and medical assistance to the aged (MAA)—while federal reimbursement was also authorized for state-paid medical care for the indigent. The federal share of public assistance spending rose steadily over this period, as federal matching formulas were made more generous and as recipient populations increased.

Social Security. Any lingering doubts about the long-term future of social security were erased within a few years after the end of World War II, as the Truman and Eisenhower administrations sponsored legislation greatly expanding and strengthening the social security system. The broad thrust toward universal coverage with "more than merely subsistence" benefit levels was sustained through the mid-1960s (see table 6.2).[17] At that point, coverage had been extended to approximately 90 percent of

Table 6.2. Major Social Security Program Changes, 1937-64

Employment Coverage

1950	Farm and domestic workers
	Self-employed (nonfarm, nonprofessional)
1954	Self-employed farmers
	Self-employed professionals (not physicians or lawyers)

Benefit Coverage

1939	Dependents and survivors (OASI)
1956	Women aged 62-64 (reduced benefits)
1956	Disabled workers--OASDI (age 50-64)
1960	Disabled workers (under 50 years of age)
1961	Men aged 62-64 (reduced benefits)

Taxable Earnings and Tax Rate
(Employee/Employer respectively)

1937	$3,000 (1.0 percent)
1950	$3,000 (1.5 percent)
1951	$3,600 (1.5 percent)
1954	$3,600 (2.0 percent)
1955	$4,200 (2.0 percent)
1957	$4,200 (2.25 percent)
1959	$4,800 (2.5 percent)
1960	$4,800 (3.0 percent)
1962	$4,800 (3.125 percent)
1963	$4,800 (3.625 percent)

Average Monthly Benefits (Worker)

1939	$22.60
1950	$43.86
1952	$49.25
1954	$59.14
1958	$66.35
1964	$77.57

SOURCE: Compiled by author.

the workforce, disability benefits had been made available through a separate trust fund, and early retirement had been authorized for women and men.

Periodic increases in social security taxes were required to support expanded eligibility and higher benefit levels. By 1965 nearly 20 million beneficiaries were receiving monthly benefits under OASDI, and annual OASDI outlays were over $15 billion. Nevertheless, the annual maximum tax for social security was still well under $200, while accumulated reserves for the OASI and DI trust funds were over $20 billion.[18]

The most important and divisive conflict during social security's first three decades came not over the basic system but rather over national health insurance. Roosevelt had indicated several times his support for some form of national health insurance but had never submitted a formal proposal to Congress, nor had he lent his full support to efforts by congressional Democrats to enact a national health bill.[19]

Truman, by comparison, strongly supported national health legislation almost from the beginning of his presidency. Late in 1945 he sent to Congress a proposal for comprehensive, pre-paid health insurance financed through higher social security taxes, but no serious action was taken on it. In 1949 Truman launched a major effort to push a national health bill through Congress. With his party back in control of both houses and a strong push by labor, the prospects for passage appeared to have improved, but the American Medical Association (AMA) and conservatives in both parties were still dominant. No national health bill reached the floor in either the House or the Senate. What Congress ultimately agreed to, in 1950, was federal reimbursement to the states for medical treatment ("vendor payments") of persons on public assistance.

The next stage in the national health policy debate was a modest Eisenhower initiative to provide federal insurance backing that would encourage private insurance companies to offer broader coverage. This proposal never progressed very far in Congress. By the late 1950s it was apparent that comprehensive national coverage for all ages was not a serious option, and the focus shifted toward coverage for the elderly as part of the old-age insurance system. The Eisenhower administration offered a noncompulsory catastrophic coverage bill in 1960, which was not adopted. The Democratic alternative, which had been the subject of intermittent hearings since 1957, proposed social security system coverage for major medical expenses through an increase in the social security payroll tax.

With the 1960 presidential election acting as a catalyst, both parties tried to capitalize on this newest version of national health policy. The

Democratic presidential candidate, John F. Kennedy, made passage of a broad social security health bill one of his legislative goals for the postconvention congressional session. Richard M. Nixon backed a plan to expand the coverage and benefits proposed earlier in the year by the Eisenhower administration. What Congress finally approved, however, were increased federal matching grants to the states and a separate grant program to reimburse the states for paying for medical care to the medically needy aged—those too poor to pay their medical bills but not sufficiently poor to qualify for old-age assistance. The medical assistance to the aged plan left decisions about coverage and benefits largely up to the states, and it was endorsed by the AMA.[20]

In 1961 and 1962 Congress raised federal reimbursement formulas for the OAA and MAA health programs, but the Kennedy administration was unable to gain approval for its full-scale medical insurance program for the aged. In 1963 the administration once again failed to add medical care to the OASI program.

Public Assistance. From 1935 to 1964 Congress repeatedly revised the formulas governing federal reimbursement grants to the states for public assistance programs.[21] These revisions included raising the percentage share and maximum reimbursement available from the federal government. Aid to the permanently and totally disabled was established in 1950, providing monthly benefits to indigent disabled individuals eighteen years of age or older. In 1956 states were authorized to receive 50 percent federal reimbursement for a variety of rehabilitative services provided for public assistance beneficiaries.[22]

From 1950 through 1962 Congress also loosened some of the ADC restrictions. Before 1950, ADC payments were made only for children, not for adults caring for those children. In 1950 and 1956 specified family members caring for ADC-eligible children were also made eligible for ADC payments. In 1961 Congress made ADC aid available for an unemployed parent; as a condition for assistance, the wage earner could not refuse a job made available through public employment offices. In 1962 the newly designated aid to families with dependent children (AFDC) program extended coverage to unemployed parents and imposed a similar requirement on beneficiaries to participate in vocational training, community work, or training projects provided by the states.

Public assistance extensions, then, were piecemeal, and the frequent boosts in federal reimbursement formulas were intended to encourage the states, not compel them, to liberalize eligibility and raise coverage. As a result, there were wide disparities among the states in the types and levels of benefits offered.

The Kennedy administration, which sponsored important changes in the basic cash assistance program, also attempted to broaden the forms of assistance available to the poor. In 1961, for example, an experimental food stamp program was implemented, allowing the poor in participating cities and counties to purchase stamps redeemable for food purchases worth more than the cost of the stamps. In 1964 the food stamp program was made permanent. An accelerated federal effort in public housing also developed during the early 1960s, along with increased attention to alternative forms of housing assistance to low-income groups.

When Lyndon Johnson first succeeded to the presidency, social welfare expansion received an even more pronounced emphasis. In 1964 Johnson gained passage of his Economic Opportunity Act, which established a variety of job training and work programs. Congressional resistance to health care assistance for the aged and the poor, however, could not be overcome.

At the time of Johnson's reelection, federal social welfare outlays totaled well over $30 billion (see table 6.3). While this sum represented a very large, long-term increase in spending, a good portion of the increase was accounted for by social security (and other retirement programs). In addition, the relative scale of federal expenditures was not very different from what it had been in 1950. For nearly a quarter century, the nature and scope of federal social welfare policy had been criticized as inadequate, but the configuration of policy had not basically changed. With the massive Democratic victory in 1964, however, the next stage in social welfare policy was soon underway.

Expanding the Base

From the mid-1960s through the late 1970s, federal social welfare spending rose dramatically. Over the fiscal 1965–80 period, real spending for payments for individuals more than tripled, accounting for more than three-fourths of all real growth in the federal budget. The share of federal outlays devoted to payments for individuals roughly doubled, to just under one-half.[23]

There were several causes for this expansion. The base of the social welfare system was enlarged and redefined. Medical care for the aged and poor was enacted. Public assistance supplements for food, housing, and varied social services were incorporated on a permanent basis. Federal aid to education became, for the first time, a general aid subsidy.

A second type of change was the repeated liberalization of eligibility and benefit levels for older social welfare programs. This expansion culminated, in several cases, with the enactment of automatic cost-of-living

Table 6.3. Federal Social Welfare Spending, Fiscal Years 1940-64 (in billions of dollars)

	Payments for Individuals Outlays				Total	
Fiscal Year	Social Security[a]	Other Retirement[b]	Public Assistance[c]	All Other[d]	Percentage of Outlays	Percentage of GNP
1940	$ --	$0.5	$0.5	$0.7	17.5%	1.7%
1945	0.2	0.9	0.6	0.4	2.4	1.0
1950	0.7	2.3	1.6	9.0	32.1	5.1
1955	4.3	3.3	2.2	4.4	20.9	3.7
1960	10.8	4.7	3.3	5.4	26.2	4.8
1964	15.8	5.9	4.5	6.0	27.2	5.1

SOURCE: *Historical Tables, Budget of the United States Government, Fiscal Year 1990*, pp. 184-208.
[a] Includes old age and survivors insurance and disability insurance trust funds.
[b] Includes railroad retirement and federal employee retirement and insurance.
[c] Includes federal support payments to states and veterans non-service-connected pensions.
[d] Includes unemployment compensation, medical care, veterans education benefits, housing assistance, food and nutrition assistance, veterans insurance and burial benefits, and refugee assistance.

adjustments to preserve real benefit gains. The most important of these was the indexing of social security in 1972, but the principle of statutory indexation was applied very broadly during the 1960s and 1970s to eligibility as well as benefit decisions.[24]

These changes comprised the basic policy decisions behind the social welfare spending expansion, but their fiscal impact turned out to be considerably greater than anticipated because of the confluence of demographic and economic factors. Budgetary constraints became very severe very quickly, drawing off much of the impetus behind social welfare policy innovation.

The Johnson Initiatives
Measured by legislative accomplishment, the Johnson presidency was prolific. Health and education programs that Truman and Kennedy had been unable to push through Congress were only part of the Johnson

record. Particularly during the Eighty-ninth Congress (1965–66), with its huge Democratic majorities, Johnson was able to secure passage for a wide range of social welfare innovations under the umbrella of his "Great Society."

The Programs: Social Security. Omnibus social security bills in 1965 and 1967 continued the practice of extending coverage and liberalizing eligibility. Benefit increases of 7 percent in 1965 and 13 percent in 1967 also were enacted, necessitating increases over previously scheduled wage base and tax rate hikes.

By far the biggest change, however, was the addition of medical care coverage for the aged. As proposed by Johnson at the outset of the 1965 congressional session, medicare was limited to a basic health plan along the lines previously proposed by Kennedy and Johnson. Coverage was provided for hospital care, nursing home care, certain outpatient diagnostic services, and home health-care visits. Financing was through an increase in the social security tax, administered through a separate trust fund. Participation was compulsory.

The American Medical Association, which had spearheaded the opposition to every previous social security health care extension, attempted to come up with a positive alternative on this occasion. Attacking the Johnson proposal for failing to cover physicians' fees, the AMA called for a comprehensive but voluntary insurance program, financed by variable premiums for participants and matching federal-state funds.

The so-called eldercare program did not attract strong support, even among Republicans, but the argument about more comprehensive coverage proved compelling. At the end of March 1965, the Ways and Means Committee reported out a bill combining the basic health care provisions of the Johnson proposal and a supplemental insurance plan (financed by premiums from participants and matching funds from general federal revenues) covering physicians' and surgeons' fees, along with other health care services. Senate changes in the House-passed bill were relatively minor, and the conference report was adopted by overwhelming margins in both the House (307–116) and the Senate (70–24).

Public Assistance. The same legislation that established medicare (PL 89–97) also revised the health care assistance program for the poor. The Johnson administration had transmitted to Congress a separate bill, extending federal matching funds to cover state medical service payments for the poor. This proposal was incorporated as Title XIX of the 1965 Social Security Act Amendments, and it extended medicaid coverage to the nonelderly poor, with the federal government providing 50 to 83 percent of the costs under a formula inversely related to a state's per capita income. The medicaid provisions also left the eligibility criteria largely to the discretion of the states, and this flexibility (along with rising health care costs) led to greater coverage and higher costs than Congress had anticipated. Additional public assistance provisions in the 1965 law included increased funding for maternal and child health-care services and more generous federal matching formulas for cash assistance programs, along with incentives to encourage states to liberalize income-eligibility criteria for public assistance programs.

Other elements of the public assistance extensions were "antipoverty" education, training, and employment programs. The scope and funding for the 1964 Economic Opportunity Act were extended significantly in 1965. In addition to its original community action programs, the Office of Economic Opportunity initiated the Head Start and Upward Bound programs. It also established funding for neighborhood legal service centers to provide free counsel on civil matters for the poor. By the end of Johnson's presidency, there were also nearly a dozen federally financed employment training programs.

Food and Housing. An important policy debate about the future direction of public assistance concerned the choice between cash or in-kind benefits. The Johnson administration's desire to extend antipoverty efforts in the areas of food and housing was caught in a cross fire between those who favored cash (in the form of a guaranteed income) and those who opposed the extensions of assistance in any form. Opposition was sufficiently widespread in key congressional committees that a program-by-program extension became all but inevitable.

Program accomplishments were nevertheless noteworthy. Spending for a variety of food assistance programs—school lunches and breakfasts, food stamps, and direct distribution—grew very rapidly. Of particular importance, the food stamp program began to acquire a broader base of political support. A series of public and private studies demonstrating the severity of hunger and malnutrition problems nationwide virtually forced the agriculture committees to treat food assistance as a welfare program rather than an agricultural policy by-product.

The administration was less successful in persuading Congress to target school feeding programs on children from low-income families and to restrict in a parallel fashion the school milk program. The cost issue was handled in a paradoxical fashion by Congress. It was difficult for the administration to obtain its requested funding for the more carefully targeted programs, such as food stamps. It was difficult also for the administration to gain agreement for offsetting the increased cost of targeted programs by restricting the availability of politically popular but less carefully targeted food programs.

With housing, the Johnson administration achieved a series of breakthroughs. In 1964 Johnson had identified housing and urban development as a cornerstone of his Great Society vision. The following year Johnson gained congressional approval for a cabinet-level department to coordinate and to highlight federal housing efforts. He also obtained enactment of an omnibus housing bill which included federal rent supplements to help low-income families otherwise unable to afford decent housing. Authorizations for other low-income housing programs were increased as well.

In 1966 and 1967 model cities and urban renewal legislation was passed, along with appropriations for rent supplements, although overall funding levels were well below Johnson's requests. In 1968 a massive housing bill was pushed through Congress which provided federal mortgage interest subsidies to low-income families for home purchases and greatly expanded mortgage subsidies for the construction of private, non-profit rental housing for the poor.

Food and housing assistance to the poor were not unprecedented, but the Johnson administration transformed them into major antipoverty programs. Despite repeated conflicts in Congress over authorizations and appropriations, the administration managed to gain increased coverage and higher benefits. In almost every instance, however, funding levels were well below those proposed by the administration.

Education. The 1965 session produced two landmark education bills—the Elementary and Secondary Education Act of 1965 and the Higher Education Act of 1965. The former established federal aid to local school districts, with funding disproportionately geared to districts with large numbers of needy children. The latter was also aimed at improving educational opportunities for the financially disadvantaged, authorizing direct federal aid to students from low-income families. A second type of assistance was also established for students with less pressing financial need. In this instance, federally guaranteed and interest-subsidized loans were to be made available through private lenders to students from families with pretax incomes of less than $15,000.

The Budgetary Impact. The entire roster of the Johnson administration's social welfare policy initiatives goes well beyond the programs reviewed here. From the perspective of budget policy, however, several points stand out. In terms of short-range cost increases, the Johnson

Table 6.4. Social Welfare Outlays, Fiscal Years 1960-69

Functional Category	Percentage of Gross National Product			
	FY 1960	FY 1965	FY 1967	FY 1969
Education, Training, Employment, and Social Services	0.19	0.32	0.81	0.81
Health	0.16	0.27	0.42	0.56
Medicare	0.00	0.00	0.35	0.61
Income Security	1.46	1.41	1.29	1.41
Social Security	2.29	2.60	2.73	2.94
Veterans Benefits and Services	1.00	0.85	0.85	0.82
Total	5.17	5.44	6.45	7.14

SOURCE: Gene Falk, *1988 Budget Perspectives: Federal Spending for the Human Resource Programs* (Washington, D.C.: Congressional Research Service, 1987), p. CRS-33.

programs had only a modest impact. Human resources outlays, for example, rose from 5.2 percent of GNP in fiscal year 1960 to 5.4 percent in fiscal 1965 and then to 7.1 percent in fiscal 1969 (see table 6.4). Much of this increase, however, was attributable to social security and medicare, which by fiscal 1969 accounted for about one-half of the total human resources outlays. Measured against total budget outlays, human resources functional categories rose from 28.4 percent of the budget in fiscal 1960 to 36.2 percent in fiscal 1969, with most of this increase concentrated during Johnson's tenure.

The social welfare policy extensions under Johnson were sharply criticized. Part of the criticism was a more or less sincere philosophical disagreement. Part was programmatic, reflecting dissatisfaction with the design and administration of particular programs and with the lack of coherence across the range of old and new public assistance programs. In fact, the stigma attached to the phrase "welfare policy" by many members of Congress had made it impossible for Johnson to go beyond piecemeal changes to a comprehensive, public assistance system. Coherence was diminished still further by the maze of committee jurisdictions through which the different programs, old and new, were funneled.

Another dimension of the attacks on social welfare policy was fiscal. While the short-term funding increases during Johnson's tenure were modest, at least in terms of subsequent spending trends, these increases took place within the context of wartime budgets. During World War II and Korea, social welfare spending had declined against the conventional measures—total outlays and GNP—and also in constant dollars. During Vietnam, social welfare spending increased against these indices and also in real terms. Moreover, the social welfare increases were about the same as the increases for defense. Thus, during wartime under Johnson, social welfare spending rose to over 7 percent of GNP, the highest level ever recorded and more than double the level registered during the Korean War years.

The traditional postwar boost in domestic spending was, in the case of Vietnam, widely anticipated despite the unique spending patterns of the Johnson years. In addition, the growing unpopularity of the war itself generated strong pressures in Congress to make up for forgone spending even before the war was over. Despite Republican control of the presidency from 1969 to 1977, the result was accelerated growth in social welfare spending. The real costs of Johnson's Great Society emerged, but only after Johnson was gone.

The Nixon-Ford Record

Over the fiscal 1969–77 period, human resources spending rose to approximately 12 percent of GNP, while the budget share for the human resources functions climbed to over 50 percent. This expansion did not result, however, from any great innovations or creativity in policy. One of the most significant and surprising outcomes of the Nixon-Ford period, in fact, was what did not occur. Despite widespread, bipartisan criticism of the patchwork public assistance "system," no major welfare reform was enacted. Further, national health insurance never made it through the House and Senate.

This period in budget policy history featured repeated, bitter battles between the executive branch and Congress over spending policy. Presidential vetoes of the annual Labor–Health, Education, and Welfare (HEW) appropriations bills were routine during Nixon's first term, and the conflicts over domestic progress escalated with the Nixon impoundments of 1973 and 1974.[25] One immediate outcome of these political and constitutional controversies was the first major reform of the budget process in more than half a century—the Congressional Budget and Impoundment Control Act of 1974.

A second and less immediately obvious outcome was the fiscal constraint emerging from the uncoordinated expansion of social welfare spending. The spending decisions of the Nixon-Ford years proved so costly that new social welfare initiatives were precluded once the Democratic party regained control of the White House. In addition, the growing imbalance between social security (and other retirement programs) and public assistance did not receive adequate attention, leaving the latter especially vulnerable to subsequent efforts at retrenchment.

Fiscal 1969–73. The beginning of the Nixon presidency appeared to hold great promise for the reform and redirection of welfare policy. Toward the end of the Johnson administration, the president had appointed a Commission on Income Maintenance Programs to consider "any and every plan, however unconventional" to improve what Johnson criticized as an outmoded welfare system.[26] On August 8, 1969, President Nixon reiterated Johnson's call for creative and unconventional welfare reform. The family assistance plan (FAP) that Nixon announced guaranteed a minimum income to every family based on size and need. For a family of four without other income, the guaranteed income was to be $1,600. Further, the working poor were also eligible for aid.

This was the type of scheme that some of the Great Society welfare planners had viewed as too radical to bring to Lyndon Johnson.[27] Nevertheless, Nixon's FAP was almost immediately attacked by congressional liberals as well as conservatives, and hopes for any dramatic breakthrough disappeared soon thereafter. With the resulting standoff on welfare reform, the focus of budget policy debates shifted to the program-by-program approach that had characterized social welfare in the past.

For social security, by comparison, the traditional political insulation that the program had enjoyed became even stronger. Benefit increases were enacted in 1969 (15 percent across the board), 1971 (10 percent), and 1972 (20 percent). These were considerably above inflation rates (as measured by the consumer price index, or CPI), and they were locked in by the indexing of social security benefits to the CPI enacted in 1972.[28] The original effective date for initial indexing was 1975, so an additional 11 percent increase was enacted in 1973, along with a revised timetable to speed up future cost-of-living adjustments.

Financing for these increases was accomplished by more than doubling the wage base (from $4,800 in 1969 to $12,000 in 1973) and increasing the tax rate (from 4.6 percent to 5.8 percent). In addition, the administration and Congress federalized eligibility standards and benefit levels for several assistance programs that were part of the social security system. Aid to the blind, the permanently and totally disabled, and the aged poor were combined into a supplemental security income (SSI) program in 1972, funded entirely by the federal government and with higher benefit levels.

The other elements of the social welfare system produced protracted and usually inconclusive conflicts between the administration and Congress. Congress blocked Nixon's efforts to combine into block grants numerous categorical grant programs in education and health. Rejected as well were Nixon's proposals to tighten need formulas for higher-education student aid and to replace food stamps with cash allowances.

Congress and the administration reached agreement on a series of liberalizations in eligibility and benefit levels for the food stamp program, but the administration failed in its attempt to restrain school lunch program costs. In 1970 national eligibility standards were applied to food stamp participation, free stamps were authorized for very poor families, and annual cost-of-living adjustments in benefit levels were mandated. The following year Congress blocked administration efforts to reduce spending and tighten eligibility for the school lunch program; and in 1972 federal assistance was raised, while eligibility was extended. The housing subsidies inaugurated by the Johnson administration were likewise expanded during the first Nixon term, although funding continued to lag behind authorizations.

The cumulative result of these decisions was to raise steadily the spending levels for all major social welfare programs, including those for the poor. Outlays for the latter roughly doubled over the fiscal 1969–73 period, reaching nearly $17 billion in fiscal 1973.[29] While these increases were significant and highly controversial, they only accounted for a small part of the upward trend in human resources spending. The increase in social security spending alone, for example, was greater than the total growth in cash and in-kind assistance programs for the poor.

The central social welfare budget trend during Nixon's first term is best illustrated by comparisons to GNP. Over the fiscal 1969–73 period, total outlays as a percentage of GNP actually dropped slightly, from 19.8 percent to 19.2 percent. Human resources outlays, by comparison, rose from 7.1 percent to 9.3 percent of GNP. This was a larger percentage point increase than had occurred over both the Kennedy and Johnson administrations, but it was not uniform across social welfare programs. Instead, about one-half of this entire increase was accounted for by retirement programs and medicare (see table 6.5).

During Nixon's first term, social welfare policy debates focused primarily on the narrow group of low-income assistance programs. The

Table 6.5. Major Sources of Growth in Human Resources Outlays, Fiscal Years 1969-73

| | As Percentages of GNP | | |
Fiscal Year	Total Human Resources	Retirement/Medicare[a]	Low-Income Assistance[b]
1969	7.14	4.18	0.92
1970	7.61	4.35	1.02
1971	8.70	4.79	1.26
1972	9.30	4.93	1.44
1973	9.33	5.29	1.30
Increase	+ 2.19	+ 1.11	+ 0.38

SOURCE: Falk, *1988 Budget Perspectives: Federal Spending for the Human Resource Programs*, pp. CRS-33, CRS-55, CRS-81.
[a] Includes social security, railroad retirement, federal civil and military retirement.
[b] Includes family support payments, supplemental security income, veterans pensions, medicaid, housing assistance, food stamps.

Nixon administration did not mount a serious attack against the Great Society's public assistance extensions, but it was stymied in its efforts to redirect these programs with a guaranteed income policy or to maintain tight control over eligibility and benefit levels. At the same time, increases in retirement programs, mainly social security, generated very little controversy, despite the comparatively greater budget-control problems posed by these programs.

The predominant policy response of this period was to avoid revisiting past decisions. After significantly raising real social security benefit levels, for example, the Nixon administration and Congress indexed the OASDI benefit provisions in 1972. This meant that the three major federal retirement programs—civil service, military, and social security—were indexed. Indexing was applied as well to food stamp eligibility and benefits, to medicaid eligibility, and to physicians' outpatient charges under medicare. The result of these changes was to compartmentalize still further the different components of an increasingly inchoate social welfare system. Moreover, the major criticism leveled at the system—excessive

Table 6.6. Major Sources of Growth in Human Resources Outlays, Fiscal Years 1973-77

	As Percentages of GNP		
Fiscal Year	Total Human Resources	Retirement/Medicare[a]	Low-Income Assistance[b]
1973	9.33	5.29	1.30
1974	9.59	5.51	1.42
1975	11.38	6.10	1.67
1976	11.99	6.33	1.72
1977	11.47	6.44	1.62
Increase			
1973-77	+ 2.14	+ 1.15	+ 0.32
1969-73	+ 2.19	+ 1.11	+ 0.38

SOURCE: Falk, *1988 Budget Perspectives: Federal Spending for the Human Resource Programs*, pp. CRS-33, CRS-55, CRS-81.
[a] Includes social security, railroad retirement, federal civil and military retirement.
[b] Includes family support payments, supplemental security income, veterans pensions, medicaid, housing assistance, food stamps.

cost—was usually directed toward the comparatively less costly public assistance programs.

Fiscal 1973–77. Whatever its prospects might otherwise have been, the budget policy offensive of the second Nixon term came to an abrupt end with the Watergate revelations. Nixon's replacement by Gerald Ford in August 1974 and the Democratic congressional gains three months later appeared to insure enactment of national health insurance along with a "liberal" version of the welfare reform Nixon had proposed to Congress years earlier. The ironic result was a further widening of the gap between retirement program outlays and public assistance. As shown in table 6.6, the changes in social welfare spending for this second fiscal period mirrored the first Nixon term. While human resources spending reached a historical peak of nearly 12 percent of GNP, the level of low-income assistance remained relatively low.

Nevertheless, the continuing criticism of public assistance costs had a

Table 6.7. Major Income and Noncash Assistance Outlays for Low-Income
Persons, Fiscal Years 1973-77

| | As Percentages of GNP | | | | | | |
| | Cash Programs | | | Noncash Programs | | | |
Fiscal Year	Family Support	Veterans Pensions	SSI	Health	Housing	Food	Total
1973	0.46	0.20	--	0.34	0.13	0.17	1.30
1974	0.38	0.18	0.14	0.39	0.13	0.20	1.42
1975	0.34	0.18	0.28	0.43	0.14	0.30	1.67
1976	0.34	0.17	0.27	0.48	0.13	0.33	1.72
1977	0.32	0.16	0.25	0.48	0.13	0.28	1.62
Change	- 0.14	- 0.04	+ 0.25	+ 0.14	0.00	+ 0.11	+ 0.32

SOURCE: Falk, *1988 Budget Perspectives: Federal Spending for the Human Resource Programs*, p. CRS-81.

pronounced effect on traditional cash assistance programs for the poor. Two of these—AFDC and related family support payments, along with veterans nonservice connected pensions—actually declined as percentages of GNP over the fiscal 1973–77 period (see table 6.7). Supplemental security income, which replaced the federal-state programs for the indigent blind, aged, and disabled, stabilized very quickly after its first year of operation. The medicaid and food stamp programs grew as percentages of GNP, albeit by very small amounts.

These anomalies in public assistance spending were particularly striking given the caseload increases. From 1960 through 1976, for example, the number of AFDC recipients increased from 800,000 families to over three million families. Over this same period, family support outlays as a percentage of GNP dropped from 0.41 percent to 0.32 percent.[30] (Veterans nonservice connected pensions dropped even more sharply over fiscal years 1960–76, despite cost-of-living benefit increases in 1973 and 1974.)[31]

The transition from Nixon to Ford cooled the rhetoric of policy debates but did not materially affect the substance or the results on social welfare. Congress continued to rebuff efforts to combine education and health programs into block grants for the states. Ford's attempts to re-

Table 6.8. Major Social Welfare Programs with Indexing Provisions, 1962-74

	Provisions Indexed	Year
Retirement and Disability Programs		
Civil Service Retirement	Benefits	1962
Military Retirement	Benefits	1963
Social Security (OASDI)	Benefits	1972
Coal Miners Disability	Benefits	1969
Railroad Retirement	Benefits	1974
Public Assistance Programs		
Food Stamps	Benefits, Eligibility	1971
Medicaid	Eligibility	1973
Supplemental Security Income	Benefits	1974

SOURCE: R. Kent Weaver, *Automatic Government, The Politics of Indexation* (Washington, D.C.: Brookings Institution, 1988), p. 43.

quire higher payments by food stamp recipients were rejected, and in 1975 mandatory coverage for the food stamp program was implemented nationwide. In 1976 Congress increased higher-education direct aid to students from low-income families, but it also raised the family income ceiling for eligibility for federal interest subsidies on guaranteed student loans.

The marginal nature of most executive branch–congressional divisions was accompanied by diminishing controls on many programs. By the end of the Ford presidency, benefits had been indexed for most retirement and disability programs. Eligibility and benefits also had been indexed for a number of low-income assistance programs (see table 6.8).

The Nixon-Ford era, then, was not exactly a stalemate. With the exception of certain housing programs, neither Nixon nor Ford was able to reverse either traditional or Great Society social welfare policies. In the case of social security, there was, of course, no attempt at reversal. With other public assistance programs, there were repeated efforts to control costs through restraints on eligibility and benefit levels and to shift greater responsibility to the states through discretionary, block grant funding.

If Congress usually prevailed on the design and direction of individual programs, it was also finding its policy options narrowing. By the mid-1970s defense outlays had dropped to less than one-fourth of the budget, while human resources spending had climbed to over one-half. The total budget had reached a peacetime peak of well over 20 percent of GNP, and deficits were reaching peacetime highs as well. The margin for an expanded social welfare system was disappearing, yet neither national health insurance nor a coherent public assistance program had been enacted. Further, within the social welfare budget, social security and medicare were beginning to expand very rapidly.

The budget battles of the Nixon-Ford era were clearly won by Congress. The implications of its victories were considerably less clear. With the Carter presidency, initial hopes for new programs soon gave way to talk of retrenchment, as cost issues became more and more pressing.

From Expansion to Retrenchment

Jimmy Carter brought to the presidency a program for adding the missing pieces to the social welfare system. The Democratic platform in 1976 endorsed "comprehensive national health insurance with universal and mandatory coverage." It pledged as well to enact a "simplified system of income maintenance" which would insure an "income floor both for the working poor and the poor not in the labor market."[32] Carter failed to add the missing pieces, and his administration spent four years revisiting many of the eligibility and funding issues that had preoccupied Nixon and Ford. Instead of comprehensive reform, piecemeal and often conflicting changes were made in existing programs, as the Carter administration and Congress struggled to contain spiraling costs.

Comprehensive reform similarly eluded Carter's successor, Ronald Reagan. What had appeared to be inexorable upward growth in the relative size of the social welfare budget was halted but not reversed by the end of the Reagan presidency, and the composition of that budget had shifted even more heavily toward social insurance and away from public assistance. Carter never achieved his programmatic objectives, while Reagan failed to gain his fiscal goals. Most important, both failed to address seriously the growing imbalance between social security (and medicare) and the remainder of the social welfare system.

Carter's Reforms

The Ninety-fifth Congress opened with clear expectations for significant advances in social welfare policy. The Carter administration's largest single change in Ford's fiscal 1978 budget was a greater than one-third boost in discretionary social welfare outlays (the education, training, employment, and social services function)—from $19.4 billion to $26.5 billion. Its recommended changes in social welfare policy, however, were developed much more slowly and against a backdrop of growing opposition in Congress.

The two major elements of Carter's social welfare program were a guaranteed income approach to public assistance and compulsory national health insurance. The former was outlined on May 2, 1977, with specific proposals unveiled three months later. The latter was delayed for eighteen months, as the administration first attempted to pass health cost-control legislation. Neither welfare reform nor national health insurance made significant progress during the Ninety-fifth Congress, and revised versions of both failed again during the Ninety-sixth.

Sources of Conflict. The social welfare record of the Carter years was a confusing one. Both the executive branch and Congress repeatedly cited budget constraints in cautioning against change. Carter insisted that national health insurance would be too expensive in the absence of a working cost-control system. Congress argued that welfare reform would be too expensive if the cash assistance system was expanded.

This focus on costs, however, affected new proposals much more than existing programs. The Food Stamp Act of 1977, for example, eliminated cash purchase requirements for food stamps, significantly increasing participation and driving program costs well above annual ceilings set by Congress. The Middle Income Student Assistance Act of 1978 greatly expanded eligibility for higher education aid, nearly doubling the income ceiling for cash assistance (Basic Education Opportunity Grants) and removing the income ceiling for participation in the subsidized guaranteed student loan program. Eligibility was expanded further the following year, along with an increase in the interest subsidy designed to encourage banks to make more loans. Extensions in eligibility and benefit formulas also occurred in housing subsidy programs.

Even when cost-control adjustments were enacted, they were often undercut. Faced with dwindling reserves in the social security retirement and disability trust funds, for example, Congress and the administration agreed on sharply increased payroll taxes for the period 1979–90. Congress also included an administration-sponsored provision which corrected the social security benefit formula, which had been overcompensating recent retirees for inflation. The 1977 social security amendments postponed the effective date of the corrected formula until 1979, however,

Table 6.9. Human Resource Outlays, Fiscal Years 1969-81

Fiscal Year	As Percentage of GNP
1969	7.1
1971	8.7
1973	9.3
1975	11.4
1977	11.5
1979	10.9
1981	12.1

SOURCE: *Historical Tables, Budget of the United States Government, Fiscal Year 1990*, pp. 49-50.

thus leaving in place artificially high benefit levels for current beneficiaries, and Congress also enacted more generous coverage for beneficiaries who were divorced or widowed.

Despite Democratic control of the White House and Congress, social welfare policy during the Carter years continued to be attacked for costs and inadequacy by congressional Democrats. Liberal congressional Democrats, such as Senator Edward M. Kennedy, criticized Carter's national health scheme as too limited, and few exhibited strong enthusiasm for welfare reform. For Kennedy, Carter's concessions to cost considerations on health care were a "failure of leadership."[33]

Support from other segments of the president's party was lukewarm at best. The House Democratic leadership set up a special Welfare Reform Subcommittee to handle Carter's welfare package in 1977, but none of the committees with direct jurisdiction (Agriculture, Education and Labor, and Ways and Means) endorsed the Carter plan. The chairman of Ways and Means, Al Ullman, declared that there was neither "the money or the experience" to make workable the job programs Carter had proposed. The chairman of Agriculture, Thomas S. Foley, objected to cash assistance in place of food stamps and declared that comprehensive reform could not "pass the Congress or the House in anything like its present form." The situation in the Senate was even less positive. Finance Committee chairman Long dismissed the basic concept of a guaranteed income, declaring that "it's my judgment that you don't need any more people on welfare."[34]

Spending Control. The lack of consensus within the Democratic

Table 6.10. Major Income and Noncash Assistance Outlays for Low-Income Persons, Fiscal Years 1977-81

| | As Percentages of GNP | | | | | | |
| | Cash Assistance | | | Noncash Benefits | | | |
Fiscal Year	Family Support	Veterans Pensions	SSI	Health	Housing	Food	Total
1977	0.32	0.16	0.25	0.48	0.13	0.28	1.62
1978	0.29	0.15	0.24	0.46	0.13	0.25	1.54
1979	0.26	0.14	0.20	0.48	0.15	0.28	1.50
1980	0.26	0.13	0.21	0.50	0.17	0.34	1.61
1981	0.26	0.13	0.22	0.53	0.19	0.38	1.70
Change	- 0.06	- 0.03	- 0.03	+ 0.05	+ 0.06	+ 0.10	+ 0.09

SOURCE: Falk, *1988 Budget Perspectives: Federal Spending for the Human Resource Programs*, p. CRS-81.

party on whether and how to control social welfare spending yielded predictably mixed budget results. During the fiscal 1977–81 period, human resources outlays increased to over 12 percent of GNP, but this actually represented a slowing down of a long-term trend (see table 6.9). A similar deceleration occurred in real spending growth for the human resources functions, although it was obscured by very high rates of inflation-generated growth.

The stabilizing of the social welfare budget, however, was not uniform. Instead, social security and medicare rose (in comparison to GNP), while other human resource functions changed very little. Of special importance, given the widespread perceptions of runaway social welfare spending under Carter, the major low-income programs accounted for approximately the same GNP percentages in fiscal 1980 and 1981 as they had at the tail end of the Ford presidency (see table 6.10). And in a continuation of the trend under Nixon and Ford, cash assistance was declining relative to GNP, while in-kind benefits were increasing.

The Carter presidency's actual contributions to social welfare policy were far removed from its initial hopes. The imbalance between social security, medicare, and the remainder of the social welfare budget widened. Instead of predominantly cash-based public assistance, the mix of cash and in-kind programs was retained, and the in-kind programs actually grew at the expense of cash programs. Cost controls on health care were not enacted, thereby foreclosing the national health insurance option and increasing the pressures to contain medicaid spending.

During the Carter years, spending for social welfare programs came under attack, but the attacks were often misguided. The sharpest criticisms were usually aimed at the Great Society's programs for the non-elderly poor. Whatever problems these might have had, soaring costs were hardly the predominant one.

Efforts to maintain, and even to increase, the real value of benefits were confined almost exclusively to programs for the elderly, and these efforts helped to reduce poverty among the elderly. Real income for the elderly grew by 23 percent between 1970 and 1980, while there was no real growth for the general population. Focusing simply on cash income, there was a nearly 40 percent decline in the poverty rate for the elderly. Counting noncash benefits, particularly medical care, the decline was even sharper.[35]

This was a remarkable achievement, but it was not accomplished by carefully targeting benefits. Instead, benefits were raised for all of the elderly, regardless of need, and the budgetary impact was enormous. By the end of fiscal 1981, social security and medicare outlays were nearly 6 percent of GNP, some 15 percent higher than the total for all human resources spending two decades earlier. With the accompanying social security tax increases, discretionary margins narrowed on both the spending and revenue sides of the budget.

The policy dilemma that existed at the end of Carter's presidency was the natural result of postponing (or avoiding) difficult social welfare decisions. There was widespread agreement that some retrenchment was necessary, but no consensus on how that should be accomplished. In particular, retrenchment had to include programs for the elderly in order to yield major savings, but these programs were obviously the strongest politically. Balancing the social welfare budget between the poor and the elderly required a new approach, and the Reagan administration started out with a dramatically different one. It soon found, however, that the unpopularity of "big government" was confined to a narrow category of relatively minor spending programs.

The Reagan Cutbacks
One of the most controversial parts of the Reagan budget program was the attempt to reduce the growth of social welfare programs. The

Reagan administration's social welfare agenda was set out in its fiscal 1982 budget revisions and consisted of three major elements:

> The first criterion is the preservation of the social safety net . . . those programs, mostly begun in the 1930's, that now constitute an agreed-upon core of protection for the elderly, the unemployed, and the poor, and . . . the people who fought for the country in times of war. . . .
>
> The second criterion is the revision of entitlements to eliminate unintended benefits. This criterion applies primarily to newer Federal entitlement programs and related income security programs that have undergone rapid growth during the last 20 years . . . [and] to certain aspects of social safety net programs that have been added unnecessarily or have grown excessively. . . .
>
> The third criterion is the reduction of benefits for people with middle to upper incomes. . . . This criterion directly challenges the drift toward the universalization of social benefit programs.[36]

There was a fairly widespread perception that these criteria, and the philosophical assumptions on which they were based, would lead to major cuts in social welfare spending. In fact, there were some important policy changes during the Reagan years, but their budgetary effects turned out to be relatively limited.

Perhaps the distinctive contribution of the Reagan presidency was what Nathan Glazer has termed the "eclipse of social engineering." The most significant revisions in public assistance, for example, were the eligibility and benefit reductions of 1981 that removed large numbers of the working poor from the benefit rolls. The principle behind these cuts, notes Glazer, was to redefine welfare as "basic charity and support, with a sufficient degree of harshness in administration and limitation of benefits that people who could work would be happy to get off it, and those who did work would try to stay off, even if working did not provide more than welfare."[37] The 1988 Family Support Act, with its work requirements for public assistance, was a further extension of this welfare redefinition.

Reagan's impact on "middle-class" benefit programs was considerably more modest. Congress never accepted the administration's wholesale advocacy of targeted benefits. Limited adjustments were enacted, for example, in college student aid programs, but the general principle of targeting benefits based on need never generated broad acceptance.

In a parallel manner, social security and medicare escaped major cutbacks. The administration's initial social security reforms, announced during May 1981, encountered fierce opposition in Congress, and the task of solving social security's funding problems was turned over to a bipartisan commission. The 1983 social security amendments did effect a small reduction in benefits for high-income beneficiaries, through provisions for taxing benefits. (In addition, the catastrophic health insurance coverage added to medicare in 1988, and repealed in 1989, was also linked to premiums based on income.)

The major social welfare legislation of the Reagan years was clustered at the beginning and the very end. Apart from several noteworthy bills—the 1981 reconciliation act, the 1983 social security amendments, and the 1988 medicare and welfare bills—the administration and Congress fought continually over marginal program changes.

Public Assistance. The most controversial social welfare policy changes of Reagan's presidency were enacted as part of an omnibus budget reconciliation act passed in 1981 (OBRA). Eligibility was restricted and benefit formulas reduced for numerous income assistance programs (see table 6.11). The composition of the "social safety net" was not altered in any meaningful way, but coverage was directed toward those at the bottom of the income scale. In particular, AFDC and food stamp benefits were scaled back and, in many instances, eliminated for numerous working poor families.

The Reagan administration was unable, however, to extend the OBRA cuts. In the fall of 1981 Reagan announced a second package of public assistance "reforms" with projected savings of $27 billion over three years. Singled out for large reductions were the food stamp, educational loan, and school feeding programs. Congress rejected almost all of the administration's second round of fiscal 1982 budget cuts, and it continued to override similar proposals in subsequent years.

Indeed, some of the 1981 cuts were later eased by Congress. Unemployment compensation extended benefits were partially restored in 1982.[38] AFDC eligibility was liberalized in 1984. Food stamp eligibility and benefits were increased in 1985.[39] Further, Reagan's 1982 "New Federalism" plan to turn AFDC and food stamps entirely over to the states in exchange for full federal funding of medicaid was quickly dropped in the face of congressional opposition.

The Family Support Act of 1988, which was hammered out over two years of negotiations between Congress and the administration, was a surprising breakthrough given these annual battles over program details. In 1986 Reagan had assigned a high priority to welfare reform as part of his State of the Union message, but his insistence that work requirements be included in any legislative package was denounced by many of the leading liberals in Congress. The following year, however, the National Governor's Association endorsed the so-called workfare requirement, so long as it was coupled to a national extension of AFDC to two-parent families in which the principal wage-earner was unemployed (AFDC-UP). As the principle of mandatory training and work requirements took on greater legitimacy, Democratic senator Daniel P. Moynihan became the prime architect for fashioning a bipartisan compromise.

The bill that was cleared by Congress on September 30, 1988, was hailed as the "most significant welfare reform in half a century."[40] Its most important conceptual change was the redirection of public assistance from income maintenance to preparation and training for work. For "employable" adults, benefits were made contingent upon participation in job training and employment programs (see table 6.12). The AFDC-UP program, which had been available in about one-half of the states, was extended nationwide, but even more stringent work requirements were imposed as a condition for its benefits. Among the bill's incentives for the transition from welfare to work were child care and medicaid benefits for twelve months after recipients' earnings made them ineligible for public assistance. Moreover, states were required to establish comprehensive child support enforcement programs, and they were also given discretion to require minor AFDC parents to live with their parents or other adult relatives as a condition for receiving assistance.

Social Security. Reagan's initial successes in cutting public assistance programs were not carried over to social security or medicare. Despite the massive social security tax increase enacted in 1977, funding shortfalls in the basic trust fund, OASI, had necessitated an emergency transfer from the disability fund just three years later, a stopgap measure. It was widely recognized that further action would be required to resolve the severe short-term funding problems faced by the social security system, along with the even more serious shortfalls being projected after the turn of the century.

The Reagan administration first proposed, on May 12, 1981, benefit changes designed to reduce projected spending growth. Included among these were a less generous benefit formula for future retirees, a substantial reduction in benefits for early retirement at age sixty-two, and more stringent eligibility standards for social security disability benefits. The administration also recommended a three-month delay in the scheduled 1982 social security COLA and the elimination of the minimum benefit for retirees with very low prior earnings.

The minimum benefit was eliminated by the 1981 reconciliation bill

Table 6.11. Major Social Welfare Changes, Omnibus Reconciliation Act of 1981 (PL 97-35)

Program/Program Category	Savings Provisions
AFDC	Eligibility standards tightened Benefits reduced (working recipients) State "workfare" programs allowed Income measurement and reporting system tightened ("monthly retrospective income accounting")
College Student Assistance	Eligibility standards tightened for guaranteed student loans (GSLs) Origination fee instituted to offset federal interest subsidy for GSLs Basic Educational Opportunity Grants (BEOGs) reduced
Elementary, Secondary School Aid	Impact aid ("category B") phased out Selected categorical grants consolidated
Federal Retirement	Semiannual cost-of-living adjustment (COLA) extended to annual adjustment
Food Stamps	Eligibility standards tightened Income measurement and reporting system tightened ("periodic retrospective income accounting") Benefit adjustments postponed
Housing	Funding level reduced for rental assistance and public housing
Medicaid	Medicaid reimbursement payments to states reduced Eligibility standards set by states allowed greater flexibility Incentive payments to states instituted for cost control and other savings Modified "freedom of choice" for recipients in selection of health care services and providers

Table 6.11. (cont'd)

Program/Program Category	Savings Provisions
Public Service Jobs	Comprehensive Employment and Training Act (CETA) jobs programs terminated CETA job training programs reduced
School Meal Programs	Federal cash and commodity subsidies reduced Inflation adjustment schedule extended for reimbursement rates Eligibility standards for "severe need" assistance tightened Income eligibility limits for students lowered
Social Services	Block grant funding levels reduced
Unemployment Compensation	Automatic extended benefits (13 weeks) for all states during high national unemployment periods eliminated State unemployment threshold for extended benefit payments raised
Veterans Benefits	Education, dental, burial benefits reduced

Source: Compiled by author.

(although it was then restored at the end of the year), as were some minor social security benefit programs. The principal social security recommendations, however, created an uproar in Congress which was fueled by interest groups representing the elderly. With no possibility of materially changing benefit formulas or the retirement age, the administration quickly conceded defeat. On September 24, 1981, Reagan announced that he would turn over the task of restoring fiscal stability to a bipartisan commission on social security. The fifteen-member panel was appointed three months later and issued its report after the 1982 elections.[41]

The social security amendments enacted early in 1983 resolved the short-term funding problems largely through tax increases. Previously scheduled increases in social security taxes were accelerated, and for the first time social security benefits were subjected to taxation for high-

Table 6.12. Major Provisions, Family Support Act of 1988 (PL 100-485)

Program	Provision
JOBS Program	States required to implement Job Opportunities and Basic Skills Training Program (JOBS) for AFDC recipients by Oct. 1, 1990. Standardized participation rate requirements and exemptions established. Child care programs (with federal matching funds) mandated to facilitate JOBS participation.
AFDC-UP	States required to operate AFDC program for two-parent families in which principal wage earner is unemployed by Oct. 1, 1990. Standardized work requirement for one parent; optional training/work requirement for second parent.
Child Care and Medicaid	Guaranteed eligibility for 12 months for child care and medicaid benefits for families whose increased earnings exceed income eligibility standard.
Child Support Enforcement	Automatic wage withholding for child support orders established. Federal standards for establishing paternity applied to states. State guidelines for child support amounts established, and periodic state review of support orders required.
Minor Parents	Permits states to deny AFDC benefits to minor parents (under age 18) not residing with parents or other adult relatives. Provides for assistance payments to be made to parent (or guardian) of a minor parent.

SOURCE: Compiled by author.

income recipients. The latter was, in effect, a benefit reduction, but it applied only to a narrow group of recipients. A broader benefit reduction, in the form of a six-month COLA delay, was adopted as well, but the basic COLA protection for social security benefits was left intact. In addition, mandatory social security coverage was extended to all new federal employees and to employees of nonprofit organizations. State and local governments, which previously had been permitted to withdraw from coverage, were prohibited from doing so in the future.

The long-term financing shortfalls were addressed through gradual increases in the retirement age—from sixty-five to sixty-six over a six-year period ending in 2009 and to sixty-seven over a six-year period ending in 2027. This solution was not popular among House Democrats, and the leadership supported an unsuccessful effort to boost payroll taxes in 2010 as an alternative to raising the retirement age. The compromise of higher taxes immediately and an upward adjustment in the retirement age over the next half century ultimately prevailed.

The Reagan administration's impact on social security, then, was very different from its original intent. The rate of growth in spending was not attacked. Rather, the short-term policy solutions Reagan finally supported were geared to supplying additional revenues that would fund current benefits and also would build a large surplus against which the system could later draw. Further, after its abortive initiatives of 1981, the administration refused to return to the issue of benefit levels. Reagan pledged in his 1984 campaign to protect social security benefits, which effectively precluded any future spending-control agreements that went beyond temporary COLA delays, and social security was also exempted from any automatic spending cuts resulting from Gramm-Rudman-Hollings.

There was a more sustained effort to reduce medicare spending growth, primarily through health provider cost controls. In 1981 Reagan proposed changes in hospital reimbursement policies as well as repeal of minor medicare benefits that had been previously enacted but had not gone into effect. The Senate Finance Committee then greatly expanded Reagan's proposals, and the final version of the reconciliation bill included higher deductibles for medicare beneficiaries, along with revised cost controls. The following year, Congress again reworked Reagan's proposals, adopting major reductions in reimbursement rates for hospitals and physicians. Congress also agreed to raise premiums for medicare Part B coverage (supplementary insurance covering physicians' services) to cover 25 percent of actual costs. The shortfall between premium revenues and costs, which was made up for out of general revenues, had gradually increased from approximately one-half to more than three-fourths of Part B program outlays. (The 25-percent requirement, initially applied to 1983 and 1984, was later extended by Congress.)

Perhaps the most intriguing medicare story during this period, however, was a series of news reports that the Reagan administration was considering a means test for medicare eligibility and benefits. The linking of medicare to financial need requirements was consistent with Reagan's initial call for reducing entitlement benefits "for people with middle to upper incomes," but it was never formally proposed. Moreover, Congress adopted, on October 1, 1982, a Senate-sponsored amendment to an appropriations bill which expressed opposition to "any proposal to impose a 'means test' on eligibility for the Medicare program or benefits provided by the Medicare program."[42]

With the medicare trust funds facing continued difficulties and with medicare spending rising rapidly, the administration and Congress returned to cost controls in 1983. A new payment plan was coupled to the social security rescue bill being considered by Congress, and both were approved several weeks later. The 1983 medicare changes did not, however, resolve the spending problems generated by an expanding beneficiary population and by rapidly rising health care costs. As a result, each year the administration and Congress were forced to return to the medicare program, and their usual approach was to limit payments to hospitals and physicians through partial freezes on cost increases. In 1987 Congress limited (but did not exempt) medicare reductions under Gramm-Rudman-Hollings, while enacting additional cost-control provisions for health care providers.

In 1988 catastrophic illness protection was added to medicare. While this provision represented the most important expansion in coverage since medicare's inception, it was tied to increased premiums based on income for those eligible for medicare. Supplemental premiums were established to cover nearly two-thirds of the new benefits, with the remainder being funded by across-the-board increases in Part B premiums. The bewildering politics of programs for the elderly was not entirely absent, as Congress added costly prescription-drug coverage to the catastrophic cost bill, while voting down long-term home care coverage. Nevertheless, the intense reaction of elderly taxpayers against the new medicare surtax led to the catastrophic program's repeal in 1989.

Spending versus Policy. The Reagan administration's impact on social welfare programs was not uniform across programs or consistent over time. In the aggregate, "payments for individuals" accounted for approximately the same percentage of the overall budget and of GNP at the end of Reagan's tenure as at the beginning (see table 6.13). In addition, these relative levels were not appreciably different from those registered during the middle and late 1970s and were roughly double the "base" at the time of the Great Society expansion.

There were, however, important changes in the composition of the

Table 6.13. Payments for Individuals Outlays, Fiscal Years 1965-89

Fiscal Year	Payments for Individuals	
	Percentage of Total Outlays	Percentage of GNP
1965	28.0	4.9
1970	33.1	6.5
1975	46.2	10.1
1980	47.0	10.4
1981	47.7	10.8
1982	47.8	11.4
1983	48.9	11.9
1984	46.9	10.8
1985	45.0	10.8
1986	45.4	10.7
1987	46.8	10.6
1988	46.9	10.4
1989 (est.)	47.0	10.4

SOURCE: *Historical Tables, Budget of the United States Government, Fiscal Year 1990*, pp. 136-40.

social welfare budget. Social security and medicare, for example, rose from less than one-half of total human resources spending in fiscal 1981 to just under 60 percent in fiscal 1989. The share for the broad grouping of programs in the education, training, employment, and social services functional category, by contrast, dropped by nearly one-half, to just over 5 percent (reflecting in large part the Reagan-sponsored cuts in public-service jobs programs).

Income and health assistance programs for the poor also declined as a percentage of overall human resources spending. The only component of public assistance to register a relative increase during Reagan's tenure was medicaid. By the late 1980s medicaid had risen to more than one-third of the total public assistance outlays.[43]

The Reagan-era social welfare budgets were not dramatic breaks with the past. For both public assistance and social insurance, individual program size (in relation to GNP) followed trends established earlier. The long-term "gainers"—social security, medicare, medicaid—continued to dominate during the 1980s. The long-term losers—cash assistance for the poor and veterans' pensions—continued their declines that had begun in the early 1970s.

Reagan capped the long-term expansion in the relative size of the social welfare budget. He influenced the policy debate and budgetary commitment associated with public assistance, by weakening the social safety net and redefining its purpose. With the much larger social insurance programs, however, Reagan's impact—both policy and budgetary—was limited.

Social Welfare and Budget Control

The bifurcated social welfare system that has evolved over the past half century presents two reasonably distinct sets of problems—fiscal and programmatic. The social insurance programs for the aged have been and remain enormously expensive. Their costs were affected only marginally by the social welfare retrenchment that began during the late 1970s and continued under the Reagan presidency.

Public assistance programs, by comparison, are considerably less costly but also more problematic. In the aggregate, their rate of real growth slowed almost to a halt during the 1980s, and current projections indicate very little growth well into the 1990s. Public assistance does not pose a major spending-control problem, although it still embraces a host of complex and unresolved programmatic issues.

The terms of debate over public assistance have changed, at least since the early 1970s. As a leading analyst recently concluded, "Although still subject to considerable controversy, arguments and evidence that [public assistance] programs have undesirable incentive effects . . . have gained considerable credibility over the past decade."[44] These arguments, however, also had enjoyed considerable credibility during much of the period between the New Deal and the Reagan presidency.[45]

The Reagan presidency revived traditional concerns about public assistance, while also imposing more stringent budgetary constraints on spending. These constraints are unlikely to loosen in the near future, and the philosophical skepticism Reagan articulated about social engineering is also unlikely to disappear. What this attitude suggests, in turn, is a stabilization of public assistance spending levels (even the Gramm-Rudman-Hollings bill, for example, will exempt most public assistance programs from automatic spending cuts) accompanied by piecemeal adjustments in programs to mitigate their negative effects.

The policy dilemmas of public assistance are underscored by the incidence and distribution of poverty. The Congressional Budget Office reports that while the overall poverty rate over the past two decades has declined slightly, the poverty rate among families with children has increased. In 1986 the adjusted poverty rate for all families was 13 percent; for families headed by single mothers, the rate was 46 percent, almost exactly what it was in 1970.[46]

The poverty problems of the nonelderly are serious and persistent. They were not resolved by expansionary public assistance policy, and, in any event, expansionary policies are not prominent on the political agenda. Policymakers are therefore faced with reconfiguring programs, not increasing budgets, in order to combat poverty.

If the spending issues associated with public assistance have, in fact, been largely resolved, those associated with social security and medicare (and, to a lesser extent, other federal retirement programs) have been barely touched upon. According to current policy estimates, social security and medicare outlays will continue to rise steadily, comprising one-third of total federal spending by the early 1990s and also accounting for nearly two-thirds of all human resources outlays at that point.[47]

The social security system has had an enormously positive impact in reducing the poverty rate among the elderly. The poverty rate for the elderly living in families, for example, dropped from 14 percent in 1970 to 4 percent in 1986. Among unrelated individuals, the rate declined from 46 percent to 20 percent over this period.[48] For both groups, however, the major parts of these decreases had occurred by the mid-1970s, and very little improvement has taken place since. What indexing has done is to prevent any erosion in real benefit levels. And, of course, indexing was implemented after real benefit levels had been increased very substantially. Indeed, one of the arguments for indexing was that it would prevent policymakers from indulging in future bidding wars to raise benefits.

Indexing social security has proved to be an effective blame-avoidance strategy, depoliticizing benefit increases and linking them to automatic tax increases. When the latter have proved to be insufficient, Congress has been willing, as in 1977 and again in 1983, to step up scheduled tax hikes to maintain the social security system's solvency. If this were the entire story, it would demonstrate heroic fiscal discipline quite at odds with prevailing theories about credit claiming.

In fact, social security tax increases have been offset by periodic cuts in other taxes, particularly for individuals. Thus, while total revenues as a percentage of GNP have remained fairly stable over the past twenty years, the proportion of those revenues available to support general government programs has declined. Social security now accounts for nearly one-third of federal tax receipts. Its annual trust fund surpluses are expected to double, from $56 billion to $116 billion, over the fiscal 1989–94 period.[49] This increase will help to mask continued, large deficits between on-budget spending and receipts, but it will not actually reduce those deficits. Instead, the social security surpluses will be held in reserve to pay for future costs.

What looks like fiscal discipline, therefore, is something quite different. Social security's solvency has been purchased by insolvency in the rest of the budget. Blame avoidance, perfectly understandable in the context of such a politically potent program, has distorted spending and tax policy. It has even adversely affected public assistance entitlements, most of which have suffered a long-term erosion in real benefit levels.

The budget-control problems associated with federal social welfare policy are largely confined to the social security programs. In Wildavsky's succinct summation, "No matter how often the problem of social security is supposed to have been solved 'once and for all,' it will keep coming back because (1) that is where the money is, and (2) other policy promises cannot be kept if it is kept whole."[50] The bipartisan agreement to insulate social security from politics simply makes it much more difficult to balance social security against other budget policy goals. Further, the confluence of indexing and projected demographic trends will likely exacerbate that difficulty, as automatic social security and medicare growth takes up an ever-increasing share of the budget. The fiscal squeeze on the old budget process is severe, and it can only be relieved by politically risky changes in social security and medicare.

7

The Old Politics of
Domestic Spending

In contrast to the entitlement status of most social welfare spending, many domestic programs are funded by annual appropriations and hence are categorized as "relatively controllable under existing law."[1] Nevertheless, outlays for the major domestic spending categories nearly quadrupled during the Nixon, Ford, and Carter presidencies—from approximately $21 billion in FY 1970 to $83 billion ten years later.[2] Over this span, the budget share for discretionary domestic programs increased by 30 percent, while domestic outlays as a percentage of GNP rose by more than 50 percent.

The rapid expansion of discretionary spending fit very well into theories premised upon an inherent prospending bias in the budget process, particularly at the congressional end. David Mayhew's portrait of a Congress dominated by the reelection imperatives of incumbents, for example, assigns a place of prominence to what he terms "particularized benefits"—tangible legislative actions that allow members to claim and to receive credit for what their constituents get.[3]

The self-interest, credit-claiming explanations for higher spending apply with special force to programs in agriculture, transportation, natural resources, and the like. These programs provide concentrated and tangible benefits for which legislators can plausibly claim credit, which would appear to make them especially susceptible to political manipulation. Further, they have been well integrated into a decentralized congressional committee system which, as Kenneth Shepsle and Barry Weingast have stressed, enables legislators "to pursue their own narrow interests." The result, they contend, is a "systematic bias that distorts public spending."[4]

In effect, traditional pork-barrel politics, an old but relatively mild congressional affliction, appeared to be turning into a much larger and more serious threat in the hands of modern legislators. President Reagan's first OMB director, David Stockman, left office in 1985, criticizing sharply Congress's "distributive tendency" in funding domestic programs.[5] In 1988 Reagan added his indictment, declaring, "Nowhere is the failure of the budget process more evident than in the annual . . . appropriations bills that establish discretionary spending levels making up just under one-half the total budget."[6]

The spending patterns of the Reagan years, however, did not conform very well to the prospending bias theories or to the Reagan administration's complaints. Domestic program outlays were, in the aggregate, at almost the same level at the end of Reagan's presidency as at the beginning. In real terms, this stasis represented a significant decline. Further, the budget share and GNP levels for domestic outlays during the 1980s were not much higher than those registered during the 1950s.

The relative decline of domestic spending under Reagan, moreover, was not unique. Spending for domestic programs over the period from the New Deal to the beginning of the Great Society was variable and volatile, unlike the steady upward climb of social welfare spending.

This area of the budget, then, has reflected a comparatively high degree of political, as well as technical, "controllability." A number of large programs have their roots in the New Deal (and some have even earlier sources), but these programs have not grown uniformly. The composition of aggregate domestic outlays has changed over time, as have some important principles about the "appropriate" responsibilities of the federal government. Most important, the domestic program budget's expansions and contractions over the past several decades strongly suggest that, at least in this area, spending control has not deteriorated.

Toward a Federal Domestic Policy

Unlike social welfare policy, where there was no federal role before the New Deal, the domestic policy initiatives of the 1930s had numerous historical antecedents. Federal public works programs, notably river and harbor projects to improve navigation, had commenced early in the nineteenth century. Federal grant-in-aid programs to support agriculture had been utilized in the 1860s, and a Federal Land Bank system had been created in 1916 to promote easier access to credit for farmers. Grant programs to the states for highway construction and for vocational rehabilitation and vocational education also predated the Roosevelt presidency. The New Deal, however, extended federal commitments to new policy areas while transforming modest federal domestic commitments into substantial and continuous ones. The New Deal made grants-in-aid a central feature of American federalism. It also legitimated direct federal support to distressed sectors of the economy and underdeveloped regions of the country.

The New Deal Expansion

Examining the New Deal's domestic policy accomplishments solely in the context of budget policy seriously understates the profound changes that took place. The size of Roosevelt's peacetime budgets, for example, hardly connotes the abrupt and permanent shift that occurred in federal economic planning and economic management. The level of economic policy activism inaugurated during the Roosevelt presidency was an exponential advance over the traditional limited and temporary approach to economic stabilization that had characterized previous administrations.

During the Harding, Coolidge, and Hoover administrations, for example, federal economic policy meant restraint rather than intervention. For the budget, this meant reducing spending, bringing revenues and spending into balance, and gradually cutting the debt incurred during World War I.[7] When Roosevelt took office, it was not immediately clear that these emphases would be abandoned, but by his second term, Roosevelt had adopted a planned deficit strategy. His 1937 budget message, for example, defended higher spending as the appropriate way to combat the Great Depression: "The programs inaugurated during the last four years to combat the depression and to initiate many needed reforms have cost large sums of money, but the benefits obtained from them are far outweighing all their costs. We shall soon be reaping the full benefits of those programs and shall have at the same time a balanced budget that will also include provision for reduction of the public debt."[8]

Roosevelt's efforts to revive the economy were not restricted to the budget, nor were budget decisions strictly governed by fiscal policy formulas. Keynesianism was not exactly conventional wisdom during the 1930s, and in any case, Roosevelt's embrace of federal economic stimulus was far from wholehearted. As described by James MacGregor Burns, "A Keynesian solution involved an almost absolute commitment, and Roosevelt was not one to commit himself absolutely to any political or economic method."[9] In addition, nonbudgetary legislative and administrative options—regulation, antitrust policy, production quotas, price controls, bank insurance, credit policy—were an integral part of Roosevelt's complex program for economic relief, recovery, and reform.

What showed up in budget numbers, then, was not necessarily the most important part of the New Deal's domestic policy expansion. (This same reservation holds true, of course, for subsequent administrations. Just as the defense budget does not equal foreign policy, the budget for domestic programs captures only one dimension of the federal government's domestic roles and responsibilities.) Parts of that expansion, how-

Table 7.1. Major Domestic Spending Categories, Fiscal Years 1932-40 (in millions of dollars)

Fiscal Year	Total Outlays	Major Domestic Categories			Percentage of Total Outlays
		Trans-portation[a]	Farm Income Stabilization	Other Natural Resources	
1932	$4,215	$ 414	$ 0	$ 161	14%
1934	5,881	812	382	700	32
1936	9,099	1,074	602	1,363	33
1938	8,278	1,030	326	1,541	35
1940	9,780	1,173	694	1,818	38

SOURCE: *Historical Statistics*, pt. 2, p. 1124.
[a] Includes direct federal expenditures for highways and air and water transportation; also includes federal intergovernmental expenditures to states for highways.

ever, were reflected in peacetime budgets much higher than those of prior administrations and heavily oriented toward domestic program spending.

During the peacetime years of the New Deal, for example, the growth of domestic spending was extremely high for programs in agriculture, transportation, and natural resources. Before Roosevelt took office, these spending categories had accounted for only a minor portion of a comparatively small federal budget. Between fiscal years 1932 and 1940, as total outlays more than doubled, funding for transportation, farm income stabilization, and natural resource programs increased at a considerably greater rate (see table 7.1). By fiscal 1940, nearly 40 percent of total spending was concentrated in these program categories.

Agriculture. In agriculture, the New Deal created the programmatic base that has defined much of federal agricultural policy over the past half century (see table 7.2). The Commodity Credit Corporation, which administers current farm loan and price support programs, was established under the 1933 Agricultural Adjustment Act. Soil conservation and domestic allotment legislation in 1935 and 1936 provided for technical assistance in developing and implementing soil conservation practices in local soil conservation districts, authorized federal payments to farmers to encourage these practices, and also limited acreage being farmed with soil-depleting crops. In 1937 the Agricultural Marketing Agreement Act au-

Table 7.2. Major Agricultural Legislation, 1933-41

Agricultural Adjustment Act of 1933

- The first major price support and acreage reduction program.
- Set parity as the goal for farm prices.
- Acreage reduction achieved through voluntary agreements with producers.
- Markets regulated through voluntary agreements with processors and others.
- Processing taxes used to offset cost of program.

Agricultural Adjustment Act Amendments of 1935

- Gave president authority to impose import quotas when imports interfered with agricultural adjustment programs.
- Designated 30 percent of customs receipts to promote agricultural exports and domestic consumption and help finance adjustment programs.

Soil Conservation and Domestic Allotment Act of 1936

- Payments to farmers authorized to encourage conservation.
- Set parity as the goal for farm income.

Agricultural Adjustment Act of 1938

- Reenacted a modified Soil Conservation and Domestic Allotment Act.
- Provided for acreage allotments, payment limits, and protection for tenants.
- First comprehensive price support legislation with nonrecourse loans.
- Marketing quotas established for several crops.

Steagall Amendment of 1941

- Required support of many nonbasic commodities at 85 percent of parity or higher.
- Soon amended to require 90 percent of parity and extended for two years after war.

SOURCE: U.S. Department of Agriculture, Economic Research Service, *History of Agricultural and Price-Support and Adjustment Programs, 1933-1984* (Washington, D.C., 1984), p. iv.

thorized the secretary of agriculture to establish production limits for producers of certain perishables (fruits and vegetables) and to set minimum prices to be paid by local processors for milk. The Agricultural Adjustment Act of 1938 went considerably further. For basic commodities (corn, wheat, and cotton), federal price supports became mandatory, with the federal government agreeing to purchase all supplies at a given support price. The secretary of agriculture also was authorized to enforce acreage allotments or marketing quotas on farmers, in combination with price supports, in order to limit supplies.

This meant, in practical terms, an annual farm plan. The federal government would predict consumption of a given crop and then would proceed to bring supply into line by determining the necessary national acreage and allotting the acreage among farmers. Farmers would be guaranteed a minimum price for their crop, but they would be restricted to planting their respective allotments.

Minimum prices, in turn, were linked to "parity," a concept that was used to gauge farm income. Base periods, during which farmers' incomes had constituted a fair or reasonable return on their costs and labor, were used to determine the relationship between current costs and current income. Price supports were then set at levels designed to provide that income and to maintain parity in accordance with intervening increases in costs. (Under the 1938 Agricultural Adjustment Act, parity levels for basic commodities were set at 52 to 75 percent. As might be anticipated, periodic disputes over parity levels and parity formulas have erupted frequently over the ensuing years.)

As the agriculture sector became tied to the federal government for supply and price management, it also became more firmly wedded for government-supplied credit. In 1933 the Commodity Credit Corporation instituted a loan program for cotton farmers, along with production controls and minimum prices. President Roosevelt also authorized a corn loan program in 1933 which was deliberately set above market prices. From these initial, emergency-based measures, there developed permanent federal crop loan programs for basic commodities. In addition, the 1933 Farm Credit Act enlarged substantially the farm credit system to support land purchases, farm improvements, and farm production. The Farm Security Administration, a New Deal creation, provided low-interest loans to small farmers unable to obtain private credit, and it was also authorized to furnish direct loans for small water-development projects. (The Farm Security Administration was later reorganized into the Farmers Home Administration, which has since supplied very large amounts of credit to finance rural housing, emergency farm loans, and watershed development.)

The cluster of New Deal agricultural programs helped to restore farm income, although 100-percent parity levels were not reached until well into World War II, when virtually all production limits were removed. From 1935 to 1939 government payments accounted for 10 percent of farm income, a level that was not reached again until the early 1960s.[10] During this period, the parity ratio averaged close to 80 percent.[11]

Two important changes, then, occurred in the federal government's relationship to the agriculture sector. First, in response to the severe depression affecting farmers, the New Deal established a system of price supports and supply controls supplemented by diverse sources of farm credit. Second, the agriculture policy structure created by the New Deal did not disappear when prosperity returned to the farms during World War II. Instead, it became a permanent fixture of federal domestic policy.

Transportation. While the 1930s did not produce a coherent, coordinated transportation policy, large spending programs were inaugurated to develop a more diversified transportation system. A considerable portion of this outlay was devoted to highways, as the rural federal highway aid program enacted in 1913 was revised to cover urban areas.

The 1913 program provided matching funds to the states for construction of rural post roads. In 1921 federal aid was redirected toward primary (interstate) and secondary (intercounty) highways. The formula for apportioning aid to the states excluded urban highways, and it was not until 1934 that this prohibition was eliminated, making available to the states more grants-in-aid for highway construction. In addition, direct federal expenditures for urban highway construction were authorized under public works legislation in 1932 and 1933. For the remainder of the decade, direct federal expenditure for highway construction outpaced the growth of grants-in-aid.

Other segments of the transportation system also received additional federal support. The 1936 Merchant Marine Act established direct federal subsidies, covering both construction and operation, of a large merchant marine fleet. The 1938 Civil Aeronautics Act placed airline safety and economic regulation under a Civil Aeronautics Authority. Federal responsibility for developing and promoting an air transportation network also was extended to operating subsidies and funding for navigation aids, safety equipment, and airport facilities.

Railroad promotion and regulation had been federally directed since the mid-1800s, but direct financial support, in the form of land and rights-of-way given to the railroads by the federal government, had ceased well before the Great Depression. In 1932, however, the Reconstruction Finance Corporation was authorized to provide loans to rail carriers unable to obtain private credit. This "temporary" assistance program ultimately lasted for more than two decades, during which time more than $1 billion in loans was approved.[12]

While the New Deal did not inaugurate federal transportation programs, it clearly expanded the federal government's involvement with particular transportation systems. For the fastest-growing modes of transportation, highways and airlines, this meant regulation, planning, and funding.

Regional and Resource Development. A host of landmark bills sponsored by the Roosevelt administration transformed entire regions through massive public works projects. The Flood Control Act of 1936 made the federal government responsible for nationwide control of flooding in river basins, giving rise to Army Corps of Engineers programs across the entire country. The Bureau of Reclamation commenced a number of major multipurpose water projects during the 1930s, including several large dams (notably the Grand Coulee) and the California Central Valley project, which was undertaken to supply water to the Sacramento and San Joaquin valleys. The New Deal's continuing advocacy of large multipurpose projects (water supply, irrigation, flood control, navigation, and hydroelectric power production) was finally and fully endorsed by the Reclamation Project Act of 1939. The funding requirements established by the 1939 act reflected the extensive federal subsidies associated with water projects for the seventeen officially designated western states. Costs of a project allocable to navigation and flood control were exclusively federal. Costs allocable to water supply and power production were paid by the federal government but were reimbursable (with interest) by local entities that purchased water or power. Reimbursement costs, however, could be spread over fifty years. Irrigation costs were similarly reimbursable but without interest.

The single most expansive New Deal creation, however, was the Tennessee Valley Authority (TVA). Its authorization embraced navigation, flood control, power production, and foresting and resource development. The TVA Act of 1933 was more than a public works or water project. Its objective was the economic development of an entire region.

A somewhat less grandiose but nonetheless important undertaking was funded under the Emergency Relief Appropriations Act of 1935. The Rural Electrification Administration (REA) received $100 million to make federal loans available to electric service providers in order to bring service to rural areas. In 1936 the Rural Electrification Act formalized the REA program and provided a ten-year authorization for the agency to lend up to $40 million annually in long-term (twenty-five-year), low-interest loans.

REA-financed systems became fixtures in the South and Southwest. The infusions of federal funding meant jobs, of course, but the electrification of vast rural areas also provided the basis for economic development. REA programs were an indirect subsidy to farmers in acquiring electrical service. Federal power projects complemented them by enlarging the pool of power sources and thereby making electricity much more affordable.

Federal conservation and environmental programs had begun long before the New Deal. The national park system, for example, started with Yellowstone in 1872. The national forest system was established in 1891. Both were periodically expanded, and federal protective regulations regarding their use became increasingly stringent. The New Deal, as a result, easily incorporated expanded conservation programs into its ambitious domestic policy agenda. The Civilian Conservation Corps combined work relief with reforestation of the national forests from 1933 to 1941. More than a dozen new national parks were established during Roosevelt's first two terms, eventually adding more than six million acres to the park system. The 1935 Historic Sites Act provided broad authorization for federal purchase and acquisition of land or structures having national significance. Federal grants-in-aid were also enacted to assist states in acquiring land for state forests.

Housing. During the 1930s the Roosevelt administration established several small direct spending programs to support housing construction.[13] Its most important contribution to the revival and expansion of the housing industry, however, was the Federal Housing Administration (FHA) mortgage guarantee program. Residential housing credit had been restricted because of large down-payment requirements and short loan maturities. The FHA program instituted federal guarantees for long-term, self-amortizing residential mortgages, encouraging private lenders to switch their residential credit policies. Within a few years, the fixed-rate and long-term mortgage had become a fixture of the housing industry, and it provided a major impetus to the private housing market's post–World War II expansion.

Domestic Reform. Roosevelt's peacetime presidency was a watershed in federal domestic policy. It incorporated activist fiscal policy as a permanent feature of federal economic stabilization. It extended regulation to every major sector of the American economy. It employed credit programs as well as direct spending programs to assist economic recovery, and it made both accepted, routine features of federal policy.

The New Deal also inaugurated the era of massive, expensive public works programs and subsidies to the agricultural, housing, and transportation sectors. While each of these began as emergency relief, each soon took on broader, long-term objectives. In particular, while World War II spurred a comprehensive economic recovery, the New Deal's extensions of federal responsibility to national policies in agriculture, transportation, and housing continued during the postwar period. In addition, the popularity and success of the New Deal's public works programs led to a major postwar boom in federal water and power projects.

Funding Domestic Policy

After World War II, Congress ratified the New Deal's extension of federal domestic responsibility. The 1946 Full Employment Act declared the "continuing policy and responsibility of the Federal Government . . . to promote maximum employment, production, and purchasing power." The 1949 Housing Act committed the federal government to "the goal of a decent home and living environment for every American, thus contributing to the development and redevelopment of communities and to the advancement of the growth, wealth, and security of the Nation."[14] These symbolic ratifications were enacted amid great controversy and had very little discernible impact on actual policy. Actual program decisions after 1945, however, continued and extended the New Deal's interventions into domestic policy areas.

The period from 1945 up to the Great Society has been termed one of "cooperative federalism," reflecting continuity with the New Deal's treatment of the states as partners in domestic recovery and development.[15] What this partnership entailed in terms of budget policy was, first, an overwhelming preponderance of aid to states rather than local governments. Second, it directed a major portion of federal funding toward capital investment projects. Third, it continued the New Deal's spending priorities for agriculture, transportation, and natural resource development.

Grants-in-Aid. The New Deal pioneered the widespread use of categorical grants-in-aid, in which the federal government defined the specific purposes for which funding would be available and the administrative and regulatory standards that states would have to meet to qualify for funding. A number of categorical aid programs were part of the federal social

Table 7.3. Federal Outlays for Grants-in-Aid, Payments for Individuals and Capital Investment, Fiscal Years 1940-70 (in billions of dollars)

Fiscal Year	Payments for Individuals		Capital Investment	
	Constant (FY 1982) Dollars	Percentage of Total Grants-in-Aid Outlays	Constant (FY 1982) Dollars	Percentage of Total Grants-in-Aid Outlays
1940	$ 2.1	28%	$ 3.8	51%
1945	2.2	39	1.0	18
1950	4.8	46	2.3	22
1955	5.5	43	3.4	27
1960	7.5	30	12.2	49
1965	10.4	29	17.3	49
1970	20.3	33	19.3	31

SOURCE: *Historical Tables, Budget of the United States Government, Fiscal Year 1990*, p. 239.

welfare expansion of the 1930s, and federal funding grew steadily, in real terms, throughout the postwar period (see table 7.3). Throughout this period, funding for capital investment projects roughly paralleled the increase in social welfare spending. In addition, by the early 1960s the actual number of project grants (107) was roughly double the number of formula-based grants (53) and funding under both was directed predominantly to state governments. From the early 1930s through the early 1960s, direct federal aid increased from less than 10 percent to nearly 25 percent of total state revenues. Aid to local governments, by comparison, was less than 2 percent for almost this entire period.[16]

The project funding provided to the states was only part of the federal government's spending on nondefense physical capital investment (see table 7.4). Most of the federal direct funding during this period was for water and power projects—Corps of Engineers and Bureau of Reclamation projects, along with funding for TVA and federal power marketing agencies. Funding to the states was largely for highway construction.

The "cooperative federalism" phase of federal policy was marked by growing federal support to the states. The amount of federal regulation applied to the states remained fairly low during the 1940s and 1950s.[17] A

Table 7.4. Federal Nondefense Outlays for Major Physical Capital Investment, Fiscal Years 1941-70 (in billions of dollars)

Fiscal Year	Direct	Grants-in-Aid
1941	$1.8	$0.3
1945	0.2	0.1
1950	1.3	0.5
1955	1.1	0.8
1960	1.9	3.3
1965	3.0	5.0
1970	2.5	7.1

SOURCE: *Historical Tables, Budget of the United States Government, Fiscal Year 1990*, pp. 165-67, 169-71.

substantial portion of federal funding, while narrowly defined in purpose, was devoted to physical capital projects. This funding was supplemented by direct federal expenditures, primarily for water and power projects, that benefited multistate areas.

Spending Programs and Spending Growth. While overall domestic program spending increased from the early 1940s through the early 1960s, relative growth indicators were mixed. As a percentage of total outlays, for example, peacetime domestic spending after World War II never reached the level of the last prewar New Deal budget (see table 7.5). Domestic outlays as a percentage of GNP were nearly identical in fiscal years 1950 and 1965 and, in both instances, below the New Deal's fiscal 1940 level.

Within spending categories, moreover, annual spending levels fluctuated from year to year. As shown in table 7.6, outlays for the major domestic spending categories usually increased over prior-year spending levels, but there were an appreciable number of annual funding decreases in every category. At the same time, the total federal budget did not increase every single year.

The period leading up to the Great Society, then, was not marked by unbridled spending growth. Peacetime spending levels for domestic programs absorbed only a portion of postwar defense declines. Further, during defense buildups, domestic programs were held steady or reduced to help finance defense increases.

Table 7.5. Domestic Program Outlays, Fiscal Years 1940-65 (in billions of dollars)

Fiscal Year	Total Outlays[a]	Percentage of GNP	Percentage of Total Budget
1940	$ 2.7	2.8%	28%
1945	3.4	1.6	4
1950	5.7	2.1	13
1955	6.2	1.6	9
1960	10.6	2.1	11
1965	15.2	2.3	13

SOURCE: *Historical Tables, Budget of the United States Government, Fiscal Year 1990*, pp. 17, 39-41.
[a] Includes outlays for the following budget functions: agriculture; commerce and housing; community and regional development; energy; natural resources and environment; and transportation.

Table 7.6. Patterns of Spending Growth, Domestic Program Categories, Fiscal Years 1945-65 (in billions of dollars)

Budget Function	Total Outlays (Current Dollars) FY 1945	FY 1955	FY 1965	Annual Outlay Changes — Increases over Prior-Year Funding	Annual Outlay Changes — Decreases under Prior-Year Funding
Agriculture	$1.6	$3.5	$4.0	12	8
Commerce and Housing Credit	- 2.6	0.1	1.2	14	6
Community and Regional Development	0.2	0.1	1.1	15	5
Energy	0.0	0.3	0.7	14	6
Natural Resources and Environment	0.5	0.9	2.5	15	5
Transportation	3.6	1.2	5.8	14	6

SOURCE: *Historical Tables, Budget of the United States Government, Fiscal Year 1990*, pp. 39-41.

At the programmatic level, there was continuity in the kinds of issues that drove domestic spending. From fiscal 1940 to fiscal 1965, approximately 85 percent of the growth in domestic spending was accounted for by transportation, agriculture, and natural resources and environment outlays. In each of these program categories, a few key policy issues were debated year after year, and funding levels responded to these debates and to the changing strength of opposing political coalitions.

Transportation outlays, for example, increased by nearly $5.4 billion between 1940 and 1965, but the growth was not steady. Instead, transportation funding (almost exclusively for highways) averaged about $1.2 billion during the early and mid-1950s. Approval of the interstate highway system, with its initial $31 billion, multiyear authorization, then led to rapid and steep increases.

The National System of Interstate Highways had been officially designated under the Federal-Aid Highway Act of 1944, but it took more than a decade to enact large-scale authorizations and appropriations. The most serious obstacle was cost. There was bipartisan agreement on the merits of a national system, but no consensus on how to fund what at the time was by far the largest and most expensive transportation program in U.S. history.

The Eisenhower administration, which formally proposed a $50 billion highway system in 1954 and which repeatedly emphasized its defense applications, initially recommended a federal public bond issue (distinct from debt-financing government securities) to finance the program. The House rejected the bond financing proposed in 1955, but it also voted down a funding mechanism based on specially earmarked highway user fees and fuel taxes.

Finally, the Highway Revenue Act of 1956 and the accompanying Federal-Aid Highway Act of 1956 resolved the impasse by establishing a trust fund, financed by user fees and fuel taxes, to supply the necessary revenues for the interstate system. Federal funding was set at 90 percent of costs, with apportionment formulas that eventually would tie each state's allocation to total system costs. The 90 to 10 federal-to-state matching ratio for approved projects was considerably more generous than previous formulas, which had required the states to pick up as much as one-half of the construction costs.[18] An additional requirement of the 1956 legislation was that the highway trust fund could not operate at a deficit, which led to tax increases in later years as the Interstate and Defense Highway System's costs rose beyond initial projections.

With the interstate system, the federal government's financial involvement in highway capital spending became much greater. The federal share of all highway capital spending was approximately 10 percent in 1950, but it expanded to about 40 percent in the 1960s.[19] What drove the spending increase, however, was not a gradual accretion of pork-barrel projects but rather a specific program for a defined objective. Moreover, the delays in approving the interstate system at a time when motor vehicle usage was growing very rapidly (and urban mass transit use was declining) were directly attributable to widespread concerns over cost.

A somewhat different scenario unfolded with federal water and power projects, because these frequently produced partisan disagreements over public-versus-private power systems and related issues. The Truman administration, which shared the New Deal's preference for large, multi-purpose public water projects, pushed for annual funding increases (and additional projects) throughout its tenure. The result was a tripling of natural resource outlays from $455 million to $1.3 billion—over the fiscal 1945–51 period—and appropriations for nearly fifty new projects by the Bureau of Reclamation alone.[20]

Federal policy in this area had been fixed, in principle, by the Reclamation Act of 1939 and the Flood Control Act of 1944. These statutes set out in detail the federal government's responsibility for a nationwide system of multipurpose water projects. Carrying out federal policy required, however, authorizations and appropriations for specific projects. Therefore, when the Eisenhower administration announced its opposition to new funding commitments, the stage was set for annual conflicts with Congress. Eisenhower's objections were framed in the context of what was termed a "new partnership," which meant in practical terms more local initiative and more local money in water resource development. It also meant a heavier reliance upon private power development.

In terms of budget policy, Eisenhower's views meant efforts to cut projects that had been started under Truman and to oppose the initiation of major new ones. There was considerable congressional resistance to the funding cutbacks for politically popular projects, reinforced by the high level of support among congressional Democrats for a federal approach which tilted clearly in favor of public power development. When the Democrats regained control of the House and Senate in 1955, they nearly tripled the number of projects Eisenhower had recommended and packaged them into an omnibus public works appropriations bill in order to discourage a presidential veto. This same pattern was repeated in later years. Congress funded the projects that the administration proposed but then added new starts or expansions that had not been recommended.

The balance of power gradually shifted to Congress. In fiscal 1956 funding had dropped by one-third from its peak under Truman, but over the next several years outlays rose appreciably. When Eisenhower left office, spending was higher than it had been a decade earlier. With a return to the traditional Democratic commitment to public power under Kennedy, funding continued its upward rise. Indeed, Kennedy had announced during his campaign a nine-point natural resources program which would reverse the Eisenhower "policy of no new starts" and would adopt budgetary practices to demonstrate that federal power projects were "wealth-creating assets that made money . . . for the taxpayer."[21]

The third principal element of the postwar domestic spending expansion was agriculture. The costs of federal price supports were extremely volatile in the postwar period, but this change was not a function of sharp reversals in federal policy. Instead, periodic shifts in demand and supply produced swings in federal spending as market prices fluctuated.

There were noteworthy policy conflicts during this period. The Truman, Kennedy, and Johnson administrations, for example, were committed to price supports and production controls that would protect small farmers and insure relatively high levels of farm income. This purpose was reflected in a Democratic predisposition toward high parity levels and comprehensive coverage of commodities.

The agriculture program statements of the Eisenhower administration and its controversial secretary of agriculture, Ezra Taft Benson, stressed the long-term superiority of returning agriculture to its pre–New Deal free market status. This policy found little sympathy in Congress, even among Republican members. So while the abstract free market debate was frequently revived, the real points of contention were parity levels, commodity controls, and production limits.

The Eisenhower administration succeeded in reducing the level of farm income support through, for example, lowering parity scales. Nevertheless, the post–Korean War period was marked by supplies that outstripped demand and by falling farm income. The administration and Congress settled upon a series of compromises on price support levels, but spending fluctuated widely regardless. Between fiscal 1958 and fiscal 1960, for example, total agricultural outlays first rose by over $2 billion and then dropped by almost the same amount. When the Kennedy administration took office, and the major policy differences with Congress were resolved, spending swings still occurred.

Centralizing Domestic Policy

During the Eighty-ninth Congress (1965–66), the number of separate grant-in-aid authorizations was increased by over 70 percent—from

221 to 379.[22] This growth was accompanied by a marked increase in overall funding, as total federal outlays for grants-in-aid roughly doubled over the fiscal 1965–69 period. Domestic spending growth in this instance was unusual in comparison to the World War II and Korean fiscal situations, when rapid expansions of defense budgets had depressed domestic outlays.

The Johnson presidency also diversified the programmatic composition of federal aid in a manner which would prove to have a continuing impact over the next decade. First, the broadened scope of aid programs mirrored the Great Society's general extension of federal domestic responsibilities to areas that previously had been reserved largely if not exclusively to the states. Second, a number of new aid programs were targeted directly at local governments, in many cases reflecting a deliberate decision to bypass what proponents of these programs perceived as politically unsympathetic and unresponsive state governments.

The Johnson administration's efforts to federalize and to centralize domestic policy-making were not confined to spending programs. Federal regulatory programs were expanded, and this expansion also had a direct impact on state and local governments. During the 1940s and 1950s broad federal mandates had accompanied grants of federal assistance. During the 1960s the number of such mandates went up dramatically, as did the numbers of partial federal preemptions of state governmental discretion and crossover regulations that made continued receipt of federal assistance in one policy area contingent upon very specific programmatic performance in another.[23]

Budgetary incentives were thus complemented by regulatory requirements as part of the federalization of domestic policy. This approach was controversial at the outset, and it became even more so under Johnson's successors. For Nixon and Ford, loosening the strings attached to federal funding was accorded a high priority as part of their efforts to establish a "New Federalism." With Carter, however, the Great Society's emphasis on targeted aid was revived. In all of these cases, federal money was being used to achieve domestic policy objectives, albeit with important variations in the discretion accorded beneficiaries.

The Johnson Programs

One of the most far-reaching domestic policy decisions of the Johnson years was the president's eventual rejection of a tax-sharing plan developed by the chairman of his Council of Economic Advisers, Walter W. Heller. Heller had long advocated a "per capita revenue-sharing" program under which the federal government would turn over to the states a fixed percentage of the taxable income reported by individuals. These funds would be made available with virtually no conditions attached and would be separate from federal grants for specific purposes.

In 1964 a presidential task force was appointed to study the feasibility and implementation of Heller's proposal, but Johnson's early promises of support evaporated. Instead, he chose to support diversified categorical aid and direct aid to cities. There was no general revenue sharing enacted under Johnson, and the use of block grants was limited as well. In 1966, for example, the Comprehensive Health Planning and Services Act substituted block grants, with modest restrictions, for a number of project and formula grants to the states for disease prevention and control programs. Two years later, a similar approach was adopted for federally supported law enforcement programs.

In general, however, revenue sharing and block grants fared poorly under Johnson, even as they gained considerable support from governors and state officials. Congressional Republicans, who also supported federal funding with less federal control, sought on a number of occasions to substitute block grants for categorical grants when periodic reauthorizations were considered. In 1967 they launched a concerted effort to convert education aid to a block grant format, but the Johnson administration successfully opposed this initiative. The administration also prevailed on other major reauthorizations.

Budgetary Diversification. Total federal domestic outlays, including grants-in-aid, roughly doubled over the fiscal 1960–70 period. Within this total, the composition of federal spending shifted only slightly as a result of Great Society programs (see table 7.7). At the end of the decade, as at its beginning, agriculture and transportation accounted for the bulk of federal spending.

This spending pattern does not conform to the legislative emphases of the Johnson years. One reason for this disjunction can be found in the comparatively low funding levels at which new federal programs began. It was during the 1970s, when authorizations and appropriations for these programs became more generous, that the full impact of the Great Society's domestic policy accomplishments emerged more fully.

Program Diversification. The Johnson administration's affinity for national policy planning was demonstrated in almost every major policy area, but it did not necessarily lead to greatly increased spending. In some instances (such as mass transit subsidies), initial authorizations were quite low. In others (such as housing), appropriations lagged behind authorizations.

Table 7.7. Composition of Domestic Spending, Fiscal Years 1960-70

Budget Function	Percentage of Total Domestic Outlays		
	FY 1960	FY 1965	FY 1970
Agriculture	25	26	25
Commerce and Housing Credit	15	8	10
Community and Regional Development	2	7	12
Energy	4	5	5
Natural Resources and Environment	15	17	15
Transportation	39	38	34

SOURCE: *Historical Tables, Budget of the United States Government, Fiscal Year 1990*, pp. 41-42.

In 1966, for example, the Department of Transportation was established to facilitate the development and implementation of coordinated, national transportation policy. The department's statutory mandate, however, was limited by Congress, and this move foreshadowed continued conflicts between the administration and Congress over transportation policy.

Congress supported, for example, a major increase in maritime ship construction subsidies, which the Johnson administration successfully blocked. Johnson's efforts to convert a minor airport safety grant-in-aid program into a $1 billion loan fund were rejected by Congress. The 1964 Urban Mass Transportation Act authorized matching grants and loans for the construction and improvement of mass transit facilities, but actual spending through FY 1970 averaged only about $60 million annually. By comparison, the interstate highway system's initial cost projections had nearly doubled by the mid-1960s, and Congress responded by stretching out the completion date and adding more mileage. Throughout the 1960s the federal highway program continued to dominate transportation spending.

Natural resources and environmental programs were assigned a high legislative priority as part of the Great Society agenda, but here again funding for new initiatives lagged well behind the statutory objectives. The Water Quality Act of 1965 and Clean Waters Restoration Act of 1966 put the federal government at the forefront of a nationwide water pollution control effort. The former set nationwide purity standards for all interstate waters, while the latter provided grant-in-aid authorizations to assist communities in meeting these standards. Approximately $3.9 billion was authorized for fiscal years 1967–71, but the bulk of the funding was scheduled for the last two years, and initial funding was reduced further by appropriations actions.

Federal air pollution control legislation was extended throughout the Johnson presidency. The Clean Air Act of 1963 was amended in 1965 to cover motor vehicle emission standards. The following year, authorizations were broadened for a variety of grant programs to assist state, regional, and local air pollution control activities. The Air Quality Act of 1967 increased authorized funding for these programs and also raised the federal share for grant-in-aid projects. Even with these extensions, however, total annual authorizations were limited to approximately $500 million annually.

A similar gap between legislative objectives and funding affected regional development programs. The Kennedy administration had sponsored limited programs of federal aid to depressed regions, and these efforts were expanded with passage of the Appalachian Regional Development Act of 1965 and the Public Works and Economic Development Act of 1965. Both authorized federal grants to local governments and other agencies for a variety of public works and development projects. Their combined authorizations were quite substantial, totaling $3.75 billion for fiscal years 1966–70. Appropriations were considerably lower, however, with large reductions below authorized levels in fiscal years 1967–69.

The urban counterpart to regional development aid was an ambitious Great Society plan to assist urban areas. The Department of Housing and Urban Development was established in 1965, and it became the administrative focal point for the housing construction and "model cities" projects that followed. The urban planning objectives of the Johnson administration went far beyond construction projects. They embraced mass transportation, urban development, jobs programs, and even police-community relations. Controversies over the design and implementation of these programs were intense, and they had a pronounced impact on funding. Outlays for housing programs and community and regional development programs increased as a result of the Great Society's legislative successes, but these increases were not nearly as dramatic as the administration or its critics claimed. From 1960 to 1970, for example, transportation outlays alone rose by nearly $3 billion. The functional totals for all commerce and housing and community and regional development programs, by comparison, grew by well under $3 billion.

Spending Control. The Johnson administration put into place the domestic program base that would later produce massive spending increases. These increases were delayed in large part until the administration had left office. Large gaps between programmatic objectives, authorizations, and appropriations occurred repeatedly under Johnson, reflecting the budget pressures stemming from the Vietnam buildup and the rise in social welfare spending. In addition, the new components of the domestic program base had to compete with older, established, and politically popular programs. There was little sentiment, especially in Congress, to forgo traditional highway and water projects in order to finance new and considerably less-focused programs. The funding consequences of the Great Society therefore were delayed until a budgetary margin was created to supplement, rather than to replace, established domestic programs.

The New Federalism

During the Nixon and Ford administrations, conflicts with Congress over domestic policy were protracted and often intense. Vetoes of authorization and appropriations measures were commonplace, and in Nixon's case policy disagreements were carried over to impoundments. These disputes were often tied to budgetary considerations, but the stakes were actually much greater. Nixon and Ford were pushing for a reversal of the domestic policy centralization that had taken place during the 1960s, and this reversal did not necessarily mean less spending. Both administrations were willing to support, for example, increased grants-in-aid to the states, but only if the states were given greater discretion in defining and implementing intergovernmental programs.

The First Term. Redefining or reallocating the respective roles of the federal and state governments was formally proposed by Nixon in 1969 with a series of legislative proposals designated as a "New Federalism." An important component was the welfare reform embodied in a federalized family assistance system. Federalization of income transfers, however, was to be complemented by a devolution of "power, funds and responsibility . . . from Washington to the states and to the people." The first set of programs defining this devolution included manpower training and jobs programs, but the centerpiece was revenue sharing. As described by Nixon, a "set portion of the revenues from federal income taxes [was to] be remitted directly to the states—with a minimum of federal restrictions on how those dollars are to be used and with a requirement that a percentage of them be channeled through for the use of local governments."[24]

By 1971 the New Federalism had become the "New American Revolution," but this grandiose rechristening did little to overcome congressional opposition to Nixon's domestic agenda. At the same time, Nixon's efforts to restrain domestic spending through vetoes and veto threats were having mixed success. In 1970, when the domestic policy battles with Congress began to get serious, Nixon vetoed three appropriations bills and two authorizations. Two of these were overridden, the first veto reversals to occur in a decade. The impact of the others was marginal. An $18 billion appropriations bill for programs administered by Housing and Urban Development, the Veterans Administration, and the National Aeronautics and Space Administration (NASA), for example, was vetoed, reduced by $300 million, and then accepted by the administration.

In 1972, when Nixon fought a months-long battle with Congress over a $250 billion spending ceiling, numerous spending measures were vetoed on purely fiscal grounds. The Labor-HEW appropriations bill for fiscal 1973 was successfully vetoed twice. A $24.7 billion authorization for the Federal Water Pollution Control Act Amendments of 1972 was attacked by Nixon as "unconscionable," "staggering," and "budget-wrecking," but his veto was easily overridden.[25] Several major authorizations, including a $3 billion public works authorization, were pocket vetoed.

The most notable domestic policy achievement of Nixon's first term was, in fact, a $30 billion, multiyear appropriation for revenue sharing. The State and Local Fiscal Assistance Act of 1972 did not conform to Nixon's original proposal. In particular, Congress directed the bulk of the funding to local governments, rather than to the state governments as Nixon had requested. There were additional congressional modifications in the revenue-sharing formula for allocating funds, but the general principle of relatively unfettered aid survived.

For the fiscal 1969–73 period, the edge in budget policy conflicts was with Congress. For domestic policy, this advantage was not as dramatic as it was elsewhere in the budget. As a percentage of GNP, for example, defense outlays dropped by almost one-third—from 8.9 percent in fiscal 1969 to 6.0 percent in fiscal 1973. The corresponding increase in non–social welfare domestic spending was almost nonexistent—from 1.9 percent to 2.0 percent. This meant, however, sustained if unspectacular growth over the period. Outlays rose by about 40 percent, with much of the growth concentrated in environmental, transportation, and community development spending.

The Second Term. The congressional advantage on domestic policy spending became considerably more pronounced with Nixon's fall and the transition to Gerald Ford. Ford continued the effort to reallocate federal responsibilities, with much of his emphasis falling on the substitution of block grants for categorical aid grants. He also revived Nixon's veto strategy, which had been largely abandoned early in 1974. Ford cast sixty-one regular vetoes during his short tenure in office, of which Congress overrode twelve. Of the fourteen major appropriations and authorizations bills that Ford vetoed for excess spending, however, Congress overrode eight.

Ford's record on block grants was unimpressive. Nixon had failed to convert categorical aid for education, law enforcement, rural community development, and transportation into block grants. Ford suffered defeats on child nutrition, education, health, and social services. Only two important block grants were approved. The Comprehensive Employment and Training Act of 1973 (CETA) converted a variety of categorical grants for job training and placement into a block grant. The Housing and Community Development Act of 1974 did the same for urban categorical aid programs, including model cities and urban renewal. Neither of these, however, was a budget-cutting measure. The trade-off was simply less federal intervention in exchange for continued, or expanded, federal funding.

As a consequence, the New Federalism in both its Nixon and Ford incarnations had a marginal effect on federal domestic policy. Federal domestic spending accelerated sharply toward the latter part of the Nixon-Ford period (see table 7.8). Moreover, the policy areas in which spending increases were especially large were generally those for which the Nixon and Ford administrations had limited enthusiasm. Natural resources and environment outlays, for example, were dominated by water resource projects in fiscal 1969, while pollution control spending accounted for only about 10 percent. In fiscal 1977, by contrast, pollution control outlays had jumped to over $4 billion and constituted the largest single component of spending in this functional category.

Federal grants-in-aid (not including payments for individuals) almost doubled, in constant dollars, from fiscal 1969 to fiscal 1977. The discretion of state and local governments in utilizing these grant funds was expanded through changes in grant design. For cities, dependence on federal dollars rose significantly. By 1976–77, the proportion of their general revenues represented by federal aid dollars was nearly 15 percent.[26] Thus, while the New Federalism did alter the nature of federal aid, it did so by enlarging substantially the funds made available to states and

Table 7.8. Federal Domestic Outlays, Fiscal Years 1969-77 (in billions of dollars)

Budget Function	FY 1969	FY 1973	FY 1977
Agriculture	$ 5.8	$ 4.8	$ 6.8
Commerce and Housing Credit	- 0.1	0.9	3.1
Community and Regional Development	1.6	4.6	7.0
Energy	1.0	1.2	5.8
Natural Resources and Environment	2.9	4.8	10.0
Transportation	6.5	9.1	14.8
General Purpose Fiscal Assistance			
(Revenue Sharing)	0.4	7.3	9.6
Total	18.1	32.7	57.1

SOURCE: *Historical Tables, Budget of the United States Government, Fiscal Year 1990*, pp. 42-43, 74-75.

localities. It did not significantly alter the categorical grants programs in most policy areas. The Nixon-Ford initiatives simply added to them.

The Carter Programs

Jimmy Carter's domestic policy proposals were, in part, a return to the Great Society's targeting of aid to distressed urban communities. For Carter, however, this return was cast in the context of a "new urban policy." As explained by his Policy Group on Urban and Regional Development, "The complexity of urban problems makes . . . a comprehensive policy approach . . . necessary."[27] Christened the "New Partnership," this ambitious undertaking quickly stalled under funding difficulties. Existing grant formulas for countercyclical fiscal and public works assistance were redrawn to target more aid to older cities with large poverty populations. The Community Development Act reauthorization in 1977 followed this same pattern, and it also set up an Urban Development Action Grant program with a $1.2 billion, three-year authorization. In general, however, a "comprehensive urban policy" never emerged during the Carter years, because of funding constraints and congressional opposition.

Carter also started out with great hopes for a "national energy policy." Gasoline and oil shortages several years previously had led to modestly upgraded federal energy supply programs, but the Carter administration raised energy policy to what the president termed, probably unfortunately, "the moral equivalent of war."[28] A complicated spending, tax, and regulatory package was proposed to Congress in 1977, and pieces of that package, usually substantially altered, along with new proposals were enacted over the next several years. The budgetary impact was considerable, as energy outlays nearly tripled, to over $15 billion, during Carter's term. The accompanying policy record was uneven. The mandatory controls and comprehensive planning that Carter repeatedly called for were finally abandoned, and much less sweeping interventionist measures were adopted. In the end, decontrol and market solutions became the preferred option.

A third Carter effort to broaden the scope of domestic policy planning was directed toward the economy. An economic stimulus package, consisting of tax rebates and spending programs, was sent to Congress during Carter's first few weeks in office. When first-quarter economic growth figures then proved to be unexpectedly high, Carter withdrew the tax rebates, infuriating Democratic congressional leaders who had reluctantly backed the proposal and establishing a reputation for uncertainty and indecision which plagued the Carter presidency for the rest of its tenure.

The economy's performance during the late 1970s was erratic. Inflation climbed even as economic growth faltered. Unemployment rates, which had improved after the 1974–75 recession, began to increase during 1979 and 1980. Interest rates soared, creating acute financing problems for key sectors of the economy, particularly automobiles and housing.

The severity of economic problems under Carter generated heated debates over the federal government's responsibility to act as an employer of last resort to combat unemployment. A second issue was economic planning to rebuild distressed industrial sectors and to direct future economic growth. In both instances, the Carter administration backed away from the full-scale commitment urged by congressional liberals, and its reluctance was largely based upon budgetary costs. One of the most highly publicized and controversial industrial rescue efforts of the Carter presidency, the assistance package for the Chrysler Corporation, was accomplished through loan guarantees rather than direct aid in order to avoid immediate budgetary costs.[29]

The Carter administration's initial hopes to refine the Great Society by introducing greater coherence and comprehensiveness to federal domestic policy were undermined and ultimately frustrated by the absence of

Table 7.9. Federal Domestic Outlays, Fiscal Years 1977-81 (in billions of dollars)

Budget Function	FY 1977	FY 1979	FY 1981
Agriculture	$ 6.8	$11.2	$11.3
Commerce and Housing Credit	3.1	4.7	8.2
Community and Regional Development	7.0	10.5	10.6
Energy	5.8	9.2	15.2
Natural Resources and Environment	10.0	12.1	13.6
Transportation	14.8	17.5	23.4
General Purpose Fiscal Assistance (Revenue Sharing)	9.6	8.4	6.8
Total	57.1	73.6	89.1

SOURCE: *Historical Tables, Budget of the United States Government, Fiscal Year 1990*, pp. 43, 75.

sufficient budgetary resources. Whatever the long-term merits of the administration's national urban policy, energy policy, full-employment policy, or industrial policy might have been, short-term costs were substantial. Further, the growth in domestic spending that had begun to gain momentum long before Carter took office had been financed to a considerable degree by shrinking defense budgets. In addition, social insurance programs were becoming much more costly as high rates of inflation heightened the budgetary impact of indexing provisions. Finally, the so-called tax revolt, signaled by the success of tax-cutting initiatives in California and other states, created an obvious political obstacle to resolving spending pressures through tax increases.

The only option left to Carter, financing domestic policy growth in priority areas by domestic cutbacks elsewhere, also proved futile. In February 1977 Carter decided to launch an attack on one of Congress' favorite pork-barrel programs, announcing his decision to work toward elimination of 19 ongoing water projects and to review the status of 300 additional ones. Congress was also informed that the administration would not award future construction contracts for any project recommended for deauthorization or cancellation. What followed was a series of fights on rescission proposals, authorization bills, and appropriations that carried over through 1979.[30] While Carter finally managed to restrain spending, the savings involved were miniscule compared to the political capital they cost him. The same difficulty arose in other traditional domestic spending areas. Congress would not accept, and the administration was unable to enforce, terminations and cutbacks of sufficient size to expand discretionary budget margins.

The domestic budget under Carter grew by more than 50 percent (see table 7.9). The increases were spread across all of the functional categories except revenue sharing (revenue sharing for cities and counties was continued in 1980, but assistance to the states was cut). This represented, in relative terms, a stabilizing of spending growth after a period of very marked increases. By the end of Carter's term, domestic policy commitments were absorbing about 2.5 percent of GNP and just under 15 percent of total outlays. For the incoming Reagan administration, these commitments were unacceptable, particularly since they were accompanied by the lowest defense budget shares and GNP levels since the late 1940s.

The Reagan Trade-offs

For the Reagan administration, the domestic policy framework it inherited was objectionable for its costs and centralization. It was also unacceptable because of the political philosophy it embodied. As a consequence, Reagan's attempts to reduce the federal government's domestic policy sphere were more encompassing than either Nixon's or Ford's. First, the Reagan agenda called for a major retrenchment in overall domestic spending. Second, it proposed turning back programs, and their funding, to the states. Third, it reduced the tax and spending margins available to support a future resurgence in domestic spending. As Richard Nathan has characterized these efforts, Reagan consistently "advanced broad-gauged and radical proposals" that were defined by a "state-centered theory of federalism."[31] And while Reagan's most ambitious undertaking—the tax and spending devolution to the states in the 1982 New Federalism proposal—was not adopted, important components of his federalism reform strategy were enacted.

Domestic Spending

The domestic spending reductions under Reagan were impressive for the extent to which they reversed previous spending patterns. Current dollar or nominal spending remained fairly stable over the fiscal 1981–89 period, and the only category in which steady spending growth occurred was agriculture (see table 7.10). Even with agriculture spending more than doubling, however, total domestic outlays rose by less than 10 percent.

Table 7.10.   Federal Domestic Outlays, Fiscal Years 1981-89 (in billions of dollars)

Budget Function	FY 1981	FY 1983	FY 1985	FY 1987	FY 1989 (est.)
Agriculture	$11.3	$22.9	$25.6	$26.6	$20.9
Commerce and Housing Credit	8.2	6.7	4.2	6.2	20.0ᵃ
Community and Regional Development	10.6	7.6	7.7	5.0	6.3
Energy	15.2	9.3	5.7	4.1	4.1
Natural Resources and Environment	13.6	12.7	13.4	13.4	16.5
Transportation	23.4	21.3	25.8	26.2	28.0
General Purpose Fiscal Assistance (Revenue Sharing)	6.8	6.4	6.3	1.6	1.9
Total	89.1	86.9	88.7	83.1	97.7

SOURCE: *Historical Tables, Budget of the United States Government, Fiscal Year 1990*, pp. 43-44, 75-77.
ᵃ Includes $12.5 billion in emergency outlays by the Federal Deposit Insurance Corporation and Federal Savings and Loan Insurance Corporation.

When measured against the usual indices, this decline was considerably more pronounced. Real spending for the domestic functions dropped by one-fourth (see table 7.11). The GNP share for domestic outlays was cut by one-third, back to a level comparable to the mid-1960s. As a portion of the entire budget, domestic program outlays fell well below 10 percent.

A sustained real spending decline in domestic programs had not occurred since the Korean War. Between FY 1950 and FY 1955, constant dollar domestic spending dropped, but only by approximately 4 percent. For each subsequent five-year period, up until FY 1980, real spending rose, usually by substantial amounts. The average increase for each of these five-year periods was over 25 percent. Thus, the 1980s retrenchment had no true parallel in recent budget policy history.

The Cutbacks. The single most important legislative impetus behind this accomplishment was the Omnibus Reconciliation Act of 1981. Its

Table 7.11. Federal Domestic Outlay Measures, Fiscal Years 1981-89

	Domestic Spending		
Fiscal Year	Percentage of GNP	Percentage of Total Outlays	FY 1982 Dollars[a] (billions of dollars)
1981	3.0%	13.1%	$95.4
1983	2.6	10.7	83.3
1985	2.2	9.4	79.6
1987	1.9	8.3	71.0
1989 (est.)	1.9	8.6	77.5

SOURCE: *Historical Tables, Budget of the United States Government, Fiscal Year 1990*, pp. 18, 20, 43-44, 75-77.
[a] Calculated using functional category totals and composite GNP deflator reported in budget tables.

changes in domestic programs were numerous. The public service jobs programs under CETA were terminated. Economic development programs were sharply reduced, with the Economic Development Administration's authorization cut from $1 billion to $290 million. Housing construction authorizations were cut, and the home-ownership assistance program phased out. Transportation subsidies for the Conrail and Amtrak rail networks were reduced, and the former was scheduled for eventual sale.

In a number of instances, such as the Economic Development Administration's programs, Reagan failed to obtain the full terminations he requested. In others, such as transportation subsidies, Congress refused to cut authorizations to the extent Reagan recommended. Nevertheless, since the authorization cuts in the reconciliation bill bound subsequent appropriations actions, the spending cuts were sweeping and substantial.

While nothing of similar magnitude came even close to passage in later years, the recurring rounds of authorizations and appropriations that governed most domestic spending allowed Reagan to protect, if not extend, these initial cuts. Economic development aid, for example, was refought each year of Reagan's first term. While Congress succeeded in maintaining the programs, spending levels were kept low. Reagan also never succeeded in eliminating mass transit subsidies or noninterstate highway aid, but here again funding levels were severely constrained.

The Department of Energy was not abolished, as Reagan had hoped, but he was able to reduce greatly the alternative energy supply programs that had been initiated under Carter. Reagan had lifted remaining federal oil price controls immediately upon taking office, and his approach to energy policy was almost diametrically opposite to the interventionist philosophy that had guided Carter. As summarized late in Reagan's second term, government intervention had been "counterproductive." The assurance of "adequate supplies of energy at reasonable prices . . . [was] best achieved through minimum Government intervention in the operation of energy markets."[32]

Revenue sharing slowly disappeared as well. In 1980 direct revenue sharing to the states had been dropped. In 1983 Reagan successfully blocked efforts to raise the annual authorizations for aid to local governments. In 1986 Congress agreed to drop future appropriations.

Reagan budgets contained dozens of program terminations that Congress never accepted. The administration also had very limited success in its "privatization" efforts, which involved selling government assets to the private sector. The wholesale dismantling of federal domestic policy responsibilities proved to be beyond Reagan's reach, but his relentless pressure to curtail funding made it impossible to pursue the national policies that had previously dominated the legislative agenda. It also effectively foreclosed new federal extensions, such as a national industrial policy, that enjoyed considerable support among congressional Democrats.

Agriculture. The conspicuous exception to Reagan's domestic curtailments was agriculture. Here again, the administration had an instinctive commitment to reducing federal intervention and to free market solutions, but it was unable to translate this commitment into a coherent program which could be sold politically. Attempts to reduce farm subsidies were sporadic. Farm-state Republicans in Congress could not be counted upon for support, particularly as the agricultural economy deteriorated markedly during the mid-1980s.

What occurred with agriculture spending during the 1980s was not a result of new policy but rather the continuation of income-support programs that had been in place for many years. The cost of these programs had fluctuated over time in response to economic conditions, but direct government payments to farmers usually had remained within politically acceptable limits. In the late 1970s, for example, farm exports rose sharply, and market prices for major crops climbed well above the government's target, or support level, prices. Farm income stabilization outlays, for example, had almost doubled between fiscal years 1977 and 1978 but then had declined without major changes in policy. While federal domestic spending had risen by more than $50 billion between fiscal years 1970 and 1980, farm income stabilization outlays had increased by less than $3 billion.

Since the budgetary impact of agriculture policy remained modest during the 1970s, there was little incentive for policymakers to tackle the broader questions concerning government intervention and support. The periodic reauthorizations for farm bills provided the opportunity for limited skirmishes over support levels and production limits, but there was no real enthusiasm in either party to risk anything more than marginal adjustments in existing policy.

The Reagan administration's initial willingness to tackle the underlying issue of federal intervention quickly eroded as the bottom fell out of the agricultural economy. Exports declined, the inflation-driven boom in farmland prices was reversed, and the agricultural credit system showed signs of collapse. Faced with the mounting budgetary costs of propping up the agricultural sector, neither the administration nor Congress could find a politically acceptable solution. In 1983 and 1984 government payments as a percentage of farm income averaged almost 25 percent, nearly four times the level under Carter.[33]

The impact of this growing dependence can be illustrated by comparing the 1981 and 1985 farm bills. The 1981 Agriculture and Food Act, while considerably less sweeping than Reagan's proposals for agriculture policy cutbacks, lowered target prices and loan levels for supported crops, relaxed income supports for dairy products, and removed production controls and supports entirely in several cases. The expectation was that these changes would reduce agriculture spending significantly. Instead, the program reductions were overwhelmed by an extraordinarily weak farm economy. Net farm income dropped, in constant dollars, to its lowest level since the Great Depression.[34] The 1982 Omnibus Budget Reconciliation Act attempted to raise crop prices and to reduce budgetary costs by a land diversion scheme which would cut production. In 1983 the administration revived a payment-in-kind (PIK) scheme from the 1960s, under which farmers would be paid with government-held commodities to reduce production. Once again, however, the farm economy performed contrary to expectations, and program costs continued to mount.

In 1984 some modest cutbacks in target prices were adopted as part of the Agricultural Programs Adjustment Act. The following year, when omnibus agriculture legislation came up for reauthorization, the Reagan administration's recommendations to phase out subsidies found little support in Congress. Despite the widespread dissatisfaction with the costs of existing farm policies, the five-year reauthorization that finally passed continued the government's commitment to income supports.

Over the past half century, agriculture policy has changed comparatively little. Support levels and production controls have been relaxed, but the ties between government and farmers remain. The inherent problem of balancing supply and demand makes it difficult to fashion predictable policy. When the farm economy is going well and government costs are modest, the incentives to eliminate supports and controls are limited. When the agricultural economy deteriorates and costs explode, the political risks of free-market solutions have proved unacceptable to both parties.

For the Reagan administration, agriculture policy was a problem from the beginning. The cost-control arguments that proved at least moderately persuasive in pushing domestic policy cutbacks in other areas were more problematical in the case of agriculture. The federal government's responsibility for agriculture, in sum, did not change very much during the 1980s.

Grants-in-Aid

The New Federalism concept of the early 1970s was revived and expanded by Reagan. In 1981 the Omnibus Reconciliation Act established six new block grants, affecting health, education, and community services. Existing block grants were also modified to accord the states greater discretion. In all, fifty-four grants carrying over $7 billion in annual funding were affected by the reconciliation statute.[35]

These grant-in-aid policy changes were not as far-reaching as Reagan had proposed, and in 1982 he presented to Congress a program for cutting through what he termed the "jungle of grants-in-aid"—the 500 categorical programs costing over $100 billion that had made the federal government "more pervasive, more intrusive, more unmanageable, more ineffective, more costly and above all more unaccountable."[36] Part of Reagan's New Federalism was a swap of welfare programs—full federal responsibility for medicaid in exchange for full state responsibility for AFDC. The domestic program component was a trust fund to provide states with funds to replace federal grants in education, transportation, and social services. States could continue programs currently in place or fund others. After 1988, full state control of several dozen major grant programs would be in place, and certain excise taxes to support these or other programs would be turned over to the states as well.

The strategy of turning over spending and taxing powers to the states

Table 7.12. Federal Grants-in-Aid Outlays, Fiscal Years 1980-89 (in billions of dollars)

| Fiscal Year | Constant FY 1982 Dollars | |
	Capital Investment	Other
1980	$24.5	$44.0
1981	22.7	38.7
1982	20.1	30.2
1983	20.3	28.6
1984	21.9	27.4
1985	22.9	28.2
1986	23.5	27.5
1987	21.1	22.4
1988	21.1	22.5
1989 (est.)	20.1	23.3

SOURCE: *Historical Tables, Budget of the United States Government, Fiscal Year 1990*, p. 240.

was never formally endorsed by Congress, but Reagan did succeed in modifying grant policies. More discretion was accorded states, both through block grants and through revisions of continuing categorical programs. Reagan's tax cuts also opened a revenue margin for the states, a number of which increased their spending commitments in areas where federal aid was cut. In many instances, Reagan's policies resulted in "states [taking] a more active part in fiscal, programmatic, and institutional affairs than they had previously taken."[37]

The budgetary impact of the Reagan program was also significant. In constant dollars, federal grants-in-aid for domestic programs dropped by nearly 40 percent during the 1980s (see table 7.12). Of equal importance, the composition of that aid shifted back to what it had been decades earlier. Capital investment outlays, which had been almost flat in real terms since the mid-1960s, were cut only slightly. Grants-in-aid for other purposes, comprising the Great Society and subsequent policy expansions, had risen by more than 600 percent in real terms between fiscal 1965 and fiscal 1980. Under Reagan, this category of aid was cut in half.

Domestic policy under Reagan, therefore, was meaningfully altered. This revision was manifested clearly in spending cutbacks. It was based on programmatic changes. As Nathan has pointed out, it was reinforced by the Reagan message: "Retrenchment involves more than money: *It sends a signal.* Reagan sent a signal to the domestic public sector that the federal government should and would do less."[38]

Controllability and Domestic Programs

Discretionary domestic programs are technically more controllable than, for example, entitlements. They are governed by the appropriations process. They are also subject to periodic adjustment during the authorization process. Where authorizations do constitute entitlements, as in the case of agricultural price support payments, spending increases have resulted from economic factors rather than policy expansions.

Controllable domestic programs still conform to the incrementalist theory of the budgetary process but with an important modification. The Reagan years, in particular, demonstrated that fiscal pressures could be used to cut domestic spending levels. Trade-offs were made from domestic programs to defense programs, just as opposite trade-offs had been made during the early 1970s.

What these trade-offs highlight is the "budgetary squeeze" noted by Wildavsky.[39] Entitlements have siphoned off resources from other domestic programs. They have also forced domestic programs to compete with defense for a shrinking share of the federal budget. Shifts in political coalitions in Congress and in control of the executive branch affect this competition, as the contrasting trends of the 1970s and 1980s illustrate. Moreover, the "old" budget process can cut spending for domestic programs, despite the credit-claiming and congressional policy decentralization hypotheses.

The dilemma for overall budget policy is that domestic programs account for only a small part of the total budget. Control in this area can be easily overwhelmed by spending increases elsewhere. If we are searching for institutional causes for the decline in spending control, discretionary programs do not provide good evidence. The characteristics of Congress that supposedly contribute most to budgetary problems—distributive tendencies, the autonomous power of committees and subcommittees, the tug of geographical interests—are especially pronounced in the legislative process governing discretionary programs. Yet, as Charles Schultze has emphasized, "whatever the budget malpractices of Congress, they did not result—at least in the past fifteen years—in an explosive growth of discretionary programs."[40]

Discretionary programs, then, have exhibited political controllability. It is this factor, rather than technical controllability, that represents the major distinction with large entitlement programs. There are points of control for both categories of programs within the existing budgetary process. Utilizing these points of control, however, demands presidential and congressional agreement to impose top-down budgeting that limits spending growth. It seems clear that fiscal discipline has been able to overcome credit-claiming incentives for domestic programs. It has been unable to overcome blame avoidance, however, for controlling entitlements.

CONCLUSION

CONCLUSION

8

Restoring Politics to Budgeting

The federal budget's elevation to a transcendent political issue has meant a lost sense of proportion about the problems it presents. The budget is important, but it is not commensurate with governance. Budget deficits are an economic concern and a political frustration, but balancing the budget is not the only legitimate objective of the budget process. Perhaps most important, major initiatives were undertaken during the 1980s to control spending growth and to reduce deficits, although the prevailing view seems to be that political obstacles have blocked "real" deficit solutions.

Indeed, debate about the federal budget often ignores the fact that highly divisive policy issues need to be resolved in order to bring the budget into balance. Late in 1987, for example, the Reagan administration and Congress established a National Economic Commission and charged it with formulating a bipartisan plan for balancing the budget. The panel included politically influential and sophisticated individuals representing Congress, the executive branch, and the private sector.[1] The apparent hope was that an independent commission would provide "political cover," allowing the White House and Congress to "adopt the commission's recommendations en bloc, arguing not only that the problem at hand must be solved but that the commission—and not the elected officials—should be blamed for the unpopular scheme."[2]

The National Economic Commission's report, originally scheduled for 1988, was finally issued on March 1, 1989, but it provided no solution. A bare majority of its fourteen members concluded that the deficit could be eliminated without raising taxes. The minority's report argued that this was highly unlikely, if not impossible.

Since George Bush already had pledged not to raise taxes during his presidential campaign, the commission's dilemma was hardly surprising. Ronald Reagan and Congress had fought for eight years over whether to balance the budget at high or low spending levels. When George Bush replaced Reagan, the policy stakes associated with the gap between spending and revenues had not disappeared. Indeed, they had become even more serious, because previous deficit-reduction agreements had implemented some of the more obvious and less painful choices available to policymakers.

It is probable that deficit reduction will continue to dominate budget policy debates, regardless of long-standing uncertainties about its economic effects. It will almost certainly remain the standard by which political experts and the media, if not the public, judge the performance of government. The central issue, then, is how to improve the capacity of policymakers either to reduce the deficit or to make clear to voters what alternative budget policy objectives have been assigned greater priority. There is no automatic or painless policy solution available at this time, nor is the commission approach an appropriate one for deciding which policies are in the national interest. The deficit problem reflects basic political disagreements. These disagreements will need to be resolved in the political arena, preferably in a manner which highlights, rather than masks, accountability.

If these observations are correct, future efforts at budget reform should directly focus upon unresolved budget policy problems. Budget reform should also proceed from a healthy recognition that politics and executive branch–congressional rivalries cannot be easily or permanently separated from the budget process. There is nothing in the recent history of budget conflict to suggest that either branch is willing to sacrifice its long-term power and influence for the short-term objective of deficit reduction, however vital that goal might appear.

The Dimensions of the Problem

There were sustained and noteworthy legislative efforts to reduce the deficit during the 1980s. The rate of growth in federal spending, for example, was cut well below the level of the 1970s. Nevertheless, the annual budget deficit when President Reagan left office was still above $150 billion, and the Congressional Budget Office was warning that the future "gap between the deficit under current policies and the [balanced] budget targets is formidable."[3]

The annual budget confrontations between Reagan and Congress produced a number of meaningful policy changes and also some important compromises. The 1981 tax cuts were scaled back, with Republicans taking the lead in shifting tax burdens from individuals to corporations. Reagan was forced to settle for no-real-growth defense budgets in his second term. Congress, for its part, accepted large reductions in discretionary domestic programs. In addition, the public assistance system was cut back, work requirements were enacted for recipients, and outlay growth was nearly flat. The 1980s also provided surprising setbacks for politically powerful interest groups. The 1986 tax reform effort overwhelmed numerous special interests, especially among business groups. Social security and medicare financing reforms were adopted despite opposition from organizations representing the elderly. The 1985 farm bill and the 1987 Omnibus Budget Reconciliation Act contained price support cutbacks opposed by most farm groups.

It should be emphasized, however, that the general parameters of what was accomplished during the 1980s were grounded in a political consensus. The prevailing public perception at the end of the 1970s was that defense budgets were too low (and the United States too weak), that income taxes were too high, and that domestic spending was out of control. Similar perceptions were widespread in Congress, which helps explain the sharp policy rebuffs to Jimmy Carter on defense and taxes. In a postelection congressional session in 1980, the chairman of the Senate Budget Committee, Ernest Hollings, took the floor to defend his committee and the budget process. The budget was not "hemorrhaging," declared Hollings, nor was the budget process "a sham and a fraud and a charade."[4] This assertion hardly constituted a ringing defense, and policymakers during the 1980s tried to resolve budget policy problems that had clearly worsened during the 1970s. The inadequacy of that response needs to be clearly understood, because it helps to explain the nature and scope of the deficit problem.

Distorted Spending Policy

In FY 1980 total outlays were approximately 22 percent of GNP. Recent baseline budget projections by the Congressional Budget Office, which are based on current policy, project a possible reduction in outlays to approximately 21 percent by FY 1994. The necessary policy assumption for these projections is no real growth in defense or nondefense discretionary spending through the mid-1990s. If this ambitious assumption holds, the total deficit by FY 1994 is projected at over $120 billion, while the on-budget deficit, excluding social security, is almost $240 billion.[5]

The short-term deficit problem, therefore, remains serious, even if discretionary spending is tightly controlled. (The long-term problem is considerably more difficult, since social security surpluses will eventually disappear, and trust fund reserves then will be used to fund benefit payments.) What complicates the short-term problem is that discretionary spending has already been tightly controlled over the past decade. The defense buildup from fiscal 1980 to fiscal 1990 (from 5 percent of GNP to nearly 6 percent) has been more than offset by the decline in nondefense discretionary spending (from 6 percent to less than 4 percent). Both categories of spending are at relatively low levels, when compared to the past three decades. With no real growth, both would decline still further as shares of GNP through the mid-1990s.

While combined defense and nondefense discretionary spending as a share of GNP dropped by almost 10 percent over the fiscal 1980–90 period, this reduction was offset by rising interest costs and by the stabilizing of entitlements and other mandatory spending at close to 11 percent of GNP. Through the mid-1990s, the current policy base for entitlements and projected interest costs will continue to absorb about 14 percent of GNP.

The spending policy problem that was not addressed adequately during the 1980s was entitlement spending, the bulk of which is indexed to inflation. In particular, indexed entitlements (primarily social security and federal civil and military retirement) as a share of GNP grew during the 1980s. By comparison, the share for nonindexed entitlements (such as AFDC and veterans pensions) was lower by the late 1980s than it had been a decade earlier. Finally, the GNP share of health entitlements has risen almost uninterruptedly over this period.[6]

The central point about indexing in this context has been stressed by Weaver: "In periods of fiscal stress, the agenda-limiting effect of indexing acts primarily to keep deficit-reduction initiatives—such as freezes in nominal benefit levels—off the agenda."[7] Policymakers generally resisted entitlement expansions during the 1980s. Even the highly controversial catastrophic health care expansion of medicare benefits, according to the CBO, represented "a major departure from previous practice" in that new benefits were "entirely financed by premiums and additional income taxes paid by participants."[8]

What policymakers refused to do was reconsider the indexing previously applied to the major entitlements. As a consequence, automatic (or current law) increases in social security and medicare alone will account for about one-half of the projected growth in total outlays through the mid-1990s. Social security benefit payments will grow, in real terms, because of the increasing number of beneficiaries and the higher initial benefit levels for new retirees. Medicare outlays are projected to grow at

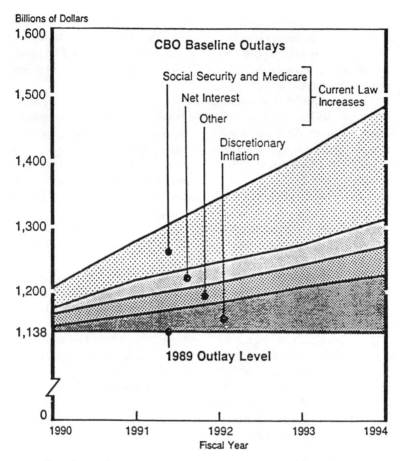

Figure 8.1. Projected sources of growth in outlays, fiscal years 1990-94. Source: Congressional Budget Office, *The Economic and Budget Outlook: Fiscal Years 1990-1994*, p. 55.

an average rate of 13 percent a year, in response to increased numbers of beneficiaries and rising health care costs.[9]

As shown in figure 8.1, the growth in indexed entitlements, net interest, and other automatically adjusted spending programs accounts for about three-fourths of the projected growth in total federal spending through the mid-1990s. Inflation adjustments for defense and nondefense discretionary programs account for the remainder. If discretionary appropriations are simply kept at current levels, with no inflation adjustment, there could be a real reduction of more than 20 percent by the mid-1990s. The policy consequences resulting from changes of this magnitude would be dramatic, but even so the impact on total spending would be limited. While the projected total deficit would be eliminated, there would still be a very large on-budget deficit.

A related problem associated with social security is that reported outlays are considerably lower than the benefits (and other costs) paid out of the trust funds. Social security trust fund payments in 1994, for example, are estimated at over $320 billion, but social security outlays are only $260 billion. The difference is accounted for by interest payments on federal securities held by the trust funds and by federal agency payments to the trust funds for employees covered by social security. These are counted as offsetting receipts, since they are intrabudgetary transactions. This accounting feature, according to the CBO, "overstates Social Security's effect on the total federal deficit and, therefore, its effect on the government's overall financing needs."[10]

The flexibility of the spending side of the budget has diminished a great deal over the past two decades, as entitlements and other mandatory spending have risen. With the most important entitlements, social security and medicare, much of this growth would have occurred anyway, since the aged population has increased. Moreover, the political influence of the elderly no doubt would have insured some inflation adjustments in benefits in the absence of indexing. Nevertheless, indexing clearly has inhibited efforts to control spending, and it has also channeled spending-control efforts toward discretionary programs. Finally, entitlement indexing also affects the revenue side of the budget, since an increasing share of revenues must be earmarked to finance the trust funds.

Skewed Revenue Policy

The relative level of tax receipts has not changed a great deal for several decades. The CBO's baseline budget projections for revenues over the next several years, for example, average approximately 19.5 percent of GNP. Only three times since World War II has the receipts-GNP ratio exceeded this level, so aggregate revenue levels are not depressed, at least by U.S. historical standards.

In addition, the level of individual income tax receipts is expected to climb close to post–World War II peaks, despite the 1981 and 1986 tax bills. For fiscal years 1992–94, individual income tax receipts are projected at about 9 percent of GNP, a level which has been exceeded only a half dozen times over the past fifty years. Individual income tax revenues are expected to outpace economic growth because of real income increases that push taxpayers into higher brackets. Over the fiscal 1990–94 period, by comparison, other sources of general tax receipts are only expected to keep pace with economic growth.[11]

The most significant long-term trend in the composition of budget receipts, however, has been the growth of social insurance taxes (mainly social security). This has occurred as a result of demographic and economic factors, such as labor force and wage rate growth. The rising level of social insurance taxes also reflects the impact of legislated tax increases necessary to finance the expanded coverage of social insurance programs.

Social security tax increases in 1977 and 1983 raised both tax rates and the wage base to which these tax rates apply. Under the 1978 social security amendments, the maximum tax rate was set at 13.4 percent, effective in 1982. Under the 1983 amendments, the tax rate was scheduled to rise to 15.3 percent in 1990. The 1983 legislation set maximum taxable earnings at $35,700. Maximum earnings in 1989 are $48,000. The maximum has been raised automatically each year based on a wage index, and it will continue to be adjusted on an annual basis.

The 1977 and 1983 amendments also shifted social security to a partial advanced funding system. Projected revenues have been set well above benefits for the next two decades, producing a growing trust fund surplus. Interest on the accumulated reserve, paid out of general revenues, will then be used as supplementary financing once the benefit payments begin to exceed revenues (currently projected around 2010). By 2020 the trust funds' assets are expected to exceed $9 trillion, with the accumulated reserve then being depleted over the next thirty years.[12]

Whatever the long-term merits of this approach, its immediate result is a heavy reliance on payroll taxes. Social security tax revenues are currently running close to $40 billion above annual benefit payments, and this surplus is expected to increase to $65 billion in FY 1994.[13] By this standard, social security "pays for itself." It does so, however, by siphoning off income tax revenues that would otherwise be available to support on-budget spending programs.

The social security program (that is, the Old Age and Survivors Insurance and Disability Insurance funds) is technically off-budget, as a result of the Gramm-Rudman-Hollings bill. The trust funds are counted, however, in calculations of the overall deficit and in determining compliance with the Gramm-Rudman-Hollings targets. Current proposals in Congress, which have widespread support, would eliminate this deficit calculation, separating social security entirely from the annual budget.

This change is defended as a means of making clear the true size of the deficit, since the current social security surpluses are used to finance the deficit through the purchase of government bonds.

Such a separation, however, would be disastrous from the standpoint of budget control, precisely because social security revenues (and benefits) affect directly and substantially the financing available for on-budget programs. Separation would further distort spending and tax policy. It would inevitably mask social security benefit and tax increases. It would make even more difficult the task of constructing a comprehensive deficit-reduction package. Indexed programs already enjoy a competitive advantage in the fight for government resources. Combining indexing with full off-budget status would simply exaggerate this advantage.

While there is no sanctity associated with the 20 percent of GNP level for revenues, the modest swings above and below this level over the past several decades indicate that it has some political and economic significance. Moreover, the changing composition of federal receipts makes it much more difficult to increase receipts significantly above current levels. An increase of 1 or 2 percent of GNP, for example, cannot be spread uniformly across revenue sources if the objective is deficit reduction. The increase would have to be limited to on-budget revenues, the largest source of which is the individual income tax. Such an increase likely would necessitate a return to income tax levels that were viewed as politically unacceptable a decade ago.

The flexibility of the revenue side of the budget, then, has declined to an even greater extent than the outlay side. Further, since the 1981 and 1986 tax bills added indexing provisions to individual income taxes, the government can no longer depend on hidden, inflation-generated tax increases to boost revenues. Combining expenditure indexing with tax indexing, as has been done, makes it much more difficult to resolve deficit problems. Since existing policy must be changed to reduce spending or to increase taxes, the president and Congress have reciprocal vetoes.

Budget Process Reforms

When he was in office, Ronald Reagan repeatedly attacked budget procedures for being cumbersome, complex, and convoluted. He was even more displeased with the results, which in his view amounted to bloated domestic budgets and inadequate defense growth. For Reagan's critics, the policy culprits were obviously different—tax cuts and defense increases that swelled deficits and starved domestic programs.

The difficulty with many procedural budget reforms is that they have little to do with the nature and scope of current deficit problems. The past decade has witnessed a marked reversal in spending priorities between defense and nondefense discretionary spending. Despite all of the delays in passing appropriations bills, and the occasional necessity of resorting to continuing resolutions in order to fund contested programs, the appropriations process has proved to be surprisingly flexible.

A line-item veto or enhanced rescission authority, both of which Reagan advocated, would increase presidential power over appropriations, but either's impact on total spending would be limited. Assuming that either can be adopted—and the former would almost certainly require a time-consuming effort for a constitutional amendment—the only types of spending that would be affected would be those where political control has already proved effective.

Despite Reagan's protestations, he and his advisers manipulated the budget process very effectively. The 1981 reconciliation strategy was extremely successful in attacking nondefense discretionary spending and, to a lesser extent, entitlement spending. The absence of similar successes in later years had less to do with the budget process than with mounting congressional opposition. Indeed, Reagan's second round of proposed spending cuts, which he sent to Congress right on the heels of the 1981 reconciliation bill's passage, generated very little support.

Nevertheless, Reagan's incessant, year-by-year attack on discretionary domestic spending yielded results. By the time Reagan left office, the nondefense discretionary share of GNP was at its lowest level since the 1950s. It is conceivable, of course, that even sharper cuts could have been made with line-item vetoes or forced rescission votes, but the amounts involved would have been insignificant when compared to the annual deficits.

Gramm-Rudman-Hollings

The Balanced Budget and Emergency Deficit Control Reaffirmation Act of 1987 restored sequestration, or automatic spending reductions, as a mechanism for reducing the deficit to zero by FY 1993. The revised Gramm-Rudman-Hollings act requires automatic percentage spending cuts (apportioned between defense and nonexempt domestic programs) if the projected deficit for a fiscal year exceeds the GRH target range. The GRH procedures have instituted some modest technical improvements in budgeting.[14] The GRH approach, however, appears to be seriously deficient.

Some problems with GRH are obvious.[15] Its deficit-reduction deadlines have been extended, and its compliance targets are skewed to the tail end of the deficit-reduction timetable. Accounting and estimating gimmicks have been used repeatedly. Costs have been shifted to future years. Most important, various evasions have forestalled any major sequestrations, leaving the true test of the GRH strategy still to come. The GRH strategy hinges on sequesters for affected programs being so severe and unacceptable that Congress and the executive branch will be forced to negotiate a more responsible and equitable deficit-reduction agreement. Presumably such an agreement would include the larger entitlements (especially social security) and taxes, both of which are exempted by GRH. Moreover, unless indexed entitlements would subsequently be subject to long-term control, real growth in the rest of the budget would once again cause deficit problems.

In truth, passage of GRH was made possible by its major flaws. It exempts tax policy from its automatic deficit-reduction formulas, thereby satisfying conservative Republicans. It also exempts social security and other large entitlements, along with discretionary public assistance programs, thereby mollifying liberal Democrats. The crux of the deficit dilemma, however, is largely tax policy and entitlement policy. Any lasting solution to budget deficits will have to require a major alteration in one or both of these areas. The only honest alternative is to admit that preserving current tax policy or entitlement policy is more important than deficit reduction.

Policy and Procedure

A great deal of time and effort is being expended on the annual budget, some of which is doubtless wasted. In particular, the annual congressional budget resolutions take months to formulate and pass, but their contribution to fiscal discipline is problematic. They are difficult to enforce, except in those areas where discretionary appropriations are already under pressure.[16] They cannot, as Reagan proved, force the president's hand on taxes. They cannot, except under extraordinary circumstances, force the hands of committees with jurisdiction over major entitlements.

The procedures now in place have made a complicated process even more complex and confusing and seemingly interminable. Reforms that were supposed to facilitate coordinated, comprehensive budget decision making have led to a declining balance across spending categories and between spending and revenue levels. It might be advisable, as some have suggested, to eliminate the budget committees, for example, and turn over

RESTORING POLITICS TO BUDGETING   241

their functions to the appropriations committees. It might be helpful to have clearer enforcement of congressional budget resolutions. It might even be wise to move to two-year budgeting cycles. Here again, however, these measures are essentially technical improvements in the budget process that are largely divorced from the policy issues that need to be addressed.

Policy Issues
The deficit levels projected over the next several years will not be eliminated without major policy changes, and there are numerous sources of information about various policy options. The Congressional Budget Office, for example, annually publishes an exhaustive analysis of spending and revenue options for reducing the deficit.[17] Private organizations and policy analysts also provide a steady stream of deficit-reduction plans.[18] No political consensus, however, has been formed behind any set of existing choices. This lack of agreement was amply demonstrated by the National Economic Commission's failure to provide a coherent plan for deficit reduction. Additional evidence is provided by the annual "budget summits" between Congress and the executive branch, which have had very limited success, the supposedly draconian Gramm-Rudman-Hollings alternatives notwithstanding.

The Scope of Decision Making
Nevertheless, one issue that deserves reconsideration is the relationship between budget decision making and the political process. In the past, a number of important decisions have been insulated from political control. This insulation has occurred through the indexing of certain spending programs, particularly the large, non-means-tested entitlements. In addition, major components of tax policy have now been indexed. The social security wage base, for example, rises annually through an indexing formula. Individual income tax brackets, exemptions, and standard deductions are adjusted each year to offset the effects of inflation. Removing these spending and tax policy decisions from the annual political agenda provides certainty and protection to beneficiaries and taxpayers. In a period of fiscal stress, however, another effect is to heighten conflict over what remains on the agenda. Since the scope of decision making is restricted, political conflict tends to be channeled toward discretionary policy. Programs and policies cannot compete on a reasonably equitable basis, since many automatically escape annual review.

It is unlikely that this imbalance will change until political control can be expanded to cover a greater portion of the annual budget. The difficulty has been in finding acceptable ways of accomplishing this expansion. Perhaps the most obvious target is indexing, where the financial stakes are enormous.

At this point, many of the obvious flaws and disparities in indexing formulas have been corrected. What remain are the basic and quite expensive indexing provisions for major benefit programs. As Weaver has concluded, "The only constituencies for change in indexing—at least a change that involves contraction—are the legislative and executive budget guardians." Even a " 'circle-the-wagons' strategy toward indexed programs, in which policy makers recognize that loss imposition is inevitable and unite on a policy to diffuse the resulting blame . . . has severe problems," he argues, "because disagreements about what to do with the budget problem are so intense."[19]

What makes indexing an attractive target from the perspective of budget control is its deficit-reduction potential. A one-year elimination of COLAs in non-means-tested benefit programs, for example, would produce cumulative savings projected at nearly $70 billion for fiscal years 1990–94. Simply limiting COLAs below consumer price index increases would, over the same period, produce roughly equivalent savings. Revenue policy indexing is also expensive. A one-year delay in indexing individual income tax schedules would yield projected additional revenues of more than $50 billion over the fiscal 1990–94 period. Outright repeal would roughly triple the revenue increases over the same five-year period.[20]

These deindexing options also create equity problems that cannot be disregarded. COLA reductions or delays, for example, obviously have a disproportionate impact on low-income beneficiaries. The deindexing of personal exemption and standard deduction amounts would have a similarly negative impact on low-income taxpayers, while the deindexing of bracket widths would have no effect at all on very high-income taxpayers. "The difficulty lies not in devising measures to limit the effects of indexing," observes Wildavsky, "but in doing so while (1) maintaining the objectives of the programs involved and (2) gaining the necessary political support."[21]

Correcting Budget Distortions

An additional difficulty arises from the type of budget deficit now being faced. The total deficit is the product of a large on-budget deficit and a substantial, growing social security surplus. Since the social security program is now officially off-budget, social security program changes cannot be incorporated into budget resolutions and reconciliation bills.[22]

This unique budgetary status makes it very difficult for policymakers to balance social security's needs against those of the rest of the budget. Yet that is precisely the kind of calculation that must occur if budget control is to be improved. Sooner or later, and preferably sooner, policymakers must decide whether competing needs require extending income taxation of social security benefits, or instituting a means test for certain benefits, or limiting or adjusting indexing for certain categories of beneficiaries.

The 1983 Social Security Amendments, for example, made social security (and railroad retirement) benefits taxable to higher-income households, but only a portion of the benefits (up to a maximum of one-half) was made taxable for individuals above specified income thresholds. Eliminating the thresholds and taxing 85 percent of benefits would yield projected additional revenues of nearly $100 billion for fiscal years 1990–94. This step would avoid many of the equity problems associated with COLA reductions while making the tax treatment of social security for high-income beneficiaries comparable to that for private contributory pensions.[23]

The point, however, is not that a particular deficit-reduction option is desirable but rather that political controls need to be reestablished over as broad a range of alternatives as possible. The options can be debated and analyzed endlessly. The issue for budget reform is how to force these options onto the political agenda and how to do so in a manner that promotes accountability on the part of elected officials. The public may ultimately decide that it prefers deficits to the alternative policy costs. The budget process cannot prevent such a choice, but it should make the preference as explicit as possible.

Presidential Budgeting and Incrementalism

The prescriptions of this study are modest—restore the importance of the president's budget and revive conditions for budgetary incrementalism in Congress. For the executive branch, a top-down budget process accords with institutional capabilities and with previous budgeting practices.[24] For Congress, the budget decision problems that must be resolved will take place under conditions of scarcity and complexity.[25] Incrementalism provides a way for decision making to be "carried on with the knowledge that few problems have to be 'solved' once and for all. . . . Problems are not so much solved as they are worn down by repeated attacks until they are no longer pressing or have been superseded by other problems."[26] In effect, reviving budgetary incrementalism means applying its decision-making strategies to the "automatic" portions of the budget.

The Reagan Lessons

The Reagan administration's accomplishments in the budget policy realm generally have been downplayed because of the deficit record it accumulated. In addition, Reagan's repeated complaints about the budget process and budget policy created the impression that Congress was impregnable. In fact, Reagan's budget record was remarkable. Reagan demonstrated that the president retains considerable influence over certain parts of the budget—tax policy, defense spending, and nondefense discretionary programs.

The impasse that developed between Reagan and Congress was not over appropriated spending. Their annual skirmishes over the defense budget resulted in unprecedented real spending levels for a peacetime era, even after Congress halted real growth. The cuts on the domestic side that Reagan advocated were never fully implemented, but discretionary domestic spending was cut back significantly. Reagan's first OMB director, David Stockman, has admitted that the "appropriated accounts are not really the problem." Reagan's cherished line-item veto, according to Stockman, would improve the president's "political control and discipline" over the budget but "would not accomplish much in terms of fixing the fiscal problem."[27]

The unresolved conflict between Reagan and Congress was ultimately over taxes and social insurance programs. After Reagan's initial efforts to reduce social security were rejected, the administration was effectively limited to stabilizing social insurance expenditures. The only significant expansion of the Reagan years, the short-lived catastrophic coverage under medicare, incorporated full beneficiary financing. Reagan could not scale back the social insurance system, because there was no political consensus in Congress, or in the country, to do so, and he was unwilling to take the political risk of trying to create one. In 1985, when Senate Republicans attempted to construct a deficit-reduction package which included a social security freeze with other spending cuts and a tax increase, Reagan refused to support them. The failure of this effort subsequently removed social security from the bargaining table during the remainder of Reagan's presidency.

At the same time, congressional Democrats were unable to correct the deficit problem through higher revenue levels. The tax increases that Reagan accepted in his first term only brought revenues to approximately

19 percent of GNP. The conventional wisdom during Reagan's second term was that he would eventually be forced to accept a much higher level in order to correct deficits. Instead, he held the line on taxes, and George Bush has promised to do the same.

What this policy means for future budgets may not be entirely clear, but the following appear to be reasonable surmises. The price that Bush and his Republican supporters must pay for keeping their antitax pledge will be continued, large on-budget deficits and, at best, no-real-growth defense budgets. The price that Democrats must pay for keeping their pledges on social insurance will be steadily shrinking resources to fund discretionary domestic programs. Interest outlays will continue to absorb a significant share of the budget, even if future deficits are reduced. Adding together interest, social insurance, and a basic defense commitment (which would have bipartisan support) yields a very small margin for discretionary domestic programs.

Budget Maladies

The problems that were corrected during the 1980s were neither illusory nor trivial. Taxpayers demanded, and received, the same protections against inflation that spending beneficiaries had been granted in the early 1970s. The defense cuts of the 1970s had created serious military deficiencies that had to be redressed. Each of these "corrections" had, and will continue to have, a negative impact on deficit levels.

Policymakers were unable to balance these corrections with corresponding cutbacks elsewhere. Indeed, social insurance costs mounted because of demographic factors, medical care costs, and the steadily increasing wage levels of new retirees. Discretionary domestic programs were reduced, but the cuts were comparatively small, given deficit levels.

The budget problems now being faced are not insuperable, but solutions to them are not supported by a political consensus. Moreover, it is not at all clear that the public's overriding preference is for deficit reduction. A survey conducted just before Reagan left office, for example, reported that nearly two-thirds of adults nationwide believed that he had done a "generally poor job" of dealing with the budget deficit. Even larger majorities (ranging from 70 to 86 percent), however, credited him for doing a good job with the economy, the military, U.S.-Soviet relations, and "restoring a sense of pride in the country." In addition, the last Gallup poll of Reagan's presidency reported that "President Reagan ended his term with the highest . . . approval rating of any president since Franklin Roosevelt."[28]

Reagan was succeeded by his vice president, the first such electoral succession in 150 years. He also left office with the Democratic party still firmly entrenched in the House and (since 1986) back in control of the Senate. Finding a clear public verdict on deficits or deficit solutions in the 1984, 1986, and 1988 election results is impossible. The public appears to have an abstract aversion to deficits but a more tangible, immediate dislike of deficit solutions.

It is futile to expect prospective guidance from public opinion given the nature and dimensions of the deficit problem. It is conceivable, however, that clearer accountability for deficit results would assist the public. The most that can be expected of the budget process is that policymakers will attempt to resolve the deficit problem in the absence of a public consensus and then will be willing to risk retrospective judgments of their efforts.

The President's Budget

The president's influence within the budget process remains formidable within certain parameters. Those parameters are defined by the normal appropriations and tax processes, where the president's legislative involvement and potential veto provide leverage. For discretionary spending and tax policy, the president's budget today is no less meaningful than it was in 1921, when the federal budget process was established. What an individual president does and how well he does it may vary a great deal, but the institutional capacity to compete with Congress has not declined within the regular budget process.

What has undercut the president's budget has been the steady rise of automatic spending. There has always been uncontrollable spending, whether for interest payments on the debt or for trust fund expenditures. What has changed dramatically over time has been the growing share of the budget taken up by automatic spending and the parallel expansion of indexing and other nondiscretionary impetuses to increased spending.

Restoring the significance of the president's budget, therefore, has little to do with line-item vetoes or rescission enhancements. Either of these changes would provide the president with a clear-cut institutional advantage over Congress in disputes over appropriated spending. It is difficult to justify such a change, however, given the overwhelming evidence that appropriated spending can be controlled quite effectively by the existing budget process.

The more glaring weakness of the budget process is its treatment of automatic spending. In particular, the president lacks the institutionalized means to integrate automatic spending with his overall budget program.

As a result, the president's budget is neither comprehensive nor coherent. This situation not only limits the opportunities for presidential leadership in budget control efforts but also weakens responsibility and accountability for the president and for Congress.

An appropriate and focused remedy for this deficiency in presidential budgeting would be a formal reconciliation addendum to the president's budget, which would then have to be acted upon by Congress as part of its budget process. A statutory, mandatory reconciliation would not alter Congress's discretionary powers. It would improve responsibility and accountability.

The Reconciliation Procedure. The congressional budget process currently provides for reconciliation instructions in concurrent budget resolutions prepared by the budget committees.[29] These instructions require committees to prepare proposals for raising revenues or for cutting spending on programs within their jurisdiction in order to comply with the spending and revenue totals in the budget resolution. The budget committees then compile these proposals into a reconciliation package, which is governed by special rules to guard against nongermane amendments and to protect the spending and revenue totals from being breached. In addition, there is a June 15 deadline for final passage of a reconciliation bill, although this deadline has not been met in recent years. However, since the Gramm-Rudman-Hollings act makes reconciliation legislation a mandatory enforcement instrument for each year's budget resolution, a reconciliation bill is, in effect, "must-pass" legislation.

Reconciliation was included in the 1974 budget act but was not fashioned into an effective weapon until considerably later. In 1980 Congress employed reconciliation to implement modest spending cuts based upon the first budget resolution for fiscal 1981. The following year, the Reagan administration, under David Stockman's direction, spearheaded a reconciliation effort which affected more than 200 programs, including entitlements, and reduced fiscal 1982 outlays by more than $35 billion.[30]

The magnitude and origin of the 1981 reconciliation process generated a congressional backlash. For example, the chairman of the House Rules Committee, Richard M. Bolling, denounced the 1981 reconciliation as the "most brutal and blunt instrument used by a president in an attempt to control the budget process since Nixon used impoundment." According to Bolling, one of the principal architects of the 1974 Budget Act, the Reagan administration was guilty of the "most excessive use of presidential power and license."[31]

When the budget committees had initiated a much less sweeping reconciliation bill in 1980, Bolling had helped to engineer its use in the spring budget resolution. Despite grumblings from the authorizing and appropriations committees about threats to their autonomy, there was widespread support for the improved flexibility and effectiveness that reconciliation added to the congressional budget process.[32] The response in 1981 was very different, at least among the congressional Democratic leadership, which was outraged that the White House had taken advantage of the very same reconciliation strategy.

Since 1981, reconciliation has been used repeatedly, but under firm congressional control. While there have been problems with extraneous provisions in reconciliation bills, and with deadlines and enforcement as well, leading budget policy experts consider reconciliation to be a powerful tool with which a disciplined majority can enforce a budget program.[33] The specific procedural advantage of reconciliation is that it allows spending not controlled by the regular appropriations process to be reduced, while avoiding the one-bill-at-a-time alternative that would in most instances be politically infeasible.

Reconciliation Limitations. In order for reconciliation to be fully integrated into the budget process, substantive and institutional limitations need to be removed. The most important substantive constraint under current law is the exemption of the off-budget social security trust funds from the reconciliation process. Reconciliation bills cannot make changes in the Old-Age and Survivors Insurance and Disability Insurance trust funds.[34] Eliminating these exemptions is a prerequisite for the review of automatic spending that must be part of any serious budget-control effort.

The institutional weakness of the current reconciliation process is the peripheral role assigned to the president. Although the president must sign the final version of any reconciliation legislation, his participation in its formulation is entirely discretionary. The president is under no obligation to submit a reconciliation proposal as part of his annual budget. Congress is under no obligation to act on one if it is submitted.

This disjunction between the regular budget of appropriated spending and extrabudget automatic spending undermines one of the basic objectives of presidential budgeting. The executive budget was adopted in 1921 in order to promote fiscal responsibility and accountability: "The annual [budget] program would be prepared by the administration and submitted to the legislature. The administration would be responsible for proposals submitted, and Congress would be responsible for considering and acting on each proposal made."[35]

As matters now stand, however, the president's budget is no longer the "initiator and driving force in the budgetary process" but rather a "tentative 'opening shot.' "[36] On appropriations and tax policy, the president's recommendations provide a clear-cut standard for measuring subsequent congressional action. On automatic spending, the president can avoid any initiative at all. Even when an administration participates in reconciliation negotiations with Congress, it can pick and choose the political issues on which it will fight, while avoiding broader leadership responsibilities for the entire package. The onus can instead be shifted to Congress, which is institutionally incapable of providing sustained policy leadership.

Making congressional action on a president's reconciliation proposal mandatory, while reserving Congress's authority to amend or to revise that proposal, would establish an automatic spending analogue to the regular appropriations process. In both instances, the president would initiate. In both instances, Congress would review and react. Responsibilities would be reasonably clear-cut. Accountability for results would be tied to objective comparisons of presidential and congressional positions.

This procedural reform would eliminate one presidential option—eschewing responsibility for preparing a comprehensive budget. It would also eliminate a congressional option—ignoring a president's reconciliation proposal. By requiring the president and Congress to act, points of agreement and disagreement would be clarified. It is possible that both sides might thereby be encouraged to negotiate full-scale budget agreements, as some have suggested, but the mandatory reconciliation procedure need not necessarily improve the prospects for agreement. It can simply establish clearer accountability for continued disagreement and for the policy results stemming from that disagreement.

Within Congress, jurisdiction over reconciliation rests with the budget committees, and there would be no need to alter this arrangement for presidential reconciliation proposals. The current congressional budget process, in sum, can easily accommodate mandatory presidential reconciliation. A routinized reconciliation procedure would simply extend to authorization entitlements many of the same top-down pressures already applied to discretionary authorizations and appropriations.

Incrementalism and Congressional Budgeting

Budgetary incrementalism is a theory about how decisions are made (and should be made). Its demise is usually attributed to political and economic changes that have made coordinated, comprehensive fiscal management imperative, thereby shifting Congress to an unwieldy top-down budget process. Its demise surely reflects as well the breakdown of consensus on budget policy goals and priorities. If the policy histories presented in this study are accurate, however, there have always been top-down pressures in the budget process, usually imposed by the president and, until the 1970s, generally adhered to through informal coordination within Congress.

The 1974 budget act has substituted formal coordination for informal coordination, and it has encouraged Congress to develop alternatives to presidential budgets. It has not, however, entirely transformed congressional decision making. The authorization and appropriations process has proved to be remarkably flexible and adaptable. It has produced fairly strong spending control. It has accommodated priorities reversals between defense and discretionary domestic spending. It has generally conformed to the incrementalist strategy of marginal change and continuing adjustment. By returning to the same policy choices year after year, Congress has avoided the problem of defining and maintaining a long-term, comprehensive ordering of preferences.

By contrast, automatic and indexed policy, whether on the spending or revenue side of the budget, creates obstacles to political control and marginal adjustment. Constituencies of beneficiaries and taxpayers pose an obvious threat to policymakers who propose cutting back on existing protections. Policymakers also have the attractive option of not acting at all, thereby leaving protections in place and running no political risk. If policymakers had to act in order to maintain real-level benefits or to maintain real-level tax liabilities, the gross imbalance between programs would moderate. The large transfer programs, such as social security, no doubt would continue to have a political advantage over most discretionary programs, but policymakers would have the option of making marginal, if unequal, shifts in both types of programs.

With income taxes, the same type of balancing between full or partial inflation adjustments could be considered without raising the specter of a tax increase. Fiscal constraints therefore could be distributed across a broader range of spending and tax policies without enormous political risks. What indexing produces, by comparison, is a procedural complement to an already formidable political advantage attached to certain policies. There is, in sum, a procedural and political block to incrementalist decision-making strategies, since some of the most important fiscal options are routinely excluded from the political agenda. These options are a de facto preference ordering, and they have such an enormous impact on the budget that they require a broad consensus to be formed as a precondition for review.

The demise of incrementalism, then, has been only partial, but this demise applies to the largest and fastest-growing portions of the budget. These are also the parts of the budget that have been insulated from politics. The optimistic notions that political insulation would improve budget control and reduce conflict have not been validated. The rise of automatic spending instead has produced, or at any rate contributed to, a prolonged period of political dissensus and budgetary warfare.

If the essence of budgeting involves choices between competing programs, certain choices cannot be permanently foreclosed. Restoring politics to budgeting depends upon a broader range of policy options in the annual budget process. A comprehensive presidential budget would reintroduce this broader range of options and, in doing so, revive the conditions for incrementalist strategies on a meaningful scale.

Assuming that Congress finally confronts automatic spending growth or automatic revenue limits, radical policy changes would be highly unlikely. Change, if it occurs at all, is going to be remedial, limited, and conditioned by existing policy. The policy issues at stake are complex, and they are being raised because of the scarcity of resources. Their resolution depends upon the blending of policy expertise with fiscal constraints, and this amalgamation is likely to be an ongoing process of adjustment and response. As Rudolph Penner, former director of the Congressional Budget Office, has stated, "When we charge some committees with setting the aggregates and others with translating them into specific programs, conflicts are bound to arise. . . . They will be less severe if policy changes are slow and marginal. That is, if one year's aggregate goals lead to only slight imperfections in the mix of micropolicies, we can easily make a correction the next year."[37]

The preservation of automatic spending growth and corresponding revenue limits, on the other hand, will continue to subvert budgetary control. In effect, the budget process cannot substitute for institutional responsibility, nor can institutional responsibility be divorced from political accountability. If, in fact, the public wants the certainty that automatic government provides, it also must accept the corollary of unbalanced and distorted budgets.

Opportunity and Results

Presidential reconciliation is not a substitute for political consensus. The imbalances that exist within and between the spending and revenue sides of the budget do not have painless solutions, and it is not helpful to insist that the budget process can magically solve the problems. At the same time, the budget process can facilitate the consideration of possible solutions by reinvigorating the separation of powers. An annual presidential reconciliation measure could force major policy options onto the political agenda. With Congress required to act on the president's proposals, important policy differences between the two branches would be clarified. Mandatory reconciliation would allow the public to understand, perhaps more clearly than at present, the policy costs of deficit reduction and to judge the differences between the two branches.

Presidential leadership, as the policy histories in this study demonstrate, is clearly the essential first step in reshaping and controlling budgets. Budget control also requires many additional steps, involving Congress and the public, over an extended period of time. The most that can be done, perhaps the best as well, is to make the links between these steps as politically honest and direct as possible. Politics and budgets are inseparable. A budget process which proceeds accordingly would provide the admixture of responsibility and accountability that lays the basis for budget control.

NOTES

INDEX

Notes

Chapter One

1. Robert Kilpatrick, chairman of the CIGNA Corporation and head of a task force on the federal budget for the Business Roundtable, quoted in *Congressional Quarterly Weekly Report* 46 (Feb. 20, 1988): 327.

2. Ibid.

3. For FY 1988, total interest on debt held by the public was $169.8 billion, of which $27.3 billion was paid to foreign holders. Twenty years earlier, the corresponding figures were $12.6 billion and $0.7 billion. The shift upward in the proportion of foreign-held debt began during the 1970s. By the early 1980s up to 20 percent of interest on debt held by the public was for foreign-held debt, with a decline to current levels starting in fiscal 1983 (*Special Analyses, Budget of the United States Government, Fiscal Year 1990* [Washington, D.C.: GPO, 1989], p. E-19).

4. These uncertainties are linked. See, for example, Robert Eisner, *How Real Is the Federal Deficit* (New York: Free Press, 1986); Brian Horrigan and Aris Protopapadakis, "Federal Deficits: A Faulty Gauge of Government's Impact on the Economy," *Business Review, Federal Reserve Bank of Philadelphia* (March/April 1982): 3–15.

5. Eisner, *How Real Is the Federal Deficit*, p. 176.

6. This does not mean that budgeting was unimportant or even uninteresting, but rather that budgeting was not treated as commensurate with governing. Howard E. Shuman calls the Budget of the United States "the country's number one political document. Presidential elections are fought over it. Congressional sessions are devoted to it. More than any other time, the 1980s and well into the 1990s are destined to be the era of the budget" (*Politics and the Budget*, 2d ed. [Englewood Cliffs, N.J.: Prentice Hall, 1988], p. 6).

7. Louis Fisher, *The Politics of Shared Power*, 2d ed. (Washington, D.C.: Congressional Quarterly, 1987), p. 6.

8. The classic study of spending policy during this period is Richard F. Fenno, Jr., *The Power of the Purse: Appropriations Politics in Congress* (Boston: Little, Brown, 1966). As described by Fenno, the decision patterns of the two appropriations committees were broadly similar: "The Senate Committee, like the House group, keeps most agency appropriations below the budget estimates. At the same time, it grants most agencies an increase over their previous year's

appropriation. It would seem that the two committees meet conflicting expectations within their chambers with a similar mixture of decisions. Economy expectations are met by keeping appropriations below estimates; program expectations
are met by allowing appropriations increases" (p. 574).

9. See Catherine E. Rudder, "Tax Policy: Structure and Choice," in *Making
Economic Policy in Congress*, ed. A. Schick (Washington, D.C.: American Enterprise Institute, 1983), pp. 196–220.

10. Fisher, *The Politics of Shared Power*, p. 215.

11. See, for example, James M. Lindsay, "Congress and Defense Policy:
1961–1986," *Armed Forces and Society* 13 (Spring 1987): 371–401.

12. The 1974 Budget Act initially required passage of two concurrent budget resolutions (spring and fall) in advance of the fiscal year, with revised resolutions possible as well. Subsequent amendments have limited the required resolutions to one per fiscal year, with an April 15 deadline for Congress to complete
action. Budget resolutions now include "appropriate levels" for the upcoming
fiscal year and planning levels for the ensuing two fiscal years for (1) total budget
authority, outlays, direct loan obligations, and primary loan guarantee commitments; (2) total revenues; (3) surplus or deficit; (4) budget authority, outlay, and
credit allocations by functional category; and (5) public debt. The major revisions
in the congressional budget process since 1974 have been the result of the two
Gramm-Rudman-Hollings bills—the Balanced Budget and Emergency Deficit
Control Act of 1985 and the Balanced Budget and Emergency Deficit Control
Reaffirmation Act of 1987.

13. Quoted in Fisher, *The Politics of Shared Power*, p. 206. Wright's re-
marks, made while he was majority leader, came during debate on a 1983 appropriations bill.

14. Aaron Wildavsky, *The New Politics of the Budgetary Process* (Glen-
view, Ill.: Scott, Foresman, 1988), p. 166.

15. James D. Savage, *Balanced Budgets and American Politics* (Ithaca,
N.Y.: Cornell University Press, 1988), p. 1.

16. *Fiscal Year 1982 Budget Revisions* (Washington, D.C.: GPO, 1981),
pp. M-1, 11.

17. Savage, *Balanced Budgets and American Politics*, p. 190.

18. The 1985 version of Gramm-Rudman-Hollings made the report of the
comptroller general (head of the General Accounting Office) the sole basis for any
sequestration order, or spending cut, issued by the president. A three-judge federal
panel in Washington, D.C., issued a ruling in February 1986 holding the sequestration procedure unconstitutional because of the comptroller general's role. The
court found the comptroller general to be an agent of Congress, not an executive
officer; hence, the procedure violated the constitutional separation of powers. Five
months later, the Supreme Court agreed: "By placing responsibility for the execu-
tion [of the GRH law] in the hands of an officer who is subject to removal only by
itself, Congress in effect has retained control over the executive function. The
Constitution does not admit such intrusion" (*Bowsher v. Synar*, 92 L Ed. 2d 583
[1986]).

19. In addition to stretching out the deficit-elimination schedule through FY 1993, the 1987 GRH revision limited the amount of permissible automatic cuts in fiscal years 1988 and 1989, regardless of the projected deficit. The potential cuts necessary to meet fiscal 1990–93 deficit ceilings were therefore significantly increased.

20. For descriptions of the current services and Gramm-Rudman-Hollings baselines, see *Special Analyses, Budget of the United States Government, Fiscal Year 1990*, pp. A-1–A-5; A-43–A-49. A third widely used baseline has been developed by the Congressional Budget Office. It is similar, but not identical, to the GRH budget baseline. The confusion stems in "scoring" cuts off baselines. The congressional budget resolution for FY 1988, for example, projected a spending increase of "$53 billion over the estimated total of $1.01 trillion. The current services baseline, however, assumes that spending will rise $61 billion to keep pace with inflation. As a result, the 1988 total was tabulated . . . as a cut of $8 billion" (Lawrence J. Haas, "Budget Focus," *National Journal* 19 [Aug. 15, 1987]: 2124).

21. "Payments for individuals" includes income transfers and in-kind benefits for individuals or families. It is an alternative measure used to aggregate various social welfare program spending. From fiscal 1981 to fiscal 1989 payments for individuals rose from less than $325 billion to over $530 billion. In constant dollars, this was an increase of 20 percent. Between 1970 and 1980 real spending for payments for individuals programs more than doubled.

22. The Social Security Amendments of 1983 had scheduled social security for off-budget status in FY 1993. The Gramm-Rudman-Hollings Act of 1985 moved this schedule up to FY 1987, at the same time terminating the off-budget status for all other programs. The Old-Age and Survivors Insurance trust fund and the Disability Insurance trust fund are classified as off-budget under function 650. The outlays and receipts of the trust funds are included in the unified budget deficit calculations under the act, but social security (and a number of other programs) is exempt from any automatic cuts, or sequestration procedure, that might be necessary to meet statutory deficit ceilings.

23. The medicare system uses an index of office expenses and earnings (MEI) as part of the fee schedule for a physician's reimbursement; hospital payments are governed by a prospective payment system (PPS) tied to hospital cost inflation. Despite these and a series of changes over the years designed to control costs, medicare spending has been one of the fastest-growing parts of the budget.

24. Indexing was first introduced in the 1981 Economic Recovery Tax Act and scheduled to take effect in 1985. The Tax Reform Act of 1986 changed marginal rate brackets, standard deductions, and personal exemptions, and a new indexing schedule was included. Income brackets and standard deductions are to be adjusted annually beginning in 1989. The personal exemption will be adjusted annually beginning in 1990.

25. Congressional Budget Office, *Reducing the Deficit: Spending and Revenue Options* (Washington, D.C.: GPO, 1989), p. 313.

26. For an insightful discussion of constitutional budget limitations, see

Aaron Wildavsky, *How to Limit Government Spending* (Berkeley: University of California Press, 1980).

27. See Louis Fisher and Neal Devins, "How Successfully Can the States' Item Veto Be Transferred to the President?" *Georgetown Law Journal* 75 (Oct. 1986): 159–97; David C. Nice, "The Item Veto and Expenditure Restraint," *Journal of Politics* 50 (May 1988): 487–99.

28. See Rudolph G. Penner and Alan J. Abramson, *Broken Purse Strings: Congressional Budgeting, 1974–1988* (Washington, D.C.: Urban Institute, 1989).

29. Dennis S. Ippolito, *Congressional Spending* (Ithaca, N.Y.: Cornell University Press, 1981), pp. 40–47.

30. Allen Schick, *Congress and Money* (Washington, D.C.: Urban Institute, 1980), pp. 72–74.

31. Quoted in Ippolito, *Congressional Spending*, p. 1.

32. Senate Committee on Rules and Administration, *Report No. 93-688, Congressional Budget Act of 1974* (Washington, D.C.: GPO, 1974), p. 4.

33. Ippolito, *Congressional Spending*, pp. 60–74.

34. Aaron Wildavsky, *The Politics of the Budgetary Process*, 3d ed. (Boston: Little, Brown, 1979), p. 62.

35. Wildavsky, *The New Politics of the Budgetary Process*, p. 424.

36. A recent quantitative study of post–World War II budget policy emphasizes this point: "The differences between Democratic and Republican budgetary policies or between administrations generally appear modest by comparison with the differences between executive and congressional policies during the postwar period. Indeed, these results suggest that separating the analysis of executive budgetary behavior from that of Congress is extremely important" (Mark S. Kamlet and David C. Mowery, "Influences on Executive and Congressional Budgetary Priorities, 1955–1981," *American Political Science Review* 81 [March 1987]: 170).

37. The differentials by policy area appear to be particularly relevant in assessing the Reagan presidency's impact on the budget (Mark S. Kamlet, David C. Mowery, and Tsai-Tsu Su, "Upsetting National Priorities? The Reagan Administration's Budgetary Strategy," ibid. 82 [Dec. 1988]: 1293–1307).

38. Wildavsky, *The New Politics of the Budgetary Process*, p. 411.

Chapter Two
1. Susan B. Hansen, *The Politics of Taxation* (New York: Praeger, 1983), p. 262.

2. See, for example, John F. Witte, *The Politics and Development of the Federal Income Tax* (Madison: University of Wisconsin Press, 1985), pp. 131–54. As Witte emphasizes, "The most important common factor in the tax policies of the Truman and Eisenhower administrations was the desire to keep deficits down and . . . control inflation. . . . The period was characterized by restraint in tax cutting" (p. 153).

3. For an insightful discussion of the Ways and Means Committee's fall from grace and the attendant effects, see Catherine E. Rudder, "Fiscal Responsibility, Fairness, and the Revenue Committees," in *Congress Reconsidered*, 4th ed., ed. L. C. Dodd and B. I. Oppenheimer (Washington, D.C.: Congressional Quarterly, 1989), pp. 225–30.

4. Ibid., p. 228.

5. Carolyn Webber and Aaron Wildavsky, *A History of Taxation and Expenditure in the Western World* (New York: Simon and Schuster, 1986), p. 530.

6. Rudder, "Fiscal Responsibility," pp. 229–30.

7. See Hansen, *The Politics of Taxation*, pp. 212–46.

8. These revenues were supplemented by sales of public lands during the pre–Civil War period. See U.S. Bureau of the Census, *Historical Statistics of the United States, Colonial Times to 1970*, pt. 2 (Washington, D.C.: GPO, 1975), p. 1106.

9. Interest costs remained the largest single outlay category until the early 1880s. By fiscal 1885 interest on the public debt had declined to less than one-fifth of total outlays (ibid., p. 1114).

10. The Civil War income taxes were terminated in 1872. An income tax was also adopted in 1894, as part of a tariff reform bill, but was then held unconstitutional by the Supreme Court the following year in *Pollock v. Farmer's Loan and Trust Company*, 157 U.S. 429 (1895).

11. A normal tax of 1 percent was levied on incomes between $20,000 and $25,000. Surcharges were then added for higher income categories, with a 6 percent maximum for incomes above $500,000. These rates and brackets remained in effect from 1913 to 1915.

12. The capital stock tax, which was equivalent to a national property tax on corporations, was finally terminated after World War II. The excess profits tax was used during the two world wars and the Korean War. It raised substantially more revenue than the regular corporate tax during World War I and II, but not during the Korean War.

13. This figure includes the corporate excess profits tax (*Historical Statistics*, pt. 2, pp. 1109–10).

14. Ibid., pp. 1095, 1111–12.

15. Witte, *Income Tax*, p. 88.

16. Quoted, ibid., p. 89.

17. Quoted in Lewis H. Kimmel, *Federal Budget and Fiscal Policy, 1789–1958* (Washington, D.C.: Brookings Institution, 1959), p. 182.

18. This phrase was contained in a special message transmitted to Congress on June 19, 1935, which offered a number of recommended tax law changes to encourage "a wider distribution of wealth" (*Congressional Record* 79 [June 19, 1935]: 9657).

19. Congressional Budget Office, *Revising the Individual Income Tax* (Washington, D.C., July 1983), p. 8.

20. Congressional Budget Office, *Revising the Corporate Income Tax* (Washington, D.C., May 1985), p. 28.

21. Congressional Budget Office, *Revising the Individual Income Tax*, p. 8.

22. Witte, *Income Tax*, p. 128.

23. *Historical Statistics*, pt. 2, p. 1091.

24. *Congressional Record* 93 (June 16, 1947): 7074.

25. The proposal was contained in Truman's 1948 State of the Union address (ibid. 94 [Jan. 7, 1948]: 36).

26. Congressional Quarterly, *Guide to U.S. Elections*, 2d ed. (Washington, D.C., 1985), p. 108.

27. *Budget of the United States Government, Fiscal Year 1961* (Washington, D.C.: GPO, 1960), p. M8.

28. Congressional Budget Office, *Revising the Individual Income Tax*, p. 9.

29. Congressional Quarterly, *Congress and the Nation, 1945–1964* (Washington, D.C., 1965), p. 417.

30. The text of Eisenhower's radio address is printed in the *Congressional Record* 100 (March 16, 1954): 3298–99.

31. Ibid. 100 (March 18, 1954): 3555–56.

32. *Budget of the United States Government, Fiscal Year 1960* (Washington, D.C.: GPO, 1959), p. M6.

33. *Budget of the United States Government, Fiscal Year 1964* (Washington, D.C.: GPO, 1963), pp. 10–11.

34. The administrative budget deficits totaled $20.7 billion, while the consolidated cash estimates (including trust funds) totaled $18.6 billion in 1963–64 deficits (ibid., p. 9).

35. Ibid., pp. 10, 9.

36. *Congress and the Nation, 1945–1964*, p. 438.

37. A third initiative was not successful. Kennedy requested in 1962 standby authority to lower temporarily income tax rates by 5 percent (subject to congressional veto), along with parallel authority to institute up to $2 billion in public works spending. Johnson did not request standby authority but did recommend background tax studies and other steps designed to speed up tax actions. Congress did not respond favorably to these requests. It is interesting that the standby authority and related proposals were a response to what was viewed as the inordinate delay in congressional action on tax law changes. The criticism in the 1975–85 period was that Congress acted too often and too hastily in changing tax law.

38. See, for example, Herbert Stein, *Presidential Economics* (New York: Simon and Schuster, 1984), pp. 101–13.

39. *Fiscal Year 1982 Budget Revisions*, p. 11. A number of economists have also gone to great pains to distinguish the economic conditions in effect at the time

of the Kennedy tax cuts from those at the outset of Reagan's administration. If the Kennedy argument about "the checkrein of taxes" has validity, however, it is clear that tax levels for individuals were much more constraining at the outset of Reagan's term. Individual income taxes were 12 percent of personal income in fiscal 1981 and climbing, compared to 10.4 percent in 1960.

40. *Budget of the United States Government, Fiscal Year 1966* (Washington, D.C.: GPO, 1965), pp. 5, 10.

41. Congressional Quarterly, *Congress and the Nation, 1965–1968* (Washington, D.C., 1969), p. 170.

42. Ibid., pp. 170, 169.

43. Congressional Budget Office, *Revising the Individual Income Tax*, p. 9.

44. Eugene Steuerle and Michael Hartzmark, "Individual Income Taxation, 1947–1979," *National Tax Journal* 34 (June 1981): 147.

45. Congressional Budget Office, *Revising the Individual Income Tax*, p. 14.

46. Ibid., pp. 3, 9.

47. See Statement of Alice M. Rivlin, Director, Congressional Budget Office, Senate Committee on the Budget, *Hearing: Tax Expenditure Limitation and Control Act of 1981* (Washington, D.C.: GPO, 1982), pp. 30–40.

48. *Weekly Compilation of Presidential Documents* 6 (Jan. 5, 1970): 7.

49. This figure does not include the effect of a once-only $100,000 capital gains exemption for home sales by taxpayers over age fifty-five.

50. Above the $10,000 level, the estimated average reductions ranged from approximately 5 to 7 percent.

51. *Congressional Quarterly Weekly Report* 36 (Oct. 21, 1978): 3035.

52. See Joseph M. Pechman, *Who Paid the Taxes, 1966–1985* (Washington, D.C.: Brookings Institution, 1985), pp. 52–58.

53. Witte, *Income Tax*, p. 315.

54. Rivlin, "Statement," p. 32.

55. Witte, *Income Tax*, p. 306.

56. *Budget of the United States Government, Fiscal Year 1981* (Washington, D.C.: GPO, 1980), pp. 612, 614. Under pressure from Democratic leaders in Congress, Carter quickly revised his budget to show an election-year surplus, primarily through manipulating outlay figures, since the initial receipt increase was already exceptionally high.

57. Ibid., p. 61.

Chapter Three
1. Webber and Wildavsky, *A History of Taxation and Expenditure in the Western World*, p. 531.

2. Witte, *Income Tax*, pp. 235, 369, 368, 22.

3. Hansen, *The Politics of Taxation*, p. 255.

4. See Alan S. Murray and Jeffrey H. Birnbaum, "Lawmakers, Lobbyists, and the Unlikely Triumph of Tax Reform," *Congress and the Presidency* 15 (Autumn 1988): 186.

5. Ibid.

6. James Tobin and Murray Weidenbaum, *Two Revolutions in Economic Policy: The First Economic Reports of Presidents Kennedy and Reagan* (Cambridge: Massachusetts Institute of Technology Press, 1988), pp. 450, 397, 420.

7. *Weekly Compilation of Presidential Documents* 17 (Feb. 23, 1981): 135.

8. *Congressional Quarterly Weekly Report* 39 (Aug. 1, 1981): 1374.

9. According to the president, "Our bill is, in short, the first real tax cut for everyone in almost 20 years" (*Weekly Compilation of Presidential Documents* 17 [Aug. 3, 1981]: 817).

10. *Fiscal Year 1982 Budget Revisions*, p. 15.

11. See Joint Committee on Taxation, *General Explanation of the Economic Recovery Tax Act of 1981* (Washington, D.C.: GPO, 1981), pp. 379–81.

12. House Speaker O'Neill was the final speaker before the vote was taken on the administration-supported substitute to the Ways and Means bill. O'Neill warned that "if the President has his way this could be a big day for the aristocracy of the world." The crucial difference between the two tax bills, O'Neill stated, was "the targeting of tax relief to middle-income Americans" (*Congressional Record* 127 [July 29, 1981]: H5327-28). After losing the vote on the 1981 tax bill, the House Democratic leadership repeatedly sought to redistribute the across-the-board cuts by eliminating or capping the cuts for upper-income taxpayers. Both the "fairness" rhetoric and the proposal for redistributed individual tax cuts were included in the 1984 Democratic party platform.

13. See Joint Economic Committee, *Hearing: Fairness and the Reagan Tax Cuts* (Washington, D.C.: GPO, June 12, 1984).

14. See James Gwartney and Richard Stroup, "Tax Cuts: Who Shoulders the Burden," *Economic Review: Federal Reserve Bank of Atlanta* 67 (March 1982): 19–27.

15. For the median taxpayer ($17,000–$19,000 for 1982 and 1983), the income tax as a percentage of adjusted gross income fell from 12.1 percent in 1981 to 11.1 percent in 1982 and to 10.1 percent in 1983(*Internal Revenue Service Statistics of Income Bulletin* 5 [Summer 1985]: 96–97).

16. *Budget of the United States Government, Fiscal Year 1984* (Washington, D.C.: GPO, 1983), p. 4-19.

17. *Weekly Compilation of Presidential Documents* 17 (Sept. 28, 1981): 1027.

18. *Congressional Quarterly Weekly Report* 40 (May 8, 1982): 1037.

19. *Weekly Compilation of Presidential Documents* 18 (Feb. 1, 1982): 78, 79.

20. *Budget of the United States Government, Fiscal Year 1983* (Washington, D.C.: GPO, 1982), p. M19.

21. Senate Committee on Finance, *Report No. 97-494*, vol. 1, *Tax Equity and Fiscal Responsibility Act of 1982* (Washington, D.C.: GPO, July 12, 1982), pp. 100–105; *Report No. 97-530, Tax Equity and Fiscal Responsibility Act of 1982* (Washington, D.C.: GPO, Aug. 17, 1982), pp. 690–96.

22. The increase for fiscal years 1984–87 averaged only about $6 billion annually. The fiscal 1988 estimate jumped to over $19 billion, and the revenue increase for the following year was projected at $25.6 billion (Congressional Budget Office, *Baseline Budget Projections for Fiscal Years 1985–1989* [Washington, D.C., 1984], p. 36).

23. *Budget of the United States Government, Fiscal Year 1986* (Washington, D.C.: GPO, 1985), p. 4-4.

24. Joint Committee on Taxation, *General Explanation of the Revenue Provisions of the Deficit Reduction Act of 1984* (Washington, D.C.: GPO, 1984), p. 1257. Estimated revenue gains for fiscal years 1988 and 1989 exceeded the 1984–87 totals.

25. These increases totaled an estimated $13.1 billion for fiscal years 1984–87, which was almost one-fourth of DEFRA's total tax increases for the period. DEFRA also contained over $5 billion in revenue cuts from a variety of tax law changes.

26. Congressional Budget Office, *An Analysis of the President's Budgetary Proposals for Fiscal Year 1985* (Washington, D.C., Feb. 1984), pp. 1–2.

27. *Congressional Quarterly Almanac, 1984* (Washington, D.C.: Congressional Quarterly, 1985), pp. 70-B, 78-B.

28. Ibid., p. 42-B.

29. *Budget of the United States Government, Fiscal Year 1989* (Washington, D.C.: GPO, 1988), p. 3a-4. The "revenue-neutral" requirement did not apply to a specific year but rather to five-year budget projections, which meant that revenue losses and gains could fluctuate from year-to-year but no net change would occur over five years. The revenue-neutral provision also did not apply to the different sources of revenues (individual versus corporate income taxes) or, of course, to individual taxpayers.

30. *Weekly Compilation of Presidential Documents* 17 (Feb. 18, 1981): 135.

31. The standby tax consisted of a surcharge equal to 1 percent of taxable income on individuals and corporations plus a $5 dollar per barrel excise tax on domestically purchased and imported oil. It was proposed for thirty-six months, beginning with fiscal year 1986, and was contingent upon economic conditions as well as congressional approval of domestic program spending cuts proposed by the administration. The tax increase was specifically limited to 1 percent or less of GNP.

32. *Weekly Compilation of Presidential Documents* 20 (Jan. 25, 1984): 96.

33. See Henry J. Aaron and Harvey Galper, *Assessing Tax Reform* (Washington, D.C.: Brookings Institution, 1985), p. 65.

34. *Budget of the United States Government, Fiscal Year 1986*, p. 4-13.

35. By 1990 it was estimated that Treasury II would increase corporate taxes by 23 percent and reduce individual taxes by 5 percent compared to prior law. The Treasury I estimates were plus 24 percent for corporations and minus 8.5 percent for individuals.

36. The procedural basis for enforcing the rule on the Senate floor was the requirement imposed by the 1974 Budget Act that a budget resolution be adopted before floor consideration of measures increasing and decreasing revenues for the fiscal year governed by the resolution. The fiscal 1987 budget resolution was in conference while the tax bill was on the floor. A majority vote of the Senate was therefore required to waive a point of order objection against any amendment that did not balance revenue increases and decreases.

37. *Congressional Record* 132 (Sept. 27, 1986): S13963.

38. The top bracket rate for unearned income never dropped below 70 percent during this period. Earned income was subject to a lower maximum marginal rate in 1971 (60 percent) and from 1972 to 1981 (50 percent).

39. There is also a 33 percent bracket for high-income taxpayers, which phases out both the 15 percent bracket and personal exemptions. For married persons with no dependents filing joint returns, the 1988 phaseout range was between $71,900 and $171,090 of taxable income. In effect, high-income taxpayers pay a 28 percent rate on all taxable income. In addition, their taxable income is not reduced by any personal exemptions. There is no surcharge above the upper-income level, since the phase-out is complete. Beginning in 1989 rate brackets, income breakpoints, and the threshold for phasing out the personal exemptions and 15 percent bracket will be adjusted annually for inflation. Annual adjustments in the standard deduction will begin in 1989, while the personal exemption adjustment will begin in 1990.

40. For a married couple filing a joint return with no dependents and a taxable income of $200,000 in 1988, the calculation would be as follows:

		Tax owed
I.	$29,750 @ 15 percent	$ 4,462.50
II.	$29,750–$71,900 @ 28 percent	11,802.00
III.	$71,900–$149,250 @ 33 percent (phase-out of 15 percent bracket saving)	25,525.50
IV.	$149,250–$171,090 @ 33 percent (phase-out of personal exemptions)	7,207.20
V.	$171,090–$200,000 @ 28 percent	8,094.80
	Total	$57,092.00

This calculation equals a flat tax of 28 percent on all taxable income ($56,000) plus an addition to taxable income of the value of personal exemptions ($1,950 per exemption × 2 exemptions = $3,900). A tax of 28 percent on the value of personal exemptions yields $1,092, which brings the total tax to $57,092.

41. *Congressional Quarterly Almanac, 1986* (Washington, D.C.: Congressional Quarterly, 1987), p. 524.

42. Congressional Budget Office, *The Effects of Tax Reform on Tax Expenditures* (Washington, D.C., 1988), pp. 12–13.

43. *Budget of the United States Government, Fiscal Year 1988* (Washington, D.C.: GPO, 1987), p. 4-15.

Chapter Four

1. A recent study by Mark S. Kamlet and David C. Mowery, for example, concluded that "executive branch budgets have been heavily influenced by top-down pressures and policy targets during much of the postwar period" ("Influences on Executive and Congressional Budgetary Priorities, 1955–1981," p. 169).

2. Wildavsky, for example, used the "huge mass and magnitude of items encountered in . . . defense" as an example of the impossibility of comprehensive, coordinated budget decision making (*The Politics of the Budgetary Process*, 3d ed., pp. 146–56). It is also noteworthy that Wildavsky's seminal study identified nothing in the size or importance of the defense budget that challenged the characteristic mode of congressional decision making.

3. See Lindsay, "Congress and Defense Policy: 1961–1986."

4. The classic pre-Vietnam distinction between the president's advantages in defense and foreign policy-making and his comparative limitations in domestic politics is found in Aaron Wildavsky, "The Two Presidencies," *Trans-Action* 4 (Dec. 1966): 7–14. Wildavsky notes that "the congressional appropriations power is potentially a significant resource, but circumstances since the end of World War II have tended to reduce its effectiveness. . . . While Congress makes its traditional small cuts in the military budget, Presidents have mostly found themselves warding off congressional attempts to increase specific items still further."

5. See James MacGregor Burns, *Roosevelt: The Lion and the Fox* (New York: Harcourt, Brace & World, 1956), pp. 400–404.

6. This difficulty has been traced, at least in part, to the lingering effects of the Nye Committee. In 1934 Senator Gerald P. Nye, along with some of the leading proponents of American isolationism, launched an investigation of the munitions industry during World War I. The dramatic charges of war profiteering and other evils that were publicized during the hearings led directly to the passing of a mandatory arms embargo. There was also a long-term boost to isolationist sentiments in Congress and the general public.

7. Burns suggests that Roosevelt's signing of the initial arms embargo, for example, was a clear trade-off: "[The embargo] legislation passed both chambers by almost unanimous votes. Roosevelt dared not stand against the tide; he had urgent domestic bills to get through, and the isolationists were threatening to filibuster" (ibid., p. 255).

8. *Congressional Record* 85 (Jan. 4, 1939): 74, 119.

9. *Historical Statistics*, pt. 2, p. 1141. The wartime peak of 12.1 million was reached in 1945.

10. Gordon A. Craig, "The Political Leader as Strategist," in *Makers of Modern Strategy,* ed. P. Paret (Princeton, N.J.: Princeton University Press, 1986), pp. 504–5.

11. Burns, *Roosevelt: The Lion and the Fox,* p. 389.

12. Ibid., pp. 397–404.

13. Kirk H. Porter and Donald B. Johnson, eds., *National Party Platforms, 1840–1968* (Urbana: University of Illinois Press, 1970), pp. 391, 369, 363.

14. *Congressional Record* 86 (Jan. 3, 1940): 9.

15. Ibid. (Jan. 4, 1940): 48.

16. *United States v. Curtiss-Wright Export Corp.,* 299 U.S. 304 (1936).

17. Samuel P. Huntington, *The Soldier and the State* (Cambridge: Harvard University Press, 1957), pp. 311–12. Burns was also editor of the *Infantry Journal,* which published posthumously the article from which this excerpt was taken.

18. Huntington, *The Soldier and the State,* p. 312.

19. This does not mean that Congress had no impact. Huntington, who describes the defense budget as "the single most important contact between the military and Congress," concludes, "It is difficult to see how this budget process could be improved upon." He is particularly positive in his assessment of the Senate Defense Appropriations Subcommittee during that period, describing discussions before it as "informed, intelligent, and focused" and as producing a hearings record that represents "one of the best sources for the general nature of military policy" (ibid., pp. 407, 412).

20. See Louis Fisher, *Presidential Spending Power* (Princeton, N.J.: Princeton University Press, 1975), pp. 158–60. See also pp. 80–93 for Fisher's informative review of reprogramming authority and practices.

21. See Richard Haass, "The Role of the Congress in American Security Policy," in *American Defense Policy,* 5th ed., ed. J. F. Reichart and S. B. Sturm (Baltimore: Johns Hopkins University Press, 1982), p. 559.

22. The fiscal 1960 Defense Appropriations Act included some 200 line items. The fiscal 1983 bill had more than 1,200, of which some two-thirds were categorized as "special interest," thereby denying the Department of Defense routine reprogramming authority (Fred Thompson, "Managing Defense Expenditures," in *Control of Federal Spending, Proceedings of the Academy of Political Science* 35 [1985]: 77).

23. Haass, "The Role of the Congress in American Security Policy," p. 559.

24. Joseph Kruzel, "The Domestic Setting," in *American Defense Annual, 1985–1986,* ed. G. E. Hudson and J. Kruzel (Lexington, Mass.: D.C. Heath, 1985), p. 5.

25. Huntington, *The Soldier and the State,* pp. 423–24.

26. *Congressional Record* 95 (Jan. 10, 1949): 138.

27. Ibid. 96 (Jan. 9, 1950): 214.

28. Ibid. 95 (April 4, 1949): 4427–28.

29. *Congress and the Nation, 1945–1964,* p. 254.

30. Truman signed the appropriations bill on Oct. 29, 1949, but then directed the secretary of defense to place the contested amount ($735 million) in reserve. His authority to impound the funds was not challenged by the chairman of either appropriations committee, Congressman Clarence Cannon or Senator Kenneth D. McKellar (Fisher, *Presidential Spending Power,* pp. 162–63).

31. See, for example, Paul Y. Hammond, "Super-Carriers and B-36 Bombers," in *American Civil-Military Decisions,* ed. H. Stein (Birmingham: University of Alabama Press, 1963).

32. Richard Smoke, "The Evolution of American Defense Policy," in *American Defense Policy,* p. 107.

33. Paul Y. Hammond, "NSC-68: Prologue to Rearmament," in *Strategy, Politics, and Defense Budgets,* ed. W. R. Schilling et al. (New York: Columbia University Press, 1962), p. 306.

34. "Radio and Television Report to the American People on the Situation in Korea," in *Public Papers of the Presidents of the United States: Harry S Truman* (Washington, D.C.: GPO, 1965), p. 612.

35. "Statement of the President upon Approving an Increase in U.S. Forces in Western Europe," ibid., p. 626.

36. *Budget of the United States Government, Fiscal Year 1961,* p. M15.

37. *Budget of the United States Government, Fiscal Year 1954* (Washington, D.C.: GPO, 1953), p. M13.

38. "Basic National Security Policies and Programs in Relation to Their Costs," in *Foreign Relations of the United States, 1952–1954,* vol. 2, *National Security Affairs* (Washington, D.C.: GPO, 1984), pp. 309–16.

39. *Congressional Record* 99 (May 20, 1953): 5180.

40. Eisenhower depicted the Soviets as deliberately trying to "force upon America and the free world an unbearable security burden leading to economic disaster" (ibid.). One of the earliest Side A versus Side B national security policy debates during Eisenhower's presidency was over whether the United States faced a primarily military threat or a dual threat: "the external threat of Soviet power; the internal threat of weakening our economy and changing our way of life" (see *Foreign Relations of the United States, 1952–1954* 2:514–34).

41. *Congressional Record* 99 (May 20, 1953): 5180.

42. His "new concept" was outlined in the fiscal 1955 budget (*Budget of the United States Government, Fiscal Year 1955* [Washington, D.C.: GPO, 1954], p. M38).

43. The doctrine was first set forth in a speech by Secretary of State John Foster Dulles to the National Press Club at Washington on Dec. 22, 1953. Dulles explained the doctrine in greater detail in a major speech to the Council on Foreign Relations at New York City the following month.

44. The doctrine helped generate a new literature and specialization on

national security policy and planning (see Smoke, "The Evolution of American Defense Policy," pp. 108–13).

45. *Foreign Relations of the United States, 1952–1954,* vol. 5, *Western European Security* (Washington, D.C.: GPO, 1983), pp. 511–12.

46. Ibid. 2:520. These paraphrased comments are contained in a memorandum of discussion for the NSC meeting prepared by the council's Deputy Executive Secretary S. Everett Gleason.

47. These figures are contained in an NSC Report ("Basic National Security Policies and Programs in Relation to Their Costs") approved April 28, 1953 (ibid. 2:311–16).

48. *Historical Tables, Budget of the United States Government, Fiscal Year 1990* (Washington, D.C.: GPO, 1989), pp. 124–25. In constant FY 1982 dollars, defense outlays totaled $211.0 billion in fiscal 1955 and $195.2 billion in fiscal 1961.

49. Comparable data were not reported for FY 1961.

50. Procurement outlays were approximately $13 billion in fiscal 1955 and $14.3 billion in fiscal 1960.

51. *Congressional Record* 104 (Jan. 9, 1958): 205.

52. Porter and Johnson, *National Party Platforms,* p. 575.

53. George F. Brown, Jr., and Lawrence J. Korb, "The Economic and Political Restraints on Force Planning," in *American Defense Policy,* p. 583.

54. *Budget of the United States Government, Fiscal Year 1963* (Washington, D.C.: GPO, 1962), p. 11.

55. Most analyses of this episode conclude that U.S. military superiority had an enormous influence on the successful outcome. Lawrence Freedman reports that "as once Khrushchev had gloated over his imminent missile superiority, the U.S. administration could now provide facts and figures on American superiority" (*The Evolution of Nuclear Strategy* [New York: St. Martin's Press, 1981], p. 265). He goes on to argue that U.S. conventional superiority in the Caribbean was the determining factor, but the fact of U.S. missile superiority at the time is not usually challenged. That the Eisenhower strategic program produced this superiority is difficult to rebut, since the U.S. forces in place during October 1962 were largely the result of fiscal 1961 and prior defense budgets. Kennedy's fiscal 1962 increases provided a modest increase in procurement schedules for strategic programs developed and put into production by Eisenhower.

56. *Budget of the United States Government, Fiscal Year 1964,* p. 17.

57. See Freedman, *The Evolution of Nuclear Strategy,* pp. 227–49.

58. *Budget of the United States Government, Fiscal Year 1965* (Washington, D.C.: GPO, 1964), pp. 8, 74.

Chapter Five
1. See Edward J. Laurance, "The Changing Role of Congress in Defense Policy-Making," *Journal of Conflict Resolution* 20 (June 1976): 213–53.

2. The pre-Vietnam stability of public opinion on defense is discussed in Lawrence J. Korb, *The Fall and Rise of the Pentagon* (Westport, Conn.: Greenwood Press, 1979), pp. 4–7. The post-Vietnam instability is examined in Ippolito, *Congressional Spending*, pp. 230–31.

3. Lindsay, "Congress and Defense Policy: 1961–1986," pp. 389, 382–85.

4. See David C. Morrison, "Chaos on Capitol Hill," *National Journal* 18 (Sept. 27, 1986): 2302–7. According to Morrison, the litany of criticisms, freely conceded by many members of Congress, includes "redundancy, legislative delays, turf building, pork barreling and micromanagement [that] increasingly characterize Congress's defense budgeting and oversight."

5. Charles W. Ostrom and Robin F. Marra, "U.S. Defense Spending and the Soviet Estimate," *American Political Science Review* 80 (Sept. 1986): 819–42. There are well-recognized pitfalls in relying on public opinion or Soviet estimates. Most adults have a grossly inaccurate view of defense spending (see Wildavsky, *The New Politics of the Budgetary Process*, p. 366). Errors in estimating Soviet military spending have been substantial (see Joshua M. Epstein, *The 1988 Defense Budget* [Washington, D.C.: Brookings Institution, 1987], p. 1). On the impact of lower growth estimates, see Ostrom and Marra, "U.S. Defense Spending and the Soviet Estimate," p. 839.

6. Estimated Vietnam expenditures accounted for $28.8 billion of the $81.0 billion FY 1969 defense budget (*Budget of the United States Government, Fiscal Year 1970* [Washington, D.C.: GPO, 1969], p. 69).

7. Johnson's fiscal 1966 defense budget request was $51.6, which represented a $600 million cut from the fiscal 1965 estimate. At the same time, the total budget was to increase by $2.3 billion. According to Johnson, this budget would begin "to grasp the opportunities of the Great Society" (*Budget of the United States Government, Fiscal Year 1966*, pp. 493, 496).

8. In presenting the fiscal 1969 defense appropriations bill, Russell had expressed to the Senate the still widespread belief that defense spending would have to be "substantially" increased "in the near future." The fiscal 1969 cuts were, for congressional military spokesmen, a deferral, not a cancellation, of scheduled weapons program spending (*Congress and the Nation, 1965–1968*, p. 830).

9. *Congressional Quarterly Almanac, 1968* (Washington, D.C.: Congressional Quarterly, 1968), p. 998.

10. See Korb, *The Fall and Rise of the Pentagon*, pp. 53–55.

11. Defense outlays were 5.1 percent of GNP in fiscal 1950. Even after Korea, this level remained close to 10 percent.

12. From a fiscal year 1950 level of $83.9 billion (in FY 1982 dollars), real defense spending nearly doubled the following year and then jumped to over $270 billion at the fiscal 1953 peak. Between Korea and Vietnam, real defense spending never dropped below $180 billion and averaged close to $200 billion annually.

13. The average annual percentage cut for this period was 6.0 percent (see ibid., p. 52).

14. On the use of reprogramming to lessen the impact of this decline, see ibid., pp. 61–66.

15. On Feb. 18, 1970, Nixon also announced that subsequent defense planning would be based on a "one-and-a-half-war" strategy, rather than the "two-and-a-half-wars" planning concept used by Johnson (*Congressional Record* 116 [Feb. 18, 1970]: 3839–40).

16. See Freedman, *The Evolution of Nuclear Strategy*, pp. 383–87.

17. The force levels on which the McGovern defense budget was based are presented in Korb, *The Fall and Rise of the Pentagon*, p. 72.

18. *Guide to U.S. Elections*, p. 126.

19. Ibid., p. 128.

20. See Ippolito, *Congressional Spending*, pp. 56–70.

21. See Schick, *Congress and Money*, pp. 72–74.

22. Quoted in Ippolito, *Congressional Spending*, p. 172.

23. The fiscal 1976 defense appropriations bill was reduced approximately $6 billion below Ford's $94.6 billion request, while the military construction appropriations bill for fiscal 1976 was cut by about $525 million.

24. The functional category breakdowns were not included in the budget resolutions for fiscal 1976, but they were part of the Budget Committee and conference reports accompanying the resolution. In both the House and Senate, the functional breakdowns in the first resolution were then used during the appropriations process. In future years, the functional breakdowns for outlays and budget authority were part of the actual resolutions.

25. Ibid., p. 176.

26. From 1961 to 1974 the number of witnesses appearing before the Senate Armed Services Committee on military procurement increased from 27 to 220, while pages of testimony published as hearings rose from 603 to 5,085. The Senate's Defense Appropriations Subcommittee published 1,709 pages of testimony in 1961 and 4,179 in 1974 (Laurance, "The Changing Role of Congress in Defense Policy-Making," pp. 227–28).

27. Part of this expansion of congressional efforts to extend fiscal and programmatic oversight was the result of greatly increased annual authorization requirements (see Robert J. Art, "Congress and the Defense Budget," *Political Science Quarterly* 100 [Summer 1985]: 228–36).

28. Comparative data for the 1957–74 period are presented in Laurance, "The Changing Role of Congress in Defense Policy-Making," p. 239. On the upward shifts in participation, see Lindsay, "Congress and Defense Policy: 1961–1986," pp. 371–401.

29. Korb, *The Fall and Rise of the Pentagon*, p. 59.

30. See Fisher, *Presidential Spending Power*, pp. 80–88.

31. See Korb, *The Fall and Rise of the Pentagon*, p. 65.

32. Congressional Budget Office, *Budget Options for Fiscal Year 1977* (Washington, D.C., 1976), p. 36.

33. Senate Committee on Armed Services, *United States/Soviet Military Balance: A Frame of Reference for Congress* (Washington, D.C.: GPO, 1976), p. 32.

34. Central Intelligence Agency, *A Dollar Comparison of Soviet and U.S. Defense Activities, 1965–1975* (Washington, D.C., Feb. 1976), pp. 2, 5.

35. See Dennis S. Ippolito, *The Budget and National Politics* (San Francisco: W. H. Freeman, 1978), p. 170.

36. For estimates, see Brown and Korb, "The Economic and Political Restraints on Force Planning," p. 584.

37. *Congressional Quarterly Almanac, 1976* (Washington, D.C.: Congressional Quarterly, 1977), p. 868.

38. The platform stated, "In order to provide for a comprehensive review of the B-1 test and evaluation program, no decision regarding B-1 production should be made prior to February 1977" (ibid., p. 869).

39. See Korb, *The Fall and Rise of the Pentagon*, p. 162.

40. See Ippolito, *Congressional Spending*, pp. 231, 177.

41. *Budget of the United States Government, Fiscal Year 1981*, p. 100.

42. *Congressional Quarterly Almanac, 1980* (Washington, D.C.: Congressional Quarterly, 1981), p. 114-B.

43. *Congressional Quarterly Weekly Report* 35 (April 30, 1977): 776–77.

44. *Budget of the United States Government, Fiscal Year 1979* (Washington, D.C.: GPO, 1978), p. 68.

45. *Congressional Quarterly Almanac, 1979* (Washington, D.C.: Congressional Quarterly, 1980), p. 179.

46. *Budget of the United States Government, Fiscal Year 1981*, p. 90.

47. The fiscal 1981 budget, for example, had procurement budget authority rising from $31.4 billion in fiscal 1979 to an estimated $54.7 billion in fiscal 1983.

48. *Department of Defense Annual Report, Fiscal Year 1980* (Washington, D.C.: GPO, 1979), p. 67.

49. Ibid., p. 5.

50. *Budget of the United States Government, Fiscal Year 1989*, p. 5-5. For slightly different estimates of the administration's program, see Congressional Budget Office, *An Analysis of the President's Budgetary Proposals for Fiscal Year 1989* (Washington, D.C., 1988), pp. 32–39.

51. *Fiscal Year 1982 Budget Revisions*, pp. 13, 124–25.

52. *Historical Tables, Budget of the United States Government, Fiscal Year 1990*, pp. 50–51.

53. Department of Defense, *Soviet Military Power: An Assessment of the Threat, 1988* (Washington, D.C.: GPO, 1988), p. 32.

54. *Department of Defense Annual Report, Fiscal Year 1982* (Washington, D.C.: GPO, 1981), p. 310; *Annual Report to the Congress, Fiscal Year 1983, Caspar W. Weinberger, Secretary of Defense* (Washington, D.C.: GPO, 1982), p. IV-7.

55. According to David A. Stockman, Reagan's first director of the Office of Management and Budget, there was an attempt by Weinberger and others to understate the real growth implications of the initial Reagan defense plan (see David A. Stockman, *The Triumph of Politics: Why the Reagan Revolution Failed* [New York: Harper & Row, 1986]).

56. *Department of Defense Annual Report, Fiscal Year 1982*, pp. 16, A-1.

57. *Annual Report to the Congress, Fiscal Year 1983*, p. A-1.

58. *Department of Defense Annual Report, Fiscal Year 1982*, p. C-4.

59. *Annual Report to the Congress, Fiscal Year 1983*, pp. B-6, I-39.

60. On the problems encountered with the B-1B during deployment, see Congressional Budget Office, *The B-1B Bomber and Options for Enhancement* (Washington, D.C., 1988).

61. Congressional Budget Office, *Future Budget Requirements for the 600-Ship Navy* (Washington, D.C., 1985), p. xii.

62. *Annual Report to the Congress, Fiscal Year 1989, Frank C. Carlucci, Secretary of Defense* (Washington, D.C.: GPO, 1988), pp. 168–69.

63. Readiness usually refers to the immediate ability to deploy and employ forces and thus embraces both equipment and trained personnel. Sustainability groups together manpower and equipment needed to maintain and sustain combat forces once employed.

64. *Department of Defense Annual Report, Fiscal Year 1982*, pp. 169–70, 175.

65. *Annual Report to the Congress, Fiscal Year 1989*, p. 15.

66. *Annual Report to the Congress, Fiscal Year 1983*, p. I-4.

67. *Congressional Quarterly Weekly Report* 39 (May 9, 1981): 785.

68. See Congressional Budget Office, *Budgeting for Defense Inflation* (Washington, D.C., 1986).

69. According to Rudolph G. Penner, director of the Congressional Budget Office from 1983 to 1987, this change in public opinion affected "congressional action on the budget in 1985, and then, of course, in 1986 and 1987, we've actually had real cuts in the defense budget." Penner also stated this relationship between the defense budget and public opinion ("as measured by the kind of polls that ask people if more or less or about the same amount should be spent on defense") showed "a very high correlation over time" (*Government Executive* 19 [Sept. 1987]: 36).

70. One of the questionable maneuvers was shifting the last military payroll

for fiscal 1987, scheduled for Sept. 30, to the following day, thus moving nearly $3 billion in outlays to fiscal 1988.

71. *National Journal* (Sept. 27, 1986): 2302.

Chapter Six

1. On the development of federal policy during this period, see Walter I. Trattner, *From Poor Law to Welfare State*, 2d ed. (New York: Free Press, 1979).

2. Wildavsky, *The New Politics of the Budgetary Process*, p. 264.

3. See U.S. General Accounting Office, *A Glossary of Terms Used in the Federal Budget Process*, 3d ed. (Washington, D.C., 1981), p. 57.

4. See R. Kent Weaver, "Controlling Entitlements," in *The New Direction in American Politics*, ed. J. E. Chubb and P. E. Peterson (Washington, D.C.: Brookings Institution, 1985), pp. 308–11.

5. Ibid., pp. 310–11.

6. See Wildavsky, *The New Politics of the Budgetary Process*, pp. 283–87.

7. Ibid., p. 346.

8. R. Kent Weaver, *Automatic Government: The Politics of Indexation* (Washington, D.C.: Brookings Institution, 1988), p. 18.

9. Ibid., pp. 29, 228.

10. Wildavsky, *The New Politics of the Budgetary Process*, pp. 346–47.

11. The unemployment compensation program, however, was a federal-state enterprise. The Social Security Act levied a federal payroll tax, which could be offset by payments to a state unemployment insurance program. By 1939 all of the states had established programs, and all utilized a trust fund to collect payroll taxes and to disburse benefits. Currently, the states handle regular benefits (usually for twenty-six weeks) and set benefit levels (within broad guidelines). Extended benefits are jointly financed by the states and the federal government, and are available for a maximum of thirteen additional weeks in states with high rates of unemployment.

12. The Social Security Act also provided small grants to the states for several programs designated as maternal and child welfare, including payments for prenatal health services, special assistance for crippled children, and social services for rural youth.

13. *Congress and the Nation, 1945–1964*, p. 1151.

14. Congressional Quarterly, *Social Security and Retirement* (Washington, D.C., 1983), p. 19.

15. *Carmichael v. Southern Coal and Coke Co.*, 301 U.S. 495 (1937); *Helvering v. Davis*, 301 U.S. 619 (1937); and *Steward Machine Co. v. Davis*, 301 U.S. 548 (1937).

16. *Congress and the Nation, 1945–1964*, pp. 1278, 1275.

17. This phrase was contained in the Senate Finance Committee's report on the original social security bill (ibid., p. 1244).

18. For data on trust fund balances, see *Historical Tables, Budget of the United States Government, Fiscal Year 1990*, pp. 300–323.

19. In 1943, for example, a compulsory national health insurance system for all persons was proposed by senators Robert F. Wagner and James E. Murray and Congressman John D. Dingell, Sr. No action was taken on their proposal during the Seventy-eighth Congress. In 1945 they reintroduced their bill but then endorsed and introduced President Truman's health-care plan, which was outlined to Congress on Nov. 19.

20. This plan was sponsored by Congressman Wilbur D. Mills, chairman of the Ways and Means Committee, and Senator Robert S. Kerr, both of whom were usually associated with the conservative bloc of congressional Democrats.

21. As federal funding became more generous, states were usually required to expand coverage and to increase benefits under their individual programs.

22. The 1956 amendments also authorized federal grants to support studies and projects aimed at reducing welfare dependency. During the 1950s and 1960s steadily increased federal support and broadened coverage made the dependency issue a more realistic concern, but there was very little sustained action taken to address it. Indeed, by the late 1960s the major policy debate was over how to integrate the working poor into the social welfare system rather than over how to combat dependency.

23. Ibid., pp. 126–28.

24. This application of indexing to the spending side of the budget is analyzed in Weaver, *Automatic Government: The Politics of Indexation*.

25. See Fisher, *Presidential Spending Power*, pp. 175–201.

26. Quoted in Leslie Lenkowsky, *Politics, Economics, and Welfare Reform* (Lanham, Md.: University Press of America, 1986), p. 42.

27. Ibid., pp. 67–69.

28. Michael J. Boskin, *Too Many Promises: The Uncertain Future of Social Security* (Homewood, Ill.: Dow Jones-Irwin, 1986), p. 178.

29. Gene Falk, *1988 Budget Perspectives: Federal Spending for the Human Resource Programs* (Washington, D.C.: Congressional Research Service, 1987), p. CRS-77.

30. Ibid., pp. CRS-71, CRS-81.

31. Ibid., p. CRS-81.

32. *Congressional Quarterly Almanac, 1976*, pp. 859–60.

33. Quoted in *Congressional Quarterly Almanac, 1978* (Washington, D.C.: Congressional Quarterly, 1979), p. 630.

34. Ibid., pp. 601–2.

35. Boskin, *Too Many Promises*, pp. 24, 27.

36. *Fiscal Year 1982 Budget Revisions*, pp. 8–9.

37. Nathan Glazer, *The Limits of Social Policy* (Cambridge: Harvard University Press, 1988), pp. 42, 44.

38. R. Kent Weaver, "Social Policy in the Reagan Era," in *The Reagan Revolution?*, ed. B. B. Kymlicka and J. V. Matthews (Chicago: Dorsey Press, 1988), p. 152.

39. Peter Gottschalk, "Retrenchment in Antipoverty Programs in the United States," ibid., p. 142.

40. *Congressional Quarterly Weekly Report* 46 (Oct. 1, 1988): 2699.

41. A review of the commission's work and recommendations is found in Paul Light, *Artful Work: The Politics of Social Security Reform* (New York: Random House, 1985).

42. Congressional Quarterly, *Congress and the Nation, 1981–1984* (Washington, D.C., 1985), p. 535.

43. Falk, *1988 Budget Perspectives*, p. CRS-85.

44. John L. Palmer, "Income Security Policies in the United States," *Journal of Public Policy* 7 (March 1987): 27.

45. See Lenkowsky, *Politics, Economics, and Welfare Reform*, pp. 11, 41.

46. Congressional Budget Office, *Trends in Family Income, 1970–1986* (Washington, D.C., 1988), p. 110.

47. Falk, *1988 Budget Perspectives*, pp. CRS-57, CRS-59.

48. Congressional Budget Office, *Trends in Family Income*, p. 110.

49. *Historical Tables, Budget of the United States Government, Fiscal Year 1990*, pp. 6, 16.

50. Wildavsky, *The New Politics of the Budgetary Process*, p. 347.

Chapter Seven
1. In fiscal year 1989, for example, slightly over $300 billion of the $1.1 trillion in spending was designated as "relatively controllable." Approximately 40 percent of this controllable total was for domestic programs. As explained by OMB, controllability indicates the "relative ease or difficulty in changing the magnitude of Federal spending through budget reductions." While spending for most purposes is ultimately controllable, the "nature or degree of controllability differs significantly among programs, particularly in the relatively short term, due to their basic design." Domestic programs categorized as relatively controllable can be reduced through annual appropriations actions (*Historical Tables, Budget of the United States Government, Fiscal Year 1990*, pp. 153–55).

2. The spending categories included here and used in this chapter to represent domestic programs are: (1) commerce and housing credit; (2) community and regional development; (3) energy; (4) natural resources and environment; (5) transportation; (6) agriculture; (7) general purpose fiscal assistance (revenue sharing). The first five of these categories comprise the "physical resources" budget category. The latter two are included under "other functions" (see ibid., pp. 39–45).

3. David R. Mayhew, *Congress: The Electoral Connection* (New Haven: Yale University Press, 1974), pp. 53–54.

4. Kenneth A. Shepsle and Barry R. Weingast, "Legislative Politics and Budget Outcomes," in *Federal Budget Policy in the 1980s*, ed. G. B. Mills and J. L. Palmer (Washington, D.C.: Urban Institute, 1984), pp. 350, 355.

5. Stockman, *The Triumph of Politics: Why the Reagan Revolution Failed.*

6. *1988 Legislative and Administrative Message: A Union of Individuals* (Washington, D.C.: The White House, Office of the Press Secretary, Jan. 25, 1988), p. 3.

7. The total public debt was reduced from a peak of $25.5 billion in FY 1919 to $16.2 billion in FY 1930. The budget was in surplus in each of the intervening years.

8. Quoted in Kimmel, *Federal Budget and Fiscal Policy, 1789–1958*, p. 182.

9. Quoted in Alonzo Hamby, *Liberalism and Its Challengers* (New York: Oxford University Press, 1985), p. 29.

10. David Rapp, *How the U.S. Got into Agriculture* (Washington, D.C.: Congressional Quarterly, 1988), p. 14.

11. *Congress and the Nation, 1945–1964*, p. 684.

12. Ibid., p. 553.

13. In 1933, for example, the Home Owners' Loan Corporation began funding direct long-term mortgage loans at low interest to individuals threatened with the loss of their homes.

14. Ibid., pp. 348, 481.

15. See Robert P. Inman, "Fiscal Allocations in a Federalist Economy: Understanding the 'New Federalism,'" in *American Domestic Priorities*, ed. J. M. Quigley and D. L. Rubinfeld (Berkeley: University of California Press, 1985), p. 3.

16. Ibid., pp. 7–8.

17. Ibid., p. 10.

18. The 1954 Federal-Aid Highway Act, for example, had changed the previous 50–50 matching formula to a 60 percent federal to 40 percent state formula.

19. Jose A. Gomez-Ibanez, "The Federal Role in Urban Transportation," ibid., p. 186.

20. *Historical Tables, Budget of the United States Government, Fiscal Year 1990*, pp. 39–40; *Congress and the Nation, 1945–1964*, p. 787.

21. Quoted in *Congress and the Nation, 1945–1964*, p. 787.

22. Kenneth T. Palmer, "The Evolution of Grant Policies," in *The Changing Politics of Federal Grants*, ed. L. D. Brown, J. W. Fossett, and K. T. Palmer (Washington, D.C.: Brookings Institution, 1984), p. 6.

23. Inman, "Fiscal Allocations in a Federalist Economy," pp. 9–10.

24. *Congressional Quarterly Almanac, 1979*, pp. 75-A, 77-A.

25. Congressional Quarterly, *Congress and the Nation, 1969–1972* (Washington, D.C., 1973), p. 104-A.

26. Palmer, "The Evolution of Grant Policies," p. 31.

27. Quoted, ibid., p. 40.

28. Congressional Quarterly, *Congress and the Nation, 1977–1980* (Washington, D.C., 1981), p. 41.

29. Dennis S. Ippolito, *Hidden Spending* (Chapel Hill: University of North Carolina Press, 1984), pp. 85–88.

30. Ippolito, *Congressional Spending,* pp. 158–60.

31. Richard P. Nathan, "Institutional Change under Reagan," in *Perspectives on the Reagan Years,* ed. J. L. Palmer (Washington, D.C.: Urban Institute, 1986), p. 134.

32. *Budget of the United States Government, Fiscal Year 1989,* p. 5-35.

33. Rapp, *How the U.S. Got into Agriculture,* p. 14.

34. U.S. Department of Agriculture, Economic Research Service, *History of Agricultural and Price-Support Adjustment Programs, 1933–1984* (Washington, D.C., 1984), p. 40.

35. Nathan, "Institutional Change under Reagan," p. 137.

36. *Congressional Quarterly Almanac, 1982* (Washington, D.C.: Congressional Quarterly, 1983), p. 5-E.

37. See Nathan, "Institutional Change under Reagan," pp. 137–41.

38. Ibid., p. 139.

39. Wildavsky, *The New Politics of the Budgetary Process,* p. 264.

40. Charles L. Schultze, "Comments," in *Federal Budget Policy in the 1980s,* p. 381.

Chapter Eight

1. The National Economic Commission's cochairmen were Robert S. Strauss, former chairman of the Democratic National Committee, and Drew Lewis, a former cabinet secretary and vice-chairman of the Republican National Committee. Its members were chosen by the congressional leaderships and the president. Two members were appointed by President-elect Bush late in 1988.

2. Lawrence J. Haas, "A Budget Commission Side Step," *National Journal* 21 (March 11, 1989): 592.

3. Congressional Budget Office, *Reducing the Deficit: Spending and Revenue Options,* p. 1.

4. *Congressional Record* 126 (Nov. 20, 1980): S14573, S14757.

5. Congressional Budget Office, *The Economic and Budget Outlook: Fiscal Years 1990–1994* (Washington, D.C., 1989), pp. xv, 46.

6. Weaver, *Automatic Government: The Politics of Indexation,* pp. 254–55.

7. Ibid., p. 256.

8. Congressional Budget Office, *The Economic and Budget Outlook: An Update* (Washington, D.C., 1988), p. 66. Given the negative response to this financing system and the subsequent repeal by Congress, the future use of similar approaches would appear to be rather unlikely. At the same time, major benefit expansions will be constrained by the lack of available financing.

9. Congressional Budget Office, *The Economic and Budget Outlook: Fiscal Years 1990–1994*, pp. 54–55.

10. Ibid., p. 49.

11. Ibid., pp. 133, 73.

12. Ibid., pp. 96–97.

13. Ibid., p. 49.

14. See Penner and Abramson, *Broken Purse Strings: Congressional Budgeting, 1974–1988*, p. 76.

15. For a comprehensive critique of the first four years of Gramm-Rudman-Hollings, see Jackie Calmes, "Gramm-Rudman-Hollings: Has Its Time Passed?" *Congressional Quarterly Weekly Report* 47 (Oct. 14, 1989): 2684–88. Alice M. Rivlin, the first director of the Congressional Budget Office, is quoted as calling Gramm-Rudman-Hollings "a well-intentioned experiment that failed." Her successor, Rudolph G. Penner, who served from 1983 to 1987, agreed that "we have reached the point where the costs outweigh the benefits."

16. See Penner and Abramson, *Broken Purse Strings: Congressional Budgeting, 1974–1988*, pp. 118–20.

17. The 1989 annual report contains nearly 150 separate recommendations for defense spending, entitlement spending, agricultural programs, nondefense discretionary spending, federal work force pay policies, and revenue policy.

18. See, for example, Joseph White and Aaron Wildavsky, "How to Fix the Deficit—Really," *Public Interest* (Winter 1989): 3–24. The American Enterprise Institute, Brookings Institution, Heritage Foundation, and Urban Institute have provided a wide variety of deficit-reduction studies.

19. Weaver, *Automatic Government: The Politics of Indexation*, p. 260.

20. Congressional Budget Office, *Reducing the Deficit: Spending and Revenue Options*, pp. 147, 313.

21. Wildavsky, *The New Politics of the Budgetary Process*, p. 283.

22. Senate Committee on the Budget, *Congressional Budget and Impoundment Control Act of 1974, As Amended* (Washington, D.C.: GPO, 1988), p. 29.

23. Congressional Budget Office, *Reducing the Deficit: Spending and Revenue Options*, pp. 343–46.

24. See Kamlet and Mowery, "Influences on Executive and Congressional Budgetary Priorities, 1955–1981," p. 169. According to Kamlet and Mowery, "Executive branch budgets have been heavily influenced by top-down pressures and policy targets during much of the postwar period."

25. On the implications of scarcity and complexity for budget theory, see

James Malachowski, Samuel Bookheimer, and David Lowery, "The Theory of the Budgetary Process in an Era of Changing Rules: FY48-FY84," *American Politics Quarterly* 15 (July 1987): 325–54.

26. Wildavsky, *The Politics of the Budgetary Process,* 3d ed., p. 60.

27. David Stockman, "The Crisis in Federal Budgeting," in *Crisis in the Budget Process,* ed. A. Schick (Washington, D.C.: American Enterprise Institute, 1986), p. 65.

28. *Polling Report* 5 (Jan. 30, 1989): 6, 1.

29. The current reconciliation procedure is outlined in Senate Committee on the Budget, *Congressional Budget and Impoundment Control Act of 1974, As Amended,* pp. 26–29.

30. See Shuman, *Politics and the Budget,* 2d ed., pp. 252–62.

31. Dennis S. Ippolito, "Reform, Congress, and the President," in *Congressional Budgeting,* ed. W. T. Wander et al. (Baltimore: Johns Hopkins University Press, 1984), p. 149.

32. See Shuman, *Politics and the Budget,* 2d ed., p. 262.

33. For an examination of the strengths and weaknesses of the reconciliation procedure, see "Reconciliation Dominates Policy-Making Process," *Congressional Quarterly Weekly Report* 47 (April 29, 1989): 964–68.

34. Senate Committee on the Budget, *Congressional Impoundment and Control Act of 1974, As Amended,* p. 29.

35. Naomi Caiden, "Paradox, Ambiguity, and Enigma: The Strange Case of the Executive Budget and the United States Constitution," *Public Administration Review* 47 (Jan./Feb. 1987): 87.

36. Ibid., p. 90.

37. Rudolph G. Penner, "An Appraisal of the Congressional Budget Process," in *Crisis in the Budget Process,* p. 70.

Index

Soviet threat and, 127–28, 133
Truman's, 99–103
Vietnam War and, 116–20
    change of shape in budget and, 120–27
    politicization of, 115–16
    procedural changes in, 115
    public attitude toward, 118
    weapons procurement and, 132
    World War II to Vietnam, 98–109
    zero growth argument in, 145
Defense policy
    ambivalence on, 127
    budget composition and, 10
    budget control and, 147–49
    congressional role in, 99, 145–49
    consensus on, 93–94, 113, 125
    military strategy and, 140–41
    presidential, 93–114
    public opinion on, 115, 118, 126, 132, 143, 272n.69
    in Reagan administration, 140–41, 145–47
    review of in 1949, 101–2
Deficit
    budget control and, 4
    Carter's defense budget and, 130
    changes in during recent decades, 2
    economic growth and, 4–6
    Economic Recovery Tax Act (1981) and, 64–65
    Gramm-Rudman-Hollings and, 239–40
    growth from 1930 to 1989, 4–5
    historical background on, 2–7
    indexing and, 242
    magnitude of, 1
    October 1987 stock crash and, 85
    political implications of, 2, 17, 232
    problems involved in, 232–38
    public opinion on, 1, 245–46
    in Reagan administration
        in 1983 and 1984, 70–72
        collapse of attempt to pass 1985 budget and, 78–79
        defense budget and, 143, 147
        projections of, 67–68
        second term, 85–87
        tax cuts in first term and, 58
    Reagan's tax policy and, 58
    in Roosevelt administration, 31
    short-term, 233–34
    social security surplus and, 88, 192, 242–43

tax burdens under Kennedy-Johnson and, 46
tax reform 1986 and, 79–80
Treasury II and, 78
between World War II and Vietnam War, 25
Deficit Reduction Act (1984), 58, 71–72
Demobilization, after World War II, 100–101
Democratic Study Group, deficit reduction and, 78
Democrats
    ambivalence on defense among, 108–9, 127, 130
    argument against proportional tax cuts by, 63
    attempt to increase personal exemption by, 38–39
    attempt to revise Reagan's tax program by, 68–69
    attitude toward Republican tax relief bill (1948), 36
    Carter's social welfare program and, 178
    Fair Tax plan of, 76
    party platform on defense, 96, 121–22
    party platform on taxes (1984), 73
    response to Economic Recovery Tax Act (1981), 60
Department of Defense
    congressional intervention in, 123, 125–27
    creation of, 101
Department of Energy, 221–22
Department of Housing and Urban Development, 212, 214
Department of Transportation, establishment of, 211
Depression, 9
    deficit spending as cure for, 195
    tax policy during, 30–32
Deterrence
    in Eisenhower's defense policy, 104–5
    mutual assured destruction and, 111
Dingell, John D., Sr., 274n.19
Disability insurance, 159
Disabled, public assistance to, 159, 162, 170, 174
Discretionary spending (nondefense), 225–26
    budget composition and, 10
    as percentage of GNP, 10, 13(illus.)
Dividends, tax treatment of, 31, 70, 76
Dole, Robert, 60–61, 69